B
PATRICK   Thompson, E. A.   C I

Who was St.
    Patrick?

LOST OR DAMAGED LIBRARY MATERIALS

THE CARE OF LIBRARY MATERIALS IS THE
RESPONSIBILITY OF THE BORROWING PATRON
TAX DOLLARS SHOULD NOT BE USED TO RE-
PLACE OR REPAIR MATERIALS ABUSED BY
INDIVIDUALS. A FEE SCHEDULE HAS BEEN
SET TO REFLECT THE COSTS TO THE LIBRARY
OF REPLACING OR SPECIAL HANDLING OF
LOST AND DAMAGED MATERIALS.

MATERIALS WERE SELECTED AS AN INTEGRAL
PART OF THE LIBRARY COLLECTION, AND
FOR THE USE OF ALL PATRONS. IF A BOOK
IS OUT OF PRINT, THE SUBJECT AREA WILL
STILL NEED TO BE RESTORED DUE TO THE
LOSS OF THE MATERIAL.

FEES WILL BE CHARGED AS FOLLOWS:

DAMAGE

1. VISIBLE DAMAGE (WATER, COFFEE,
   INK, ETC.) WHICH REDUCES LIFE
   OF MATERIAL BUT STILL CAN CIR-
   CULATE....................$2.00
2. DAMAGE REQUIRING ANY SPECIAL
   HANDLING (SAND, PENCIL MARKS,
   ETC.)....................$3.00
3. DAMAGE REQUIRING THE BOOK BE
   REBOUND..................$6.00

Loss

THE REPLACEMENT COST OF THE MATERIAL
WILL BE CHARGED, PLUS A $2.00
MATERIALS AND HANDLING FEE.

IF THE MATERIAL ITSELF CANNOT BE
REPLACED: 1.) THE PRICE WE PAID WILL
BE CHARGED PLUS A $2.00 PROCESSING
AND HANDLING FEE FOR A NEW BOOK.
2.) A FLAT FEE OF $10.00 WILL BE
CHARGED TO REPLACE THE LOSS TO THE
COLLECTION.
(THE AVERAGE PER-VOLUME COST OF A BOOK
IS $23.00)

WHO WAS SAINT PATRICK?

Page from the *Book of Armagh* (f.24v.) showing the end of the *Confessio* and the scribe's epilogue. (Trinity College, Dublin).

Who Was Saint Patrick?

E. A. Thompson

St. Martin's Press   New York

© E. A. Thompson 1985

First published in the United States of America in 1986

ISBN 0−312−87084−1

Library of Congress Cataloging-in-Publication
Data
Thompson, E. A.
  Who was Saint Patrick?

  Bibliography: p.
  Includes index.
  1. Patrick, Saint, 373?−463? 2. Christian
Saints — Ireland — Biography. I. Title.
BR1720.P26T48   1986   270.2′092′4   [B]
85−14624
ISBN 0−312−87084−1

Printed in Great Britain by St Edmundsbury Press,
Bury St Edmunds, Suffolk

c 1

CONTENTS

v

ABBREVIATIONS

AB   *Analecta Bollandiana*
CSEL   *Corpus Scriptorum Ecclesiasticorum Latinorum*
IER   *Irish Ecclesiastical Record*
IHS   *Irish Historical Studies*
JRSAI   *Journal of the Royal Society of Antiquaries in Ireland*
PRIA   *Proceedings of the Royal Irish Academy*

Note   I quote Patrick's works by the number of the section (or chapter) followed in brackets by the number of the page and line as set out in the editions of Newport White and Bieler, which are identical in this respect

LIST OF PLATES

Preface

The terms 'Western Roman Empire' and 'Eastern Roman Empire' do not imply that there were two Roman Empires. They merely mean respectively the western and the eastern parts of the Empire. The Western Empire included all the European provinces except those lying in the Balkan peninsula south of the Balkan range of mountains. It also included the north African coastal lands west of the Tripolitanian desert. Throughout this area Latin was the language of the educated classes, whereas these classes spoke Greek in the Eastern provinces. The term 'Later Roman Empire' was coined by J. B. Bury, and is used to denote Roman history in (roughly speaking) the fourth, fifth, and sixth centuries. In this book the term 'Roman' is used to denote any free person born inside the Empire, whereas a 'barbarian' means anyone born outside the frontier. The *solidus* (plural, *solidi*) was a splendid gold coin first minted about 309 by Constantine the Great (306–37). It continued to be minted without being debased until the time of the Crusades. A poor man could exist on less than 2 *solidi* a year, but a really rich senator might have an annual income of several hundred thousands of *solidi* in St Patrick's time.

It was a great help to me when writing this book to be able to spend several days in University College, Swansea, browsing through the journals relating to Celtic studies which that College possesses. My warm thanks are due to the Librarian. I am also grateful to the Editor of the *Journal of Theological Studies* who has given me permission to re-print some paragraphs from an article which appeared in that journal in 1980. Not least, I am very grateful to the Leverhulme Trust, which awarded me an Emeritus Fellowship for the year 1984. This enabled me to pay several visits to outlying places such as Swansea and London.

Nottingham   E. A. THOMPSON
March 1985

I would also like to thank my friend, Dr. R. S. Smith, Emeritus Librarian of the University of Nottingham, who corrected the proofs and in several places the contents of this book.

August 1985   E.A.T.

Introduction

Not long ago I asked six British University teachers and one Knight of the Realm what was the nationality of St Patrick. By a coincidence they all answered in the same words: 'Irish, of course.' That was a surprise. It suggested that there is room for a book about Patrick which could be read and understood by persons who know no Latin. The present book, then, is intended for those who have not had a Classical education, who do not know the difference between *amo* and *amas*, and who have never even heard of Lesbia's sparrow or the fountain of Bandusia.

Patrick was not Irish. He was a Briton, the only ancient Briton whom we really know. We have the names of scores of Britons who lived in the time of the Roman Empire, and we have a fact or two about many of them. But we do not know anything of significance about the personality of any one of them with the single exception of Patrick. And we know Patrick because of an almost unbelievable stroke of good luck: two little books which he wrote have managed to survive the centuries! He was not writing for the benefit of posterity. He wrote each of his books — they should really be called 'letters' — in a given situation, one in a time of controversy, the other after a brutal crime. He had no thought of future generations as he penned them. Yet they survived the fifth and sixth centuries in wholly unknown conditions in the darkness of barbarian Ireland, far from the cities and the libraries of the civilised world. They are the only existing Latin books of the time of the Roman Empire which were written outside the Imperial Roman frontier in one of the lands of the barbarians. They are tiny books. Together they fill no more than sixteen pages of Latin in the latest printed edition, but their value and interest are limitless. And what is more, their authorship is not open to doubt. We can be sure that they are Patrick's own work. It would be an exaggeration, but not a gross exaggeration, to say that it is as certain that Patrick wrote these two books as it is that Jonathan Swift wrote *Gulliver's Travels* and that W. B. Yeats wrote *The Wild Swans at Coole*.

The two books are known as the *Epistle to the Soldiers of Coroticus* and the *Confession*. The *Epistle* is an angry, outraged protest to the soldiers of the otherwise unknown 'tyrant' Coroticus. These men had attacked a group of Patrick's newly baptised Christians, killing some and carrying off others into slavery. Patrick excommunicates the thugs who perpetrated this outrage — they were Christians — and demands the return of the enslaved. The *Epistle* tells us some matter of the utmost interest about Patrick, but it is the *Confession* which is of capital value and gives us most of what we know about him. The word 'confession' here is not used in its modern sense. It means rather a defence or justification of his life or at any rate of some episodes and aspects of his life. He wrote the *Epistle* before the *Confession*, but not very long before: several phrases which he had used in the *Epistle* were still running through his head when he came to write the *Confession*. He wrote the *Epistle* late in his career in Ireland when he had already won many converts there. He was still active when he wrote the *Epistle*, but he wrote the *Confession* in his old age when he felt that his career was almost over.

In this century several good biographies of Patrick have been written in English; but they were written by scholars for other scholars to read. With one exception — R. P. C. Hanson's *The Life and Writings of the Historical St Patrick* — they can hardly be understood except by those who know Latin; and nowadays these are distressingly few. Most of these books give a good deal of space to two questions of importance but hardly of electrifying interest: what are the exact dates of Patrick, and what is the value of the *Lives* of him which were written in the seventh and later mediaeval centuries? In this book there is practically no discussion of these dismal conundrums. As for his date, it is agreed on all sides that he lived in the fifth century. But when we ask, in the first half of the century or the second? we are at once floundering and out of our depth, and have hardly a straw to clutch at. My own view, which I have banished to an appendix, is that he was not appointed as bishop until after the year 434. How long after? Nobody knows. Let us say simply (without being too mathematical about it) that his career fell in the 'middle' of the fifth century. And if you insist, in however thunderous a voice, that there *must* be *some* means of narrowing the limits and of defining the word 'middle' in this connexion, I can only repeat that there is not: 'after 434' is as much as we can say.

The value of the *Lives* and the Irish annals and other late documents? An easy question, at any rate by Patrician standards. It is the great service of D. A. Binchy to have shown that for the career of Patrick (and of Coroticus, he might have added) they have no value at all. They add nothing whatever (except fiction) to what we learn from Patrick's own writings. It is true that an Irishman called Tirachan, who wrote about Patrick towards the end of the seventh century, seems able to identify Patrick's one and only Irish place-name, the Wood of Voclut — indeed, Tirachan himself may have been born in its vicinity. But that is quite a different thing from having independent knowledge of Patrick's life and career. The place-name survived unchanged, no doubt, for generations; but if a man about the year 700 knew where the place was situated it does not follow that he also knew something about a slave who had toiled there, hungry and cold, nearly three centuries earlier. It cannot be stressed too often that Patrick's own writings contain *all* the valid evidence about his life and thought which we possess. In the seventh and later centuries a small mountain of guesswork, mythology, and political and ecclesiastical propaganda — especially in favour of the primacy of Armagh over the other Irish churches — grew up about his name, but for our purposes it is irrelevant and worthless. We are not concerned with the struggles of later generations or with how they used the name of Patrick. They had no more valid evidence at their disposal than we have. Our aim is simply and solely to interpret the evidence of his own two books. That means that we must abandon all the stories which take Patrick to Auxerre, Lérins, and Rome, and which bring him into contact with St Germanus of Auxerre and Pope Leo the Great. And we have no help from archaeology. What R. A. S. Macalister said half a century ago seems still to be true: archaeology presents 'an almost death-like silence' for this period of Irish history.[1]

If by some hideous mischance Patrick's writings had been lost and we had to rely solely on the mediaeval *Lives*, annals, and so forth, we

---

1 Macalister, *Ancient Ireland*, p. 176. Patrick's alleged connexion with Auxerre and Lérins was destroyed by Binchy, 'Patrick and His Biographers', pp. 80−90.

should know more about him, I suppose, than we know about Agamemnon, king of Mycenae, but not much more; and it is not out of the question that if we had to rely wholly on the mediaeval *Lives* — and John Gwynn described part of the best one among them as 'a very phantasmogoria of miracle' — we should wonder whether Patrick had ever really lived or whether he was not one of those betwixt-and-between figures like King Arthur and Hamlet and Robin Hood, who may or may not have lived but who seem to be beyond the reach of historians. The *Life* by Muirchu contains some grains of truth taken from the *Confession*; but if the *Confession* had been lost to us, is it certain that we should have been able to recognise these grains for what they are? Should we have been able to dig them out from the mountain of miracle and other claptrap in which Muirchu has buried them? It would have been hard work.[2]

Patrick was almost completely unknown on the Continent in his lifetime and for centuries after it. That the Church had won successes in Ireland seems to have been news for a moment in the fifth century, but only for a moment. In the second half of the century the Western Roman Empire crashed in one of the greatest convulsions of history, and men had other things to think about than the conversion to Christianity of some of the remotest barbarians known to the geography books. No European mentions Patrick by name until early in the eighth century, and indeed no manuscript of his writings reached the Continent until late in the eighth century or early in the ninth.[3]

A more surprising fact is that he was almost completely forgotten in Ireland itself. True, his name was remembered with a dim, uncomprehending veneration, and somehow or other, somewhere or other, a manuscript of his writings escaped destruction. A copy was made of the manuscript somewhat before 630 — the date is very doubtful; but by that time every fact about him which was not contained in his books had already been forgotten. After those who had known him personally died off one by one, no traditions about him were preserved. There were his writings (which in the early years nobody seems to have read), and there was nothing else. The inference is, I think, that in his own lifetime and for many years after it men did not recognise his significance. If they had done so, there would have been stories worth the telling and re-telling, and anecdotes which would illustrate his greatness. But in fact there were none, and soon it was

2 John Gwynn, *Liber Ardmachanus*, p. XXXIX.
3 Grosjean, 'Notes 7', p. 173; Bieler, *Libri Epistolarum*, I. p. 18.

too late: those who had known him and could have told were silent for ever. I have said that it was surprising that men should have forgotten him, but when we come to look at the facts, we shall see that it is not very surprising after all.[4]

Our attempt to understand Patrick is not made easier by his extraordinary use of the Latin language. Almost alone among the famous authors of the Roman Empire he writes more or less as he spoke. He writes something like colloquial Latin, spoken Latin. But even writing this kind of Latin did not come easily to him. Although he had been educated up to the age of sixteen, he writes laboriously. In spite of all his efforts, he often cannot make his meaning clear. When the late Dr Bieler wrote that Patrick 'is never very anxious to give us a lucid exposition of facts', he is saying what is almost as far from the truth as it would be possible for a literary critic to reach. Patrick struggles unceasingly, painfully, even agonisingly, to explain his point of view to his readers. But often the task is beyond him, and he fails. And since he often assumes his readers to know the situation in which he was writing, the room for disagreement and dispute about the meaning of his words is wide, all too very wide.[5]

But nothing can outweigh the fact that we have his own authentic and personal writings, his very own words, his very own thoughts. With the help of the information which he gives us we can state many of the problems. Some we cannot answer; some we can. Some we can almost answer — almost, but not quite. The complete answer is sometimes just out of our reach, just round the corner where we cannot quite see it. But in 1905 J. B. Bury of Co Monaghan published his epoch-making biography of Patrick and for the first time applied modern methods to the study of Patrick. And in 1962 D. A. Binchy brought out a spectacularly brilliant paper about him, showing that all the secondary works throw no light whatever on Patrick. As a result of these two works the right questions can more and more be formulated, and the search for the right answers is more and more rewarding.

---

4 Bieler, op. cit., I. pp. 27−9. See p. 88f. below.
5 Bieler, *The Life and Legend*, p. 65.

CHAPTER ONE

Birth and Family

Here is a translation of the first paragraph of the *Confession*:

> I, Patrick, a most uneducated sinner and the least of all the faithful and the most contemptible in the eyes of many, am the son of Calpurnius, a deacon, son of Potitus, a priest, who was from the village of Bannaventa Burniae [or Bannavem Taburniae, or the like], for he had an estate near it, where I was taken captive. At that time I was about sixteen years of age. I did not know the true God, and I was carried away to captivity in Ireland with so many thousands of persons — as we deserved, because we departed away from God and did not keep his commandments and were not obedient to our bishops, who used to remind us of our salvation. And the Lord brought upon us the fury of his anger and scattered us among many nations as far as the end of the earth, where now my insignificant self lives among foreigners.

1. — *Enslavement*

That seems to be a straightforward and candid opening. There are several Biblical references and echoes in it. This sort of self-disparagement is a convention in many other writers of the time, but not here. Patrick's words go beyond what convention required. He is acutely aware throughout the *Confession* of what he thought was his inadequate education, inadequate when compared with the education which others of his age and class had enjoyed. This is a matter to which he returns again and again in the *Confession*, so much so that we shall have to examine it later on.

We must not blame Patrick for beginning his little book by saying in effect, 'I, Patrick, the least of all the faithful, am a well-to-do landowner's son,' etc. He is not at all boasting of his descent. He is simply telling us who he is. He is identifying himself. He is writing the title-page, as it were, of his book. He is far from boasting of his social position, and indeed his readers would take it for granted that a bishop, or anyone who could write a book in the fifth century and circulate it, was likely to be a man of some means and leisure. There was no need for him to labour that point.[1]

But this apparently candid and limpid opening is not so simple to understand as it may seem (quite apart from the problems connected with the place-name). In fact, this seemingly innocent opening passage is one of the less reliable parts of the *Confession*. Patrick was on his father's estate outside Bannaventa, he says, when Irish raiders caught him and 'thousands' of others, and shipped them across the Irish Sea into slavery. (It would seem that his parents and relatives were not caught: they may well have been in the neighbouring town at the time of the raid, and there the town walls would protect them.) But Patrick goes on to say that the prisoners all deserved their fate because they had departed away from God and did not heed their bishops. Now, this generalisation, in which Patrick condemns the impiety of the 'thousands' who were carried off with him, is rash and doubtless inaccurate. He ascribes his own shortcomings (or what he afterwards came to think were shortcomings) to thousands of other people whose beliefs and attitudes he cannot possibly have known anything about. He cannot have been acquainted with more than a tiny minority of the thousands who were shipped away. And at the time of the calamity he was aged sixteen and, as he admits, was indifferent to religion. How then could he have come to this conclusion at this date about his fellow-sufferers' disgraceful impiety? In fact, of course, we do not know what he thought of them at the time of his capture. We have only his opinion as he looked back across half a century of time. But it is even harder to see how he could have had evidence about the prisoners' religion or lack of it at the time when he was writing. Even as a bishop years afterwards, travelling this way

---

1 For the view that Patrick is boasting of his social position see (if you think that life is long enough) a fantastic passage of Zimmer, *The Celtic Church*, p. 39.

and that in Ireland, he could not possibly have met with more than a tiny handful of these unfortunates, if indeed he met with any of them. They had been dispersed to different owners as soon as they reached the Irish slave-markets long ago. Doubtless by the time when he returned as bishop many of them, perhaps all of them, were dead, the expectation of life being short in the ancient world for freemen, shorter still for slaves. Some of the raiders' victims were slaves even before they were carried off — for example, the slaves of his own father Calpurnius, and these he is not known ever to have tried to find. (The word which he uses to describe what the raiders did to the household slaves has been taken to mean that they massacred many of them, and that is probably right.) Did these slaves deserve to be kidnapped for their irreligion? Whose fault was it if these men and women slaves were less than enthusiastic Christians at the time of the raid? What kind of example had their owners set them? In Patrick's household the householder and his son set them an example of a non-Christian life. So when Patrick invites us to think that those whom the Irish raiders carried off deserved their fate, we shall hesitate to follow him. He is an inexperienced writer, and in this case he generalises too readily.[2]

But our difficulties do not end there. Patrick describes those 'thousands' who were forced away across the sea as though they were all Christians — not very devout Christians, to be sure, but Christians all the same, nominal Christians, 'We had departed away from God', he says of them all in general. He does not say that 'some of us' had departed away from God: we all had done so. Now, this is not a phrase which he would use of pagans who had never been associated with the Christian God and so could not be said to have departed away from him. The criticism that the victims of the raiders had not been obedient to the bishops is also one which he would not level against pagans: no one would expect pagans to be obedient to Christian bishops as such. But is it likely that all or most of the prisoners were Christians? No: if it were so, we should be presented with something of a problem. In the years immediately after 400 there appear to have been a considerable number of Christians among the city-dwellers and the villa-owners throughout the Western Roman provinces, but that was not true of the countryfolk in general. That is to say, Christianity (in so far as it existed) was an urban, and in the countryside an upper-class, phenomenon, the

2 Epistle, §10 (256. 10), *deuastauerunt*.

religion of the landowners, in the last years of Roman Britain and in the following decades; and we should expect that those who were toiling in the fields were still pagan almost to a man. But the sort of person whom the Irish raiders are most likely to have rounded up and driven away to their ships are those found working in the fields and going about their business in the unfortified villages. The townsmen hearing of the approach of barbarian raiders would shut their town gates, and the town walls would protect them, for Western barbarians were notoriously bad at siege warfare. But the countryfolk had no defence except flight, and if the raiders had penetrated inland from their ships without being spotted and could take them by surprise, the possibility of flight was gone. So it was essentially a pagan part of the population which was likely to end up in the Irish ships and to be sold miserably in the Irish slave-markets.

How then does Patrick come to suggest that the bulk of the captives were Christian? In fact, the phrase in which he says that 'we departed away from God' is an echo of Isaiah, lix. 13; and we might be tempted to think that perhaps he hastily chose to quote a verse of the prophet which did not exactly suit his context. But I doubt if his Scriptural quotations were as carelessly chosen as that would imply. And he is certainly not quoting any prophet when he says that they were carried off 'according to their deserts' and that 'we were not obedient to our bishops'. It is hard to resist the impression that he has misrepresented or misunderstood — or rather (let us say) that he has forgotten — the true situation here and that he has justified the enslavement of these people — they deserved their fate, he says — when in fact they did not deserve it at all. By his own standards after his conversion, it was he himself who deserved it: he himself had been irreligious, and he is generalising from his own case. The fact is that Patrick seems to have distorted the truth here. He has done so carelessly, perhaps, and unthinkingly: he is certainly not trying consciously to mislead us. He is guilty of one of those facile generalisations to which sermon-preachers are prone (how often have we been assured that 'We are all miserable sinners'?). But there is no reason to think that the Irish raiders' victims were all of them sinners, whether miserable or hilarious.

According to Patrick, the prisoners had not been obedient to their bishops. Does it follow that the raiders had carried off people from a number of different bishoprics? If he was referring only to a single bishopric, that in which Bannaventa lay, would he not have said that 'we were not obedient to the bishop' rather than 'to the bishops'? The point is a small one, and perhaps it would be a mistake to draw too many inferences from it.[3]

But even if the raid was a big one, there is yet a further problem. When Patrick says that he was carried off to Ireland 'with so many thousands of persons', we must again hesitate to believe him, or at the very least we shall keep an open mind. Little is known about Irish ships and their capacity at this date; but it would hardly be fanciful to suppose that if the raiders really carried off 'so many thousands of persons', they must have left Britain in a fleet which was smaller, but not very much smaller, than the fleet which sailed with Agamemnon on the voyage to Troy! But that is not the point. The point is that Patrick could not possibly have known even approximately how many Britons had been carried away, especially if they had been taken from several dioceses and several city-states. He would have had other things to worry about than the difficulty of estimating the number of the enslaved. And the raiders would hardly feel themselves called upon to hand out exact statistical information to their prisoners. Indeed, it is not likely that even for their own purposes they ever grossed up the total of the day's takings. Each crew would know how many prisoners they had themselves shipped home, and perhaps how many their closest neighbours had caught. But would they have troubled to tot up the over-all catch of the entire fleet of independent pirate ships? We must bear in mind, then, that when Patrick uses the word 'thousands' he means no more than we mean when we use the word 'crowds' or even 'hundreds', which need not mean more than a few score or even a few dozen. But no doubt hundreds of Britons entered into slavery on that fateful day.

In a number of ways, then, we can find fault with Patrick's apparently clear and simple description of the Irish slave-raid which brought about such a catastrophic change in his life. He says quite without justification that the victims of the raiders deserved their fate, when in fact there were no reasons for condemning them so harshly. He describes the enslaved Britons as in general Christians, when the vast majority of them are likely to have been pagans. He gives their numbers as amounting to 'thousands', which may have been right or may have been wrong but which he could not possibly have known to be right. This is a generous number of mistakes to find in so few lines of the printed text.

3   For the meaning of *sacerdos* at this date see Hanson, *St Patrick : His Origins*, pp. 33f.; but Bieler, 'St Patrick and the British Church', p. 129 n. 5, holds that the word *may* mean 'priest', and in that case the argument falls to the ground.

But if we try to imagine what happened it is easy enough to visualise how some (though not all) of his mistakes arose. Imagine Patrick and the family household slaves going about their normal business in his father's comfortable house during what appeared to be a normal comfortable day. Suddenly the hideous Irish raiders burst in, overpower all the occupants, kill some of them (doubtless the adult males in particular), secure the women and children, loot the house, and drive the frightened survivors roughly to their boats. Although Patrick reports the fate of the household slaves, he does not mention what happened to the field-workers when the raiders came: he may not have known their fate at the time. All the captives alike would be stunned by the horror and brutality of what was happening to them. At the boats Patrick would see all along the beach lines of other prisoners from other estates being loaded on to the other pirates' vessels, and soon would begin the horrifying journey across the open sea, the prisoners packed tightly on the bottom of the tossing curachs. The only persons apart from his captors with whom he had any contact would be his own household slaves (in so far as they had survived) when they were being driven from the villa to the shore and loaded into the boats like himself. If we may suppose that the slaves of the household were Christians, at any rate in name, he could easily take away in his mind the impression that the throngs of prisoners whom he had glimpsed with stunned eyes on the beach amounted to 'thousands' and were Christians like the people immediately around him. After all, in the *Confession* he is recollecting the happenings of that day of pandemonium and panic after an interval of some fifty years.

I have called the Irish raiders 'hideous'. According to the British author Gildas, writing in the early sixth century, the Irish raiders who so often vexed Britain in the first half of the fifth century made an unprepossessing sight, not at all to the taste of their victims. Carried across the sea in their curachs they were like 'dark squadrons of maggots <emerging> from their narrow slits in the ground as the heat of the sun grows warm.' (The British are not always flattering when they try to describe the Irish.) The Irish resembled the Pictish raiders (who were also harrying Britain at this date) in that they covered their faces with bushy beards, as Gildas goes on to say, but exposed their private parts and the surrounding regions of their bodies naked to the shocked eyes of the Britons. A Greek historian of the second century B.C. remarks that a Celtic army went into battle naked for the sake of efficiency: some of the ground about them was overgrown with brambles, and otherwise these might catch in their clothes and impede the use of their weapons. (One might think that if parts of their naked bodies were caught in the brambles, their efficiency would be even further reduced.) In the year 297 a Gallic orator had described Irish raiders as 'semi-nude'. Let us hope that it was moderates such as these who captured Patrick rather than the extremists of whom Gildas speaks. Patrick as a civilised Briton would certainly have thought the latter to be underdressed, but in fact he is too refined even to mention such an indelicacy.[4]

2. — Family

Before Patrick was carried off by the Irish slave-raiders he was not greatly troubled by religion. True, he came of a clerical family. His father Calpurnius was a deacon of the Church, and his grandfather Potitus was a priest. They were both evidently married. Yet the popes at this time, not least Pope Siricius (385—90), and some of the Councils of the Church were insisting on the celibacy of the clergy. They were supported by such ecclesiastical titans as St Ambrose, St Jerome, and St Augustine. The popes and councils and titans were aware, of course, that a married clergy existed and was indeed the norm. There was nothing unusual or exceptional in a married cleric. What the popes and councils aimed at was to change this situation. But celibacy fought a losing battle against Calpurnius and Potitus and countless others. In Britain and afterwards in Ireland for several generations the clergy found that the appeal of celibacy was by no means irresistible. Nor did the deacon Calpurnius or the priest Potitus carry their general religious fervour to such lengths as to hand it on to Patrick. Until he was sixteen years of age he turned aside from God, he tells us, did not keep the commandments, and did not obey the bishops. When he was fifteen, that is, on the eve of his capture by the pirates, 'I did not believe in the living God, no, not from my infancy, but I remained in death and unbelief'. So the first British clergyman's household known to us included a wholly irreligious son.[5]

---

4 Polybius, *History*, II. 28, 8 (ed. and transl. Paton, I, p. 310); Gildas, *De Excidio*, §19 (ed. and transl. Winterbottom, p. 94); *Panegyrici Latini*, iv (viii). 11, 4 (ed. and French transl. Galletier, I, 91).
5 *Confession*, §1 (235. 4), §27 (244. 4). For celibacy in the earliest Irish Church see Hughes, *The Church*, pp. 51—3.

But perhaps the attitude of the father and grandfather was even more deplorable than their rejection of celibacy might suggest. The father Calpurnius was a town-councillor in the local town; and since this office tended to be hereditary, Potitus was probably one, too. Now, when Constantine the Great was converted to Christianity early in the fourth century, he decided in the first rash outburst of enthusiasm for his new religion to exempt the Christian clergy from the duties of the city councils, which were heavy and could be expensive. His aim was that this exemption should leave the well-to-do clergy free to give their full attention to the service of God. (I say 'well-to-do clergy', but in fact A. H. M. Jones tells us that the great majority of the clergy were drawn from the class of city-councillors.) What actually happened, however, was not exactly what Constantine had in mind: there was an instant rush of city-councillors and their families into holy orders, not so as to give their undivided attention to God but so as to avoid the financial risks and charges of the councils. The law had to be modified again and again over the next two centuries and more, in order to balance the interests of the city councils and those of the clergy. Thus, in 364 the emperors of the day enacted that a city-councillor who took orders must make over his property to his sons or relatives. This would put his religious convictions to the test, for the emperors had some doubts about the sincerity of many of the new swarm of ordinands; and if Calpurnius's religion was of the same luke-warm quality as his young son's, the emperors' doubts were not altogether misplaced in his case. Patrick makes no comment on the matter. He certainly does not mention that his father had made over the family property to him. Indeed, it is clear from what he says that his father did nothing of the sort: the family country house continued to be owned by the father, not by himself. It may be, then, that Calpurnius's religious reasons for holding office in the Church (if he had religious reasons) were reinforced by more earthly ones. Be that as it may, Patrick's references to his parents and relatives are uniformly affectionate.[6]

It was one of the duties of the councillors to collect the amount of the taxes which the central government demanded from their localities. If they collected less than the government had demanded, the law compelled them to make up the deficit out of their own pockets. It is hardly surprising that they did their utmost to make sure that there would be no deficit. They exacted the sums due to the government so

---

6 *Epistle*, §10 (256. 12), §27 (244. 4); cf. Jones, *The Later Roman Empire*, II, p. 925.

ruthlessly that, according to a priest of Marseilles writing in the 440s, 'there are as many tyrants as there are town-councillors'. We have no reason to think that the British 'exactors' (as the officials who actually went round and collected the revenues were aptly named) were more kindly or more soft-hearted than those of Gaul or that Calpurnius's behaviour was a good-natured exception to the general rule. At any rate, Patrick makes no claim that it was. But the power of Imperial Rome collapsed in Britain in the year 409 and was never restored there. We do not know for how long the city-councils survived after the collapse. Presumably the councillors continued to collect the taxes not in order to forward them to the appropriate authorities, who no longer existed so far as they were concerned, but so as to pocket the revenues themselves. The opportunity must have seemed far too good to throw away. So when Patrick says that his father was a town councillor, he is not necessarily referring to the years before 409. The city councils may well have lingered on, at any rate in some parts of the country, for years after that date. The fact of his father's being a councillor gives us no help with the insoluble problem of Patrick's chronology. What it does teach us is that Patrick was anything but a man of the people. He was a member of a narrow class of landowners, useful to their superiors but cruelly oppressive to those below them.[7]

3. — Birth

No one has ever been able to identify the town where Calpurnius acted as a councillor. Its site was a matter of discussion and conjecture among Irish scholars even before the year 700. Near it lay a village which Patrick appears to say was called Bannaventa Burniae (or the like). His words are not quite clear, but if Bannaventa Burniae is a *village* name, we have little hope of ever being able to identify it, for Romano-British village names which can be located on the map are few and far between. When Patrick says that his father or grandfather was 'from' the village, he may mean no more than that he was a resident in the country house which he owned outside the village. And this village was administered from the town where Calpurnius acted as councillor.

---

7 Salvian, *De Gubernatione Dei*, V.18 (ed. Halm, p.. 107).

We know and can identify dozens of Romano-British place-names other than those of villages, and it is exasperating that when Patrick explicitly records this one, we cannot locate it. One possible explanation — and 'possible' may be too optimistic a word — is that the place is identical with the Bannaventa named in one of the Itineraries. (These Itineraries are lists of the stations on some of the great Roman roads: they are a sort of skeleton road-map.) A Bannaventa appears on Watling Street, and more than one of the routes from London passed through it. A traveller on the main road from London to Chester or to Lincoln or to York had to make its acquaintance. It must therefore have been fairly well known to travellers. It was situated at Whilton Lodge outside Daventry in Northamptonshire. The main objection to identifying it with Patrick's Bannaventa is that it lies far to the east of the likely range of Irish pirates. It is true that when a Roman army of reinforcements from the Continent landed at Richborough in Kent in the crisis year of 368 and marched to London, it encountered Pictish raiders along its line of march; and these Picts had come down from north of the Firth of Forth. But these Pictish raiders had doubtless come down the east coast of Britain by sea, and they were not at all so far from their ships as Irish raiders would have been if they had penetrated to Whilton Lodge from, say, the Bristol Channel. The Irish pirates' journey overland from their ships in the Bristol Channel (or wherever they may have left them) would have been long and therefore dangerous. Their ships, too, would have been open to attack when they were so far inland. And why go such a distance into the interior when there were plenty of rich villas and villages nearer the western coast? So scholars have turned away from Whilton Lodge and have put forward guesses about the situation of Bannaventa ranging from the unlikely neighbourhood of Carlisle and Hadrian's Wall to the rich lands in the vicinity of the Bristol Channel. Some of the wilder spirits have actually claimed that Patrick was an Italian or a Spaniard or even a Scotsman! (The most distinguished subscriber to that last school is Tobias Smollett, and he, though something of an historian, is better known for writing coarse and lively fiction than for expertise in Roman history.) In mediaeval times there were those who thought that Patrick was a Jew from Armorica, but these have found few followers. We can be sure only that Patrick was a Briton, probably from the west country. More than this we cannot say.[8]

8 For a review of the problem of Bannaventa see Hanson, *St Patrick : His Origins*, pp. 113–6, and Thomas, *Christianity*, pp. 310–4. I am sceptical of Carlisle and the

The importance of identifying the site of Bannaventa could be exaggerated. To record a man's birthplace in the western Roman Empire would convey relatively little information to readers. If we say today that three persons were born respectively in York, Lyons, and Milan, we tell an enormous amount about them. We tell their language, probably their religion (if any), and in some degree their upbringing, education, and outlook as well as the fact that one would describe himself proudly as an Englishman, another as a Frenchman, the third as an Italian, and so on. (I say nothing of the vulgar belief that there is such a thing as a 'national character'.) But if we say that three persons came respectively from Eboracum, Lugudunum, and Mediolanum, we tell very much less. We imply simply that, like practically everybody else born in a Western Roman city, they all alike spoke Latin, were of much the same religion and education (if any), read the same books if they read any books at all, and we imply little in the way of patriotism. When we use the modern place-names we stress the differences between the three. When we use the Roman place-names we stress the similarities between them. West Roman cultural and material life hardly varied from one region to another (apart from the fact, admittedly an important fact, that in the south men cultivated vines and olives and in the north they did not). An outstanding characteristic of Roman life all over western Europe was its uniformity.

Now, St Patrick does not say that he was born in Bannaventa Burniae (or Berniae or whatever the correct form may have been); but it is usually thought — I do not know why — that that was his birthplace. Whether it was or was not does not affect our opinion of him: his education and outlook would have been much the same if he had been in Gloucester or London or Cirencester or any other of the Romano-British cities. But if a Western Roman's precise birthplace was a matter of indifference to readers, why does Patrick mention Bannaventa at all? He gives no hint that he had been born there. His purpose is simply to let us know where he was when disaster struck him down. But does it let us know even that? What is gained by naming so obscure a place? What Roman reader of Patrick would

---

neighbourhood of Hadrian's Wall as the site of the place because slave-raiders are unlikely to have launched a major raid under the very noses of the garrison troops, when so many undefended places were available elsewhere. And even if there were no longer any garrison troops there at the relevant time, the raiders would know that the empty forts could be used as impregnable places of refuge by the natives. Patrick as an Armorican Jew: Bieler, *Four Latin Lives*, p. 50. For Smollett's opinion see *Humphrey Clinker*, Letter of 28 August. For other fantastic guesses see the collection in Bieler, 'Patrician Studies', p. 360 n. 4.

know where Bannaventa lay? None of his Irish converts would ever have heard of the place. We could understand his procedure better if he had added that the place was situated near Chester or Gloucester or some other great centre well known in the British Isles. But he gives no such information. What was his reason, then, for telling his readers that his father owned an estate, and that he himself had been kidnapped, in a place which, we may guess, not one of them in a hundred, Irish and perhaps British, had ever heard of? (Incidentally, I do not wish to imply by that phrase that Patrick had so many as a hundred readers in his own day.) It is as if a modern writer, without comment or explanation, were to inform the world at large that his father had a country house at Cappoquin or Mullinavat — or indeed at Whilton Lodge — and that he was kidnapped there. Where are Cappoquin or Mullinavat? Where is Bannaventa? Without a word or two of explanation the names are meaningless. The passage in which Patrick mentions Bannaventa by name does not even suggest that the place lay in Britain! In fact, it *was* in Britain. We can infer that with certainty from later passages in the *Confession*, but we do not learn it and could not infer it from the passage which gives us the place-name. We must conclude that the all but meaningless reference to Bannaventa is simply an example of Patrick's lack of experience and skill as a writer. At all events, there are not one but two problems connected with the name of the saint's birthplace (if it *was* his birth-place): where did Bannaventa lie? And what was the point of mentioning so obscure a place-name without giving readers any indication of where the place was to be found?[9]

The date of a holy man's birth was of even less interest to fifth-century readers than his place of birth; and we would rummage for a long time through the fifth-century *Lives* of the saints and through the secular chronicles without finding a single date of birth, whether of a bishop or of a politician or of an army-commander, of a holy man or of an unholy man. Patrick's birth-date is unknown, the day of the year as well as the year itself. We do not even know whether he was born in the fourth century or in the fifth. The ancient attitude on this matter is not hard to understand. It is important to know that W. B. Yeats was alive and writing poetry in 1916 — 'A terrible beauty is born', etc. — but it is decidedly less important to know that

9 That Bannaventa lay in Britain is clear from *Confession*, §23 (242. 12), §43 (248. 24). Long ago the suggestion was made that the mysterious *Burniae* or *Berniae* is a corruption of *Britanniae*, but no one has accepted it. For understandable reasons no one has accepted the bizarre suggestion that it is a corruption of <*Hi*>*berniae*, reported by Haverfield, 'English Topographical Notes', p. 711.

he was born in 1865. Would our estimate of Julius Caesar's career be significantly changed if we knew the year of his birth? Would our admiration for the sublime poetry of the *Iliad* intensify or evaporate if we knew where, when, or even *whether* Homer was born?

So an ancient reader would have been interested to know that Patrick (if he had ever heard of him) was a Briton. He would hardly have been interested to know in addition the name of the actual town in which he had been born. Perhaps we should regard the name Bannaventa as something of a windfall, a piece of gratuitous information which in fact tells us nothing at all.

4. — His Boyhood Sin

Besides his enslavement another event took place during Patrick's boyhood which reverberated throughout the rest of his life; but its nature is wholly unknown. Here is a translation of the main passage in which he speaks of it: when he had become deacon 'because of anxiety, in a sad mood, I made known to my closest friend things which I had done in my boyhood one day, or rather in a single hour, because I had no strength yet. I do not know (God knows) if I was fifteen years of age at the time, and I did not believe in the living God and had not done so from my infancy, but I remained in death and in unbelief until I was severely punished and in truth was humiliated by hunger and nakedness, and that every day'.[10]

The thing which he did that day worried him even when he was writing the *Confession* perhaps as much as fifty years after he had done it. We cannot even begin to guess what this sin was. The way in which he refers to it could apply to falsehood, dishonesty, violence as well as what John Gwynn terms 'impurity'. But impurity — let us call it 'sex' — is almost (though not quite) as remote as humour from the words and thoughts of St Patrick. It was evidently the sort of sin which would debar, or which could be used to debar, a man from being appointed as bishop later on in his life. Of its nature he gives no hint whatever. In the end, in circumstances which he deeply deplored, it became widely known, all too widely known, to his contemporaries, but not to us. We know nothing of it. Macalister writes with Presbyterian warmth — he was organist in a Presbyterian

10 *Confession*, §27 (244. 2). He refers to the sin also *ibid.*, §32 (245. 5).

chapel in Dublin for many years: 'What it may have been we do not know, have no right to know, and should not wish to know'! But even Macalister would probably allow us to point out that Patrick nowhere shows the slightest inclination to belittle the sin in question or to pooh-pooh it. He never tries to defend himself on this score. He never claims that reports of it had been exaggerated or that its colours had been heightened. He never hints that it was a minor slip, a mere peccadillo. It was clearly a very serious sin indeed by the standards of earnest Christians, or at any rate of earnest clergy, at that time. It weighed on Patrick's mind; and when he returned to Britain after six years of slavery in Ireland and some further years (it seems) of labour in Gaul, it was still in the front of his thoughts. He then told his closest friend about it, perhaps as much as ten years after he had committed it. It was clearly a matter of urgent importance even when the possibility of his being made a bishop, if it had been mentioned to him, would have seemed utterly incredible, even grotesque. When Patrick writes that those who sat in judgement on him later on counted 'my sins against my episcopate', he is telling us that the sin (to which he returns on two further occasions) was the decisive reason for his being criticised on that occasion. It is clear that this sin had been no merry prank such as robbing his neighbour's orchard of its apples. It was something very much more grim. All that Patrick can do when writing about it is to stress his youth and inexperience at the time when he so lamentably committed it.[11]

So the saint began his life comfortably as the son of a member of the oppressive gentry, a boy whose father owned land, houses, and slaves. By the standards of his locality Patrick as a lad was well fed and well heeled. His father was a married deacon, his grandfather a married priest. Neither deacon nor priest was much troubled by the increasing volume of the appeals for celibacy among the clergy uttered half way across the world by the pope in distant Italy. And neither father nor grandfather injected much religion into Patrick. The boy led an easy and irreligious life which later on he deplored. But we must not overstate his attitude towards his boyhood. To say that he afterwards looked back on his early life with 'bitter remorse' shows a misunderstanding of his character. He could display regret and anger, but he is never bitter. In normal circumstances the boy could have looked forward to receiving a higher education at the

---

11 Macalister, *Ancient Ireland*, p. 173; John Gwynn, *Liber Ardmachanus*, p. lxxxiv n. 5. I cannot imagine why Thomas, *Christianity*, p. 332, gravely suggests that Patrick may have stolen some Church candles!

school of the nearest professor or 'rhetor'. But as it turned out, a higher education never came his way, and this misfortune — a social loss, as we shall see, as well as an educational one — he never ceased to regret. Indeed, if it had not been for those Irish raiders who sold him off to Co Mayo when he was still irreligious and still unfamiliar with the Latin Bible, we should probably never have heard of this rich, young, perhaps idle youth. There must have been scores of such lads in Britain at this time, but he is the only one of whom we hear. No one could have guessed that one day his name would be more widely known throughout the world than the names of Jerome and Augustine and even Constantine the Great himself.[12]

12 The quotation is from Bieler, 'St Patrick and the British Church', p. 129.

CHAPTER TWO

Slavery and Escape

So Irish marauders carried Patrick off forcibly from his home — or one of his homes — in Britain when he was sixteen years of age. In Ireland they sold him and their other prisoners as slaves to different purchasers, and the prisoners were transported as far from Britain as possible: in this way their chances of escape were reduced.

1. — A Slave in Ireland

Patrick himself was sold to a slave-owner who lived in what is now Co Mayo 'near the Wood of Voclut' (his second place-name with Bannaventa, and his only Irish place-name). This name is commonly thought to survive in the modern Foghill (Fochoill). The place lies in the extreme north-east of the county near Killala on the borders of Co Sligo. Here he was put to work as a shepherd in woods and on a mountain in a remote part of the countryside. There is no indication that he suffered the barbaric cruelties which are the normal lot of slaves. But unfortunately he tells us nothing about the man who had bought him or about the life which his owner led. He laboured for him for six years, and it was during these lonely years that he became a Christian in more than name. Like many another anguished soul *in extremis*, he turned to heaven as a last resort. There was no other direction in which he could turn. Here is how he describes his conversion:

And there the Lord opened my perception of my heart's unbelief so that I remembered my sins even though late, and turned with all my heart to the Lord my God who had regard to my humiliation and pitied my youth and ignorance and guarded me before I knew him and before I had wisdom and distinguished between good and bad and fortified me and consoled me as a father his son.[1]

Patrick says that in his opinion it was due to the fact that he had 'sought and found' God that he had been saved from all maltreatment, and he has no ill to say of his owner (though in fact it is not his way to speak ill of any individual). Although he refers to II Corinthians, xi. 27 'hunger and nakedness', he says that his chief recollection was of suffering from exposure to the elements — snow, frost, rain — but that he felt no other hardship. It may be that he suffered more from neglect than from his owner's whip. He showed some energy in his work. He laboured without indolence or laziness, he says, 'as I now see, because the spirit then was aglow within me.' Indeed, he goes so far as to express thanks for the great kindnesses which God bestowed on him 'in the land of my captivity'. That is to say, he appears to have been something of an Uncle Tom — an abjectly religious and obedient, submissive slave, whose owner in the novel rewarded him by beating him brutally to death, though happily for himself Patrick's master was no Simon Legree, and he did not meet the tear-jerking fate of Uncle Tom. Perhaps he remembered Ephesians, vi. 5 — 7, where slaves are given (by a freeman, perhaps a slave-owner) the numbing advice to obey their masters, 'with fear and trembling'. At all events, it is not often that we hear from the ancient world the voice of an ex-slave speaking of his slavery. We may doubt whether Patrick's unprotesting comments and his attitude of acceptance and submission were typical of what slaves in general thought.[2]

At any rate, in a single day he would say up to a hundred prayers and almost as many at night. He was awake before dawn, whatever the weather, in order to pray. His love of God grew more and more profound, and his fear of him, and his faith.[3]

But his attitude towards slavery as an institution was not affected

---

1 *Confession*, §2 (235.14); Voclut, *ibid.*, §23 (242.21); shepherd, *ibid.*, §16 (239.14); saved from hardship, *ibid.*, §3, §33 (*ibid.*, 236.4; 245.9); energy as a slave, *ibid.*, §16 (239.20). O'Rahilly, *The Two Patricks*, p. 61, thought the resemblance between Voclut and Foghill to be a coincidence.
2 *Confession*, §16 (239.17), §27 (244.6).
3 *Ibid.*, §16 (239.17).

by his experiences as a slave. He is one of the few extant authors of the ancient world who had first-hand knowledge of slavery in that he not only owned slaves but had himself worked and suffered as one. Later on, when he was a bishop, converted slave-women were terror-ised and threatened by their owners, a fact which he deplored. He was furiously angry with the followers of Coroticus who kidnapped newly baptised Christians and sold them to pagan and apostate slave-owners. But it is not at all clear that he would have been equally enraged if those who were kidnapped and sold had been pagans. What seems to anger him is that it was Christians who had suffered so brutally. He does not express anger at kidnapping and murder in themselves. Would he have been so angry at the terrorising of the slave-women if they had not been converted? He never once hints that slavery is a vile, degrading, and inefficient institution. The idea that the structure of society could be changed so as to abolish slavery does not occur to him. He twice refers to his own enslave-ment as an 'humiliation'; but he does not say that his father's slaves suffered any humiliation. Evidently there was no humiliation in being a slave in the villa outside Bannaventa. That is to say, he is like every other Christian writer of the ancient world in this respect. Without exception they raise no question about the abolition of slavery.[4]

But after six years his slavery came to an end.

2. — *The Escape to the Sea*

The account of how he managed to escape from slavery in Ireland is Patrick's longest piece of continuous narrative, and I translate it in full. Vivid and valuable though the story may be, how gladly we should exchange it for an equally long description of his life as a slave in western Ireland, or of the society which he saw around him when he was a slave there, or even of life at his home in Britain, or of his reasons for not trying to convert the countless pagans in Britain before sailing off to Ireland as bishop, and so on and on. But that, of course, is to wish that he was a different man and that he had written a different book in a different world. What we have here is a narra-tive — a long and yet an incomplete narrative — of how he escaped

4 *Ibid.*, §42 (248.20−22); *humilio, ibid.*, §12 (238.17), §27 (244.5). See the brilliant pages of de Ste. Croix, 'Early Christian Attitudes', pp. 15−24.

from slavery. Of course, the absence of place-names from the narrative of his escape needs no explanation. Patrick did not know the names of the Irish places through which he passed in his flight to the coast; and it would be unwise of a runaway slave to stop very often to ask the way — the way to where? How could he know? And why should he try to find out the name of such-and-such a river or lake or settlement? It would be just as hard to slip safely past it, no matter what its name might be. And even if he somehow found out the place-names, he would not have recorded them, since to the vast majority of his readers — let us say, to all of them — they would have been meaningless, a mere jumble of meaningless letters.

Here is what he says:[5]

One night I heard in my sleep a voice saying to me, 'You do well to fast, since you are soon about to go to your own country'; and again after a little while I heard a message telling me, 'Look, your ship is ready.' And it was not near, but there were about two hundred miles, and I had never been there, and I had no men there whom I knew. And then afterwards I turned to flight and left the man with whom I had been for six years, and I came in the strength of God who kept directing my journey towards good, and I feared nothing until I reached that ship.

And on that day on which I reached it the ship started from its place [i.e., probably, was dragged off the beach and set afloat] and I said that I had the means of subsistence wherewith to sail with them; and the captain, he disliked it and replied sharply and angrily, 'Don't you try to go with us.' And when I heard this I parted from them so as to go to the miserable hut where I was lodging, and on the road I began to pray, and before I finished the prayer I heard one of them and he was shouting out loudly behind me, 'Come quickly, because these men are calling you', and I returned at once and they began to say to me, 'Come because we are receiving you in good faith. Make friendship with us in whatever way you wish.' And on that day accordingly I refused to suck their nipples through fear of God. But nonetheless I hoped of them that they would come to faith in Jesus Christ because they were pagans — and so I won my way with them, and we sailed at once.

Before we follow him overseas let us pause for breath. What an extraordinary number of short sentences connected by 'and' after 'and'! It is the Latin of a man speaking rather than writing. It is hard

5   The following is a translation of *Confession*, §17−18 (239.22−240.17).

to think of anything like it in all the rest of Latin literature. If it was Patrick's ambition to compete with the writings of educated men, he had indeed good reason to blush! And what a peculiar and un-Roman phrase, 'to suck their nipples'! It appears to be a Celtic Irish expression meaning, 'to enter a formal appeal for protection and friendly consideration' or simply 'to swear friendship'. The practice was Irish and confirms what we should otherwise have assumed — that the ship was Irish and manned by a pagan Irish crew. It also confirms what we should *not* otherwise have assumed — that Patrick is writing this passage either for Irish readers or at any rate for readers who were in close touch with Irish customs, for he gives no word of explanation of that strange phrase.[6]

Almost at the end of the *Confession* he refers again to his escape from slavery and his journey across Ireland, and he remarks in a single monosyllable that he had escaped 'with difficulty': he 'scarcely' escaped. That is one reason why I said that this is an incomplete narrative. He gives no hint at the nature of the difficulties and dangers and hardships which he overcame on his flight, and indeed we may doubt whether such scenes of low life would have been of much interest to his readers. Ancient writers, Christian as well as pagan, do not often linger over the lives and sorrows of slaves: such subjects were of minimal interest. Presumably, for some at least of the way Patrick was pursued by his owner, though the fact that he had been working in the remote countryside with the flocks when he decided to run may well have meant that his disappearance was not noticed immediately, so that he may have had something of a start over his pursuers. As Carney says, 'travelling from Co Mayo . . . negotiating forest, bog, mountain, and river, undertaking unavoidable detours, and all the time using necessary fugitive caution, must have taken considerably more than a week.' True, but the view that Patrick spent 'years' wandering across Ireland is singularly improbable; and to think that he spent a few years in Ireland 'looking for the ship', suggests a certain vagueness, not to say a superhuman inefficiency, in the divine guidance. Once a slave decides to run, he cannot afford to stop from his flight for a single minute until he reaches a land where he can no longer be enslaved, if any such exists.[7]

How did Patrick find his way to a suitable port? It is wrong to

---

6 On this phrase see Ryan, 'A Difficult Phrase', pp. 293–9, and O'Brien, 'Miscellania Hibernica', p. 373.
7 *Confession*, §61 (253.9), *uix.* Carney, *The Problem*, p. 56; Powell, 'The Textual Integrity', 398f.

think that the voice in his dream *named* a port. How could he have recognised the name of any Irish port even if the divine voice had spelled one out to him letter by letter? But Patrick does not say that the voice named a port. Presumably, he had to set off into the unknown: but how he decided in which direction to run, we do not know. He says simply that God 'kept directing my journey towards good', which means in effect, I suppose, that good luck and good judgement led him to an appropriate harbour in the end. And how did he feed himself on that long journey of two hundred Roman miles? (A Roman mile was about 1,500 metres.) It would be optimistic to suppose that he got help and hospitality on many occasions. In a slave-owning society runaway slaves rarely meet with help and hospitality from freemen. Slaves are never cheap, and to help one to run away is to help rob his owner of a valuable piece of property and is likely to be mercilessly punished. And to think that a Christian freeman would be more likely than a pagan to help a runaway slave would be a howling mistake — to say nothing of the fact that Patrick is exceedingly unlikely to have come within miles of a Christian at that date. So far from asking the way or begging for help, the runaway's best course is to keep out of sight, to lie low in the daytime, and to travel by night only. There is only one way in which Patrick could have fed himself: he must have stolen food as he went his way, even if pious scholars think such a procedure to be impossible in any saint, above all in so holy a saint as British St Patrick! But in fact I do not know how anyone (other than a slave-owner) could describe as 'immoral' a slave's theft of food and other necessities to help him on his flight to freedom (unless he were to steal them from someone as hungry and helpless as himself). If that is 'immoral', then every runaway slave is immoral by virtue of running away, for by running away he has stolen from his owner a valuable piece of property, namely, one slave — himself. Patrick, then, had already robbed one slave-owner — the man who had owned himself — by the mere fact of running away and so depriving him of his property for which he had doubtless paid a fair market price. When Patrick writes in the passage translated above, 'I said that I had the means of subsistence wherewith to sail with them', he suggests that he had stolen enough food to enable him to lay up a small reserve, a little more than was necessary for his immediate support and for other needs on the overland journey, a reserve which would sustain him to the end of his voyage across the sea.[8]

8 Carney, *op. cit.*, p. 55, 'named a port'.

3. — The Voyage and the Desert

The saint goes on:

> And after three days we reached land and for twenty-eight days we made our way through a desert and they lacked food, and hunger prevailed over them, and one day the captain began to speak to me: 'What then, Christian? You say your god is great and all-powerful; then why are you not able to pray for us? For we are in danger from hunger. We shall hardly be able to see any men again.' I spoke to them boldly, 'With confidence and with all your heart be converted to the Lord my God because nothing is impossible for him, so that this day he may send food for you into your path until you are sated, for he has an abundance everywhere', and with God's help so it was done. Look, a herd of pigs appeared on the road before our eyes, and they killed many of them, and they stayed there for two nights and were refreshed and relieved by their meat, because many of them had fainted and were left half-dead by the roadside, and after this they gave the deepest thanks to God, and I was honoured in their eyes, and from this day they had food in plenty. They also found woodland honey, and they offered part of it to me, and one of them said, 'It is consecrated to the gods'. Thank God, I tasted none of it.'[9]

To say that discussion of this passage has been extensive would be a laughable understatement. Two relatively minor questions which we cannot even begin to answer are, What was the nature of the voyage, trade or piracy, for it was hardly a cross-Channel passenger service transporting Irishmen to the Empire in return for their fare (and Patrick seems to have been charged no fare)? Was this a regular or exceptional voyage? And secondly, why did the ill-mannered and surly captain navigate his ship towards a desert which was uninhabited? Seamen usually sail towards a port rather than towards an empty and desolate wilderness. The old view that the men were traders carrying a cargo of dogs, perhaps Irish wolf-hounds, for sale in the Roman provinces, has been exploded: it depended on a false reading of Patrick's manuscripts.[10]

But these are relative details. Far more basic is the question, At the end of the three-day voyage did they land in Britain or in Gaul? Above all, how was it possible to find anywhere in the Western

9 The translation is of *Confession*, §19 (240.18−241.13).
10 The view about the dogs was based on the false reading *canes*, 'dogs', for *carne*, 'flesh', in *Confession*, §19 (241.6): see Hanson and Blanc, *Saint Patrick*, p. 92 n. 1, but Bieler, 'Interpretationes Patricianae', pp. 5−7, retains the dogs.

Roman Empire a desert so vast that able-bodied men could march through it for twenty-eight days without meeting a single inhabitant? And why does Patrick tell us twice, as in fact he does, that this journey took twenty-eight days when he has given us no hint whatever at the time he took to escape from Co Mayo and reach the Irish port where he embarked? And why not mention the length of time involved in reaching home after he left the sailors? The fact is that he gives precise times when dealing with his journey with the sailors and no basis whatever for estimating any other time-lapse. Why?

Let us suppose first that the travellers landed in Gaul. The immediate question is whether an Irish ship of that period could have covered the distance — say, 270 miles — from the south-eastern tip of Ireland to the north-western tip of Brittany (as it was not yet called) in three days, even bearing in mind that it would cross that open and ferocious sea with no stop and no shelter? And would an ancient ship make a dash straight across the open ocean rather than hop from Ireland to Wales and on to Cornwall and further on to Brittany, so lengthening the time taken by the voyage considerably? This voyage would certainly be impossible for men crewing a boat propelled by oars only. No crew would or could row continuously, night and day, for three days without a break. But a modern student of Irish navigation in the early Middle Ages remarks that the curach of mediaeval times 'unlike the modern curach, was essentially a sailing vessel. The normal means of propulsion being the sail, it followed that the freeboard could be made greater than that of an oared vessel. A comparatively large crew and cargo could be carried . . . Such are the buoyancy and handiness of the <modern> vessel that it is said to be almost unsinkable so long as the courage and strength of the crew hold out. Centuries of sea-experience have bred a most marvellous skill.'[11]

We know that hide-covered ships propelled not only by oars but by a sail as well were available to the Irish long before Patrick's day. The most spectacular piece of archaeological evidence, dating from about the beginning of the Christian era, is the beaten gold model of a ship measuring $7\frac{1}{2}$" x 3" with nine benches for rowers, a mast, and two yards, found at Broighter in Co Derry. There was also a steering

11 Marcus, 'Irish Pioneers', pp. 356f., 359, and 93−100. It is a pity that Ionas, *Vita Columbani* I. 23 (Bruno Krusch, *Ionae Vitae Sanctorum Columbani, Vedastis, Iohannis* (Hannover and Leipzig 1905), pp. 205f.) does not specify the cargo on board the Irish merchantman which put in at Nantes in 610. Observe that O Raifeartaigh, 'St Patrick's Twenty-Eight Days', 405f., argues strongly against the ability of any Irish ship of the time to make the journey in the space of three days.

oar, and the full crew numbered at least nineteen men. And Gildas, writing in the early sixth century but referring to the raids of the Picts and Irish early in the fifth century, mentions both the oars and the sails of their curachs. Such a skin-covered sailing-ship could have travelled about ninety miles a day. And so, with a sail Patrick's ship could indeed have carried him 250−300 miles to Gaul from the south-east of Ireland in three days. If Patrick means that the ship carried him to Gaul, there is nothing impossible in his story.[12]

What then of the huge and empty desert? In 1905 J. B. Bury put forward a famous theory to account for it. He suggested that Patrick and the crewmen landed in Gaul at the time of the enormous invasion of the Vandals, Alans, and Sueves, who burst over the Rhine frontier into the Roman Empire on 31 December 406 and continued ravaging Gaul until they crossed the Pyrenees into Spain in the autumn of 409. Bury thought that Patrick and his companions arrived when the invasion was at its height and that the travellers deliberately avoided the roads, and perhaps made considerable halts and often lay low in order not to fall in with the marauders. If that is really what happened, we must describe Patrick as possibly the feeblest war-reporter who has ever lived. Ought he not at least to have thanked God most piously for preserving him and his companions from the swords of the invaders? And no methods of warfare known to the world in the fifth century could have emptied so vast an area so completely of its inhabitants. Worse still (from the point of view of Bury and his followers) later study of the course of this invasion has shown that the barbarians ravaged a huge swathe of land in central Gaul running from the Pas de Calais to the western end of the Pyrenees, leaving north-western Gaul, where Patrick would have landed, more or less untouched. So far as the Vandals and their associates were concerned, the seafarers could have put in safely in what is now Brittany and could have walked openly and light-heartedly singing at the top of their voices (if they had so wished) for endless miles in complete safety. In that region there was no risk of a Vandal ever clapping an eye on them. Patrick's narrative gives no hint that he and the members of the ship's crew were trying

12 The find was first reported by A. J. Evans, 'On a Votive Deposit', where Evans remarks on p. 405 that 'the farmer on whose land the find was made . . . is a shrewd hard-headed Presbyterian upon whose word Mr Day [a Cork dealer who acquired the boat] could thoroughly rely'. That is re-assuring. Had the farmer been a soft-headed Roman Catholic Mr Day could hardly have believed a word he said! For later bibliography see Farrell and Penny, 'The Broighter Boat'. Mr Day sold the treasure to the British Museum for £600, and the Irish were obliged to undertake an expensive law-suit before they could recover it. It is now in the National Museum, Dublin. See Praeger, *The Way*, p. 63.

to avoid human settlements or roving bands of marauders. On the contrary, when they began to starve, the narrative leaves us with the impression that they would have been more than glad to come upon any settlement of any kind. [13]

Some scholars have tried to reduce the size of the problem by suggesting that the travellers marched away from the sea for fourteen days and spent the other fourteen coming back again. This theory does indeed cut the size of the desert in half, but it by no means cuts the size of the problem by half. A desert which strong seamen could not cross in fourteen days is as much of a mystery in the Western Roman Empire as a desert which they only crossed in twenty-eight days.

Let us turn to the alternative theory: when St Patrick escaped from slavery in Ireland, his ship took him not to Gaul but to Britain. Gaul or Britain? Opinion among scholars is divided about fifty-fifty, though the big guns favour Britain. Now, the voice which Patrick had heard in his sleep had said, 'You do well to fast since you are soon about to go to your own country.' Observe that word 'soon'. The word suggests an immediate voyage to Britain rather than a voyage to Gaul and a further voyage some years later from Gaul to the shores of Britain and then a walk to his home. The word 'soon' is not wholly decisive, but it should not be overlooked. And again, on the hypothesis of an escape to Britain, there is no problem with the ship's ability to cover the distance in three days. Even the most ramshackle curach without a shred of sail, crewed by the most drunken of ship's companies, roaring 'Yo ho ho' the whole way across, would be able to complete such a journey, some seventy miles or less, in far fewer than seventy-two hours. And if you ask why, when he was aiming to travel to Britain, did Patrick embark on a ship bound for Gaul, the answer is that he had no choice in the matter: he took the only ship available. There are no other reasonable theories concerning his destination. We certainly cannot follow those scholars who suppose that the ship sailed to the 'Caledonian Forest'. Such scholars never tell us what possible motive could have led the captain to sail to a land where trade, loot, and slaves were all alike unobtainable. But there is this to be said for such an opinion: the problem would indeed be easier to solve if we could suppose that the captain was out of his mind and did not know what he was doing or where he was going.

There are two reasons why we should hesitate to accept Britain as

---

13 Bury, *The Life of St Patrick*, pp. 34f., 338–42. For the actual course of the invasion see Courtois, *Les Vandales*, pp. 42–51.

25

the land to which the ship sailed. Bury pointed out that Patrick's words really rule out a voyage to Britain. The saint says (in a passage which I shall translate later on), 'Again after a few years I was in Britain with my parents.' Bury rightly remarked that the words 'after a few years' cannot reasonably mean 'a few years after my capture' by the Irish raiders at Bannaventa. He has just referred to this time as being 'after many years', that is, many years after his capture by the Irish; and it is not easy to believe that he would refer to the one period of time as 'many years' and also as 'a few years' within ten lines of the printed text. He is indeed a bad writer but he is not an out-and-out crackpot. Secondly, Bury goes on to say that if the sea-farers had landed in Britain, Patrick could have reached his home in a few days. A march of twenty-eight days through an uninhabited wilderness is even more wildly improbable in Britain than in Gaul. In fact, a few days at most would have brought him to Gloucester or Chester or London or to some place where he might well have contacted persons who knew his relatives or knew of them. But no such contacts would be possible in Gaul. It is unlikely that anyone in Gaul would know a town-councillor of a small town in Britain: inter-provincial travel by such persons was infrequent in the fifth century. The great Gallic landowner, Sidonius Apollinaris, had better opportunities for travel than any British town-councillor; yet it is clear from his correspondence that he knew hardly anyone in Spain and no one at all in Britain. And if Patrick had landed in Britain in the first place, it is improbable that he would have reached home only 'after a few years'. The distances in Britain are too short and the obstacles too slight for an absence of some years after leaving Ireland. Indeed, if he and the crew had landed anywhere on the west coast of Britain and had marched eastwards for twenty-eight days covering, let us say, no more than ten miles a day, they would probably have found themselves many miles from land in the chilly waters of the North Sea at the end of their tramp. And it has never been suggested that they were trying to walk to Denmark.

It seems fairly clear that when Patrick escaped from Ireland his ship took him not to Britain but to Gaul. But we may well complain that he ought at least to have made this point explicitly. A contemporary reader would have been less troubled than we are by his failure to identify the desert, for in the absence of an atlas in every home the name of the desert, if it had one and if Patrick had recorded it, would have meant even less than Gobi and Kalahari mean to us. (Is the Gobi desert in the USSR or in China? It is in neither. Is the

Kalahari in South Africa, South-West Africa, or in Angola? It is in none of the three.) Apart from the absence of geography the narrative of the escape is extraordinarily vivid and realistic. But can we in fact believe it?

4. — The Second Enslavement

At the end of the episode Patrick eventually left the seafarers, and they marched on we do not know to what goal or to what fate. They did not dream that after fifteen hundred years men would still be enquiring into their (probably routine) voyage and its purpose and outcome, and would still dislike the captain's surly and unpleasant manner. In Gaul (if that is where he found himself) Patrick himself must have been obliged to work to keep himself alive and to earn enough resources to allow him to travel in the direction of his home. What is certain is that his personal position was now one of extreme danger whether he landed in Gaul or in Britain. This danger threatened from Roman slave-dealers.

After the passage translated on p. 22 above Patrick goes on to describe an extraordinary dream which he dreamt in the night following his refusal to eat the honey consecrated to pagan gods. This dream will occupy us later on. Having described the dream Patrick continues his narrative: 'And again after many years I was taken captive once more.' [He uses the same unusual phrase which he had twice used of the Irish raiders who took him captive at Bannaventa.] 'And so on that first night I remained with them. But I heard a divine message telling me, "For two months you will be with them". So it turned out: on that sixtieth night the Lord set me free from their hands.' Now without any warning he returns to his main narrative. 'He also during our march provided for us food and fire and dry weather every day until on the tenth day we reached men. As I indicated above, we made our way through the desert for twenty-eight days, and on that night on which we reached men we had nothing left of our food. And after a few years I was in Britain again with my parents.'[14]

This second captivity is an event of baffling obscurity. As a result of their finding the pork and the honey, the sailors thought highly of

14 *Confession*, §21f. (242.3−12). For the dream see p. 48. below.

Patrick. But then without warning or introduction he says, 'And again after many years I was taken captive once more.' Who took him captive? What persons is he referring to when he says, 'on that first night I stayed with them'? It cannot be the inhabitants of the settlement which they eventually reached, for he and the sailors had not yet reached the settlement at this stage of the story. Throughout this narrative Patrick constantly refers to the ship's crew as 'they' and 'them'. He seems to mean — and indeed there is no other possibility — that he stayed with the crew on that first night after being captured again. But it was he alone who was captured: the crew did not suffer the same fate. The most natural interpretation of the episode, I think, is that the sailors rounded on him and sold him in the settlement when at last they reached it. Having said this, he goes on with the narrative of his escape and takes up the story where he had left it a few moments before. If this is the correct interpretation of the strange event, then when he says that he was enslaved 'after many years', he is referring to the six years which had elapsed since his capture by the Irish raiders at Bannaventa: six years after the calamity at Bannaventa he was enslaved again. Now, when he last mentioned the sailors, they were full of his praise. But they had not become Christian. They were still pagan. And however deep their gratitude to him for apparently providing them with food when they were starving, yet they knew his circumstances. They knew that he was an escaped slave, friendless and without resources or influence, an ideal subject for a kidnap. The windfall was irresistible, and so they overpowered him.[15]

The Imperial Roman law was that a Roman who escaped or was ransomed from captivity among the barbarians outside the frontier resumed at once his full citizen status and all his rights as a citizen as soon as he set foot inside the frontier. But there were Roman slave-dealers whose purpose in life was not so much to enforce the law in this respect as to make an easy profit at the expense of the returning citizen. In Gaul Patrick was penniless. He had no friends and knew nobody. If the crew were to sell him to the local slave-dealers, nobody would be any the wiser. His family in Britain would never know that he had managed to escape from Ireland. Patrick does not tell us why the unpleasant captain changed his mind when they were still in port in Ireland. At first he would not accept Patrick as a

---

15 For a different translation of *post paucos annos* see O Raifeartaigh, Review of Hanson and Blanc, p. 221; and the various ways of understanding *Confession*, §21, are summarised by Bieler, *The Life and Legend*, p. 62.

passenger, but then after discussion with his men (apparently) he changed his mind and took him on board. It may be — the suggestion is only a guess — that he did so because even at that time, before they left Ireland, the captain and his men saw the possibility of selling the runaway. Patrick does not say that this is what happened. We may guess (if this is the explanation of how he became a slave for the second time) that he omitted to explain the reasons for it because of his reluctance to reveal clearly the treachery and ingratitude of the sailors, for whom he utters no word of blame or criticism (just as he utters no word of blame or criticism of the Irish raiders who had carried him off from Britain). I must stress that this account of how Patrick was enslaved a second time is nothing more than a guess, but I would claim that at least it is not so startlingly improbable as Bury's view that 'the sentence [telling of this enslavement] is a parenthetical reference to his lifework in Ireland, considered as a second enslavement.' Patrick wrote in order to be understood, but who — other than Bury — could possibly understand such an impenetrable parable as that? But Bury's explanation is lucidity itself when compared with Bieler's view that the whole paragraph is 'inserted merely for the sake of argument as being further proof of divine assistance,' and the incident 'may have taken place many years later.' If that is so, then Patrick was in dire need of divine assistance not only as a Christian and as a runaway slave but also and especially as a writer. I mention these two strange opinions only in order to illustrate the straits to which even the greatest of scholars have been reduced in order to explain the desperate obscurities of Patrick's writings.[16]

As for the extreme awkwardness of the paragraph in which Patrick tells of the second enslavement, the explanation may be that it is a later insertion of Patrick's. He had finished writing the *Confession*, or at any rate this part of it, when it occurred to him that he ought to have mentioned this incident. He therefore inserted it briefly in the margin (or wherever writers of the fifth century inserted their addenda), and a later copyist included it clumsily in the text.

Before we consider the episode of the desert as a whole it is worth lingering for a moment over Patrick's refusal to taste the honey when he was told that it had been consecrated to pagan gods. Evidently, even at this date he was familiar with I Corinthians, x. 28, 'But if any

16 Bury, *The Life of St Patrick*, p. 294, Bieler, *The Life and Legend*, p. 62. In general see Thompson, 'Barbarian Raiders'. Enslavement of free persons inside the Empire at about this date was even more extensive than we had thought, as is made clear by one of the newly discovered letters of St Augustine: see his *Epistle*, 10*, ed. J. Divjak, pp. 46—51.

man say unto you, This is offered in sacrifice unto idols, eat not for his sake that shewed it, and for conscience sake', etc. The avoidance of food which could be said to have been dedicated to pagan gods was a very serious matter to the early Christians living in a pagan environment.

5. — An Adventurous Theory

It is a general rule of Patrick's *Confession*, or at any rate the first half of it, that incidents are related in chronological order. There is no certain case where the author clearly disregards this wholesome practice. The incident of the second enslavement is told towards the end of the narrative of his escape from Ireland and therefore, we might think, took place at the time of that escape. In fact, it comes into the narrative from nowhere and vanishes again, like the ship's crew, without leaving any echo behind. The second period of slavery lasted for sixty days and so, while doubtless seeming calamitous at the time, can hardly have been of major importance in so eventful a life as Patrick's when he looked back over the years half a century later. If it was of importance, he has certainly not told us wherein its importance lay. He could not have told us less about it. When he was bishop later on, he was enslaved in Ireland many times and feared enslavement often. Why did he single out this case for special mention? But this is only part of a wider problem. Why he should have told us of his escape as a whole in such detail is not at all easy to understand. Carney rightly emphasises that 'he devoted here so much space to incidents that otherwise must seem trivial when compared with the great acts of his life that he has failed to mention'. When he was a bishop years later, how did it affect his relations with his fellow-Christians to state that his ship had taken three days to carry him across the sea from Ireland some fifty years previously? What was the relevance to his life in his old age, when he was writing the *Confession*, of the fact that he and his companions marched for neither twenty-seven nor twenty-nine days through the desert but for precisely twenty-eight days? Why was the story of the march through the wilderness so much more important than an account of how he reached home after parting from the sailors, or than an account of how he prepared himself for a career as an ecclesiastic? And if the story of the journey was of major importance, why not explain why the ship's captain steered towards such an unproductive coast?[17]

Nobody has ever been able to give a satisfactory explanation of these vexing problems. MacNeill makes some good points when he writes crisply: 'If they landed on the coast of Gaul, left their ship there, and started off to travel overland, it was because they knew where they were going. If they travelled without sufficient food for the journey, it was because they had reason to expect that ample food could be found during the journey.' O Raifeartaigh has also made some relevant remarks: short of their ship being blown off course to Gaul, 'there is no rational explanation of either their beaching on an unfamiliar or uninhabited coast or of their having struck inland fireless, exposed to the elements, short of provisions . . . and that on a wildgoose chase through an unknown wilderness at the end of which their best prospect was the hostility of any inhabitants they might eventually come upon.' I do not know what is the answer to these observations: each of them makes a valid point, and each of them applies to a landing in Britain just as much as to a landing in Gaul. Their only effect is to make Patrick's story even more difficult and puzzling than we had already thought it to be. But O Raifeartaigh is on firmer ground when he asks why, if the men were mere traders, they should have undertaken a very dangerous voyage to Gaul. 'For half the trouble and at very much less risk their wares would have fetched a good price in Britain.' That last point is decisive, I think, against the view that the men were traders who traded with Gaul — unless they traded in some commodity which was in demand in Gaul but not in Britain, and that is unlikely in view of the uniformity of Roman civilisation all over the West. But O Raifeartaigh's points do not tell against the view that the men were marauders who planned to plunder Gaul.[18]

We must not wholly rule out the possibility that the solution may be an unpleasant one. The blunt truth is that the story of the march through the vast desert, whether it took place in Gaul or in Britain, is impossible as Patrick tells it. It could not have happened. There was no such desert, whether caused by nature or by warfare, in any

17 Carney, *The Problem*, p. 60.
18 MacNeill, 'The Hymn of St Secundinus', p. 138; O Raifeartaigh, 'St. Patrick's Twenty-Eight Days', p. 412f.; Carney, *The Problem*, pp. 67−9. O Raifeartaigh, art. cit. pp. 397−405, argues that the chapters in question have come to be in the wrong order in Patrick's manuscripts: they ought to be read in the order §19, 22, 21, 20, 23. But that, I think, is too complicated to be explicable. He would have done better to place §21 in a new position — but where? — and leave the order of the other chapters unchanged.

province of the Western Roman Empire, whether in Britain, Gaul, or anywhere else, whether needing fourteen or twenty-eight days to cross. It is not open to doubt that Patrick and the ship's company did not march, and could not have marched, anywhere in the Western provinces for twenty-eight days, or even for fourteen days, without meeting a soul. They may have lost their way a dozen times, and they may have walked round in circles, but they still could not have spent twenty-eight days spinning round like a top or in any other rotary motion anywhere in the Western Empire without meeting somebody or other, friend or foe, man or woman, slave or free, barbarian or Roman.

But why then does Patrick tell the tale? Was he muddled and fuddled in his old age about an incident which had happened some fifty years before? There is a touch of incoherence in his story of his second enslavement (unless he inserted it in the margin as an afterthought), but it is impossible to detect any sign of the fuddy-duddy in the rest of his book. When he wrote the *Confession* he was anything but senile. Are we driven then to conclude that he was deliberately misleading his readers? But what motive could he possibly have had for perpetrating such a deception? It would undoubtedly have been difficult for his readers to detect any such deception, for few readers in Britain, if any, and no readers at all in Ireland would know that such a desert as he describes did not exist anywhere in the West. To that extent he had his readers at his mercy: not one of them owned an atlas. But what could his aim have been if the story is not true?

The only answer to that question which is at all worth considering — though that is not to say that it is the correct one — is a remarkable suggestion thrown out tentatively by James Carney (who himself does not accept the theory). In the *Confession* Patrick was defending his career against critics who alleged that he had gone to Ireland as bishop for the sake of personal gain: he was there to make money (or whatever passed for money at that date). Now, suppose that the ship's company was in fact a band of pirates or at any rate that they had turned to marauding and were searching for loot inside the falling Empire. If they engaged in actual plundering while Patrick was one of their number, his critics, if they had learned of this (and, by the way, if the alleged looting took place in Britain they could hardly have failed to uncover the fact) would have had a devastating weapon with which to destroy his career for ever. If such information were true and were to become known, Patrick could never have been appointed to the bishopric, and it would have had a most damaging effect if it became known even in his old age. Patrick, then, on this theory, is 'explaining' why his association with these men came into being, what the nature of the association was, and why he stayed with the sailors for so long after they reached land. This is why he leaves in obscurity the subsequent events, including the manner in which he parted from them in the end. 'Patrick would see an adequate defence in the facts of his aloofness from their every act and his efforts to bring them to Christ.' Perhaps indeed questions had already been asked, and he devotes so much space to the incident so as to make quite clear that there was nothing criminal in this part of his life and that the men with whom he sailed were vaguely 'travellers' and nothing more.[19]

There are obvious shortcomings in this notable theory. First, it rests on sheer guesswork; but, of course, in the nature of the matter there could be no evidence to support it. Secondly, Patrick's defence of what had happened some fifty years previously is published rather late in the day. And yet we cannot be quite sure that at the time when he was about to write the *Confession* doubt had not been thrown on the nature of his association with those unforgotten sailors who had crossed the ocean so long ago. Above all, the theory ascribes to Patrick a deceit which seems to be inconsistent with everything else that we know of his character. But the fact remains that no one seems to have suggested anything more convincing — or rather, less unconvincing — to explain his strange story. Beyond any doubt, there is something puzzling, if not outright incredible, in the episode of the escape from Ireland as Patrick tells it. The mechanics of the escape, as O Raifeartaigh rightly remarks, 'would not normally be expected to call for more than the most perfunctory mention'. Whatever criticisms had been made of this part of his life, surely after *fifty years* his best course would have been to let sleeping dogs snooze on. On the theory which we are discussing, the more circumstantial the narrative the more convincing it could be made to appear. If the narrative was intended to answer a criticism, it was important to make it detailed, vivid, and convincing.

If we accept that the story is a cover-up, that it is a fiction, we need not trouble ourselves with the question whether the ship reached Britain or Gaul at the end of the three days. To pore over the details of the narrative so as to answer this question would be a waste of time. If the story as a whole is fiction, the details are presumably

19 I have developed the hint which can be found in Carney, *The Problem*, pp. 67–9. Who are those who disbelieve Patrick in *Confession*, §10 (237.25)?

fiction, too. On this theory, we can never find out whether the ship eventually berthed in Gaul or Britain.

That is the problem, then. As Bury mildly put it, 'There is something very strange about the whole story.' There are two main questions. First, why does Patrick go into such detail about his escape from Ireland? Secondly, why does he present us with a story which is simply incredible, a story which has led one able scholar to suggest that it is nothing but a hint from God that Patrick was treading in the footsteps of St Paul? Whatever the explanation may be, the theory that Patrick has published an elaborate deception is one which a wise man would mention only in a whisper and only after dark, when nobody is looking.[20]

20 Bury, *The Life of St Patrick*, p. 32.

CHAPTER THREE

The Return Home

At the beginning of Chapter One it looked as though Patrick's account of his capture at his father's villa was misleading in several respects, though it was easy enough to see how his mistakes could have arisen. At the end of Chapter Two he seemed to be guilty of something worse. He seemed to make a deliberate attempt to lead us astray on his activities with the ship's crew (though there can be no certainty in the matter). But that is all. We shall never again have reason to doubt the literal truth of what he tells us. We cannot question a single syllable written by him throughout the rest of his work.

1. — The Return Home

So Patrick spent some years in Gaul before he could get home. He was aged twenty-two when he escaped from Ireland, and since he returned to Britain 'after a few years', he would have stayed in Gaul until he was, say, twenty-five or twenty-six. He must have spent his time in Gaul in circumstances of considerable hardship. There is neither evidence nor likelihood that he spent these years improving his education or raising his cultural level or idling in a monastery or meeting or hobnobbing with the leading Gallic churchmen of the day. To suppose that, if he wanted to receive an education and then a safe and free passage home, he had nothing to do but to go to

Auxerre and knock on the door of the bishop Germanus (if he was alive at the time) is to idealise life as it was lived in the Later Roman Empire. At this time he would continue to speak colloquial Latin, as he had done at home in Britain; but he could obtain no practice or instruction in literary Latin, nor at this stage had he any reason for wanting it. No doubt he felt himself lucky enough to be alive and free. But once he managed to reach Britain, a few days would probably take him from the coast to his home (though in Britain, too, he would have to be on the watch for slave-dealers).[1]

But he did reach home at last, and was warmly welcomed by his parents. He then began a period of his life of which he tells us practically nothing except in a few, a very few, scattered hints and incidental remarks. Now in his middle twenties, he had become a very different person from the boy who had been swept away by the slave-raiders. Instead of a carefree, sinful lad, he was now deeply, even obsessively Christian, though as yet he cannot have known much about the sombre dogmas and heresies of the Church. Indeed, we have no evidence that he ever came to know much about these, although he certainly knew enough to dissociate himself (at any rate, by implication) from the heresy of Arianism which had racked the Christians both of the Eastern Empire and of the Western for most of the fourth century. And even towards the end of his life he had never heard of Pelagianism, or at any rate (as we shall see) he did not think it worth mentioning, although it was a Briton who had initiated it and although it was flourishing in Britain — at any rate, in parts of Britain — at least as late as the 430s. Although four popes had thundered against it, it seems to have passed Patrick by. If he had any substantial knowledge of it, how could he have omitted all reference to it from the *Confession* as a whole and especially from his statement of faith near the beginning of it? But, as Binchy remarked, 'the Celtic Church contributed little to theology: its writers shared the general incapacity for abstract thought'. Patrick was no exception. He never had original opinions about the teachings of the Church. His mind was never tainted by theological thought. Throughout his life his Christianity seems to have been wholly conventional, low-brow, and commonplace except in two respects — its intense sincerity, and his determination to export Christianity

---

1 *Confession*, §23 (242.12), where *post paucos annos* means 'a few years after' the events which he has just been narrating and must be distinguished from *post annos multos* of §21 (242.3). For a thoughtful but in my view unsuccessful attempt to interpret the passage differently see O Raifeartaigh, 'The Reading *nec a me orietur*', pp. 189–92.

beyond the Roman frontier. He had read little or nothing, and he must have appeared to possess few of those qualities which cause a man to be remembered for fifteen or sixteen hundred years. But at this date he did not foresee that one day he would return to Ireland as a churchman: he did not hope for any such thing nor did he even think of it. So he felt no great need for a higher education. As it turned out, he was never to acquire the ability to compose the Latin of the great Continental writers of his day or of British educated men or of British Gildas in the following century. Throughout the rest of his life, as we shall see, he never ceased to be acutely conscious of this shortcoming (as he conceived it to be) and to lament it rather too loudly and too often.[2]

But no doubt when at last he reached his home and his parents, a young men in his middle twenties, his mind was filled with relief and gratitude for his survival rather than with misgivings about the state of his education. His parents welcomed him as their son, as he is careful to tell us. Whether they also welcomed his new-found Christianity he does not reveal. Presumably in their joy at the recovery of their boy they would overlook such an unexpected aberration.

We do not know how long he had been at home when he dreamed a dream which altered the course of his life. 'I saw in a vision of the night a man coming as it were from Ireland, whose name was Victoricus, with countless letters, and he gave me one of them, and I read the beginning of the letter containing the words "The Voice of the Irish", and when I was reading the beginning of the letter I was thinking that in that moment I was hearing the voice of those who were beside the Wood of Voclut, which is near the western sea, and they cried out thus as if with one voice, "We are asking you, holy boy, to come and continue to walk among us", and I was very moved in my heart and I could not read on, and so I woke up. Thank God, that after many years the Lord gave to them according to their cry'.[3]

We do not know who Victoricus was: presumably Patrick had known him in Ireland. Presumably, too, the Wood of Voclut was the place where he had worked in Ireland: if not, the point of mentioning it is meaningless. At any rate, this vision was one of the turning-points of Patrick's life, perhaps the most crucial of all. It was this which decided him to go back to Ireland and win the inhabitants to

---

2 *Confession*, §4 (236.11), §15 (239.13), cf. Binchy, Review of Hughes, *The Church*, pp. 217–19.
3 *Confession*, §23 (242.16).

his own religion. To the end of his life he considered himself to be God's chosen man to do this work. No doubt, soon after seeing this vision he earnestly set about preparing himself for ordination and for life as a priest of the Church and for an eventual return to the land of his captivity.

Many, many years must have elapsed between his return to Britain and the Church authorities' consideration of him as a possible bishop — years, probably decades. He had to change from being an ecclesiastical illiterate into the fairly highly qualified person who eventually set out for Ireland. The reason why he has little to say about this enormous period of his life from his mid-twenties to at least his mid-forties and perhaps his fifties, I suppose, is that it did not come under the fire of his critics. We must never forget that one purpose of the *Confession* seems to be to rebut his critics; and in general Patrick does not deal in it with subjects which had not been criticised. This was a period of preparation rather than of action.

In this period we know that Patrick became a deacon; and by the time he became a deacon he had admitted to his closest friend the sin of which he had been guilty when still a boy of fifteen and which was still weighing on his mind. We know further that late in this period he was living abroad and not in Britain. I have little doubt that he was in Ireland. There are three hints in his writings that this was so. (i) Years later, when he had long been a bishop, he speaks of a priest whom he had himself educated 'from infancy'. This priest must have been over thirty years of age at the time — otherwise he would hardly have been a priest — and Patrick must have been in Ireland for some twenty years at least if he was able to say that he had educated 'from infancy' a man of that age. We shall see that he was hardly bishop for twenty years. (ii) His use of the word 'proselyte' points to this conclusion. I translate this word as 'sojourner': it always means 'visitor', 'stranger', 'alien', never a 'convert', as Christine Mohrmann pointed out. So, at the beginning of the *Epistle* Patrick calls himself 'sojourner and exile for the love of God' at a time when he was certainly in Ireland. Towards the end of the *Confession* he expresses the hope that he will become a martyr 'with those sojourners and captives' with whom he is working in Ireland. But he uses the word a third time. He says explicitly that he was not in Britain at the time when the seniors (whom we shall meet presently) rejected him and when 'the Lord spared a sojourner and foreigner for his name's sake'. The phrase shows, in my view, that he means that he was in Ireland at the time rather than, say, in Christian Gaul, for to use such a phrase of a visit to Christian communities in Gaul would be hardly less than offensive. (iii) Thirdly, Patrick as bishop years later tells the Christians in Ireland that he had been associated with them 'from my young manhood', 'from the time when I was a young man'. Now, he refers to the period before his enslavement as his 'boyhood'. The period of his slavery as his 'adolescence'. After his escape to Britain he is in his 'young manhood': he was then in his middle or late twenties. It follows that he had been working among his converts for a very long time, 'since my young manhood', or 'since I became an adult'. It is not out of the question, then, that much of his life *after* his escape from Ireland and his return home was spent in Ireland, though he will have passed a period of some years in Britain first immediately after his return from slavery. In my opinion, these facts or probabilities appear to give us fairly firm grounds for thinking that Patrick was in Ireland *after* he had escaped from slavery there but *before* he returned as bishop of the Irish Christians. How long this stay in Ireland lasted, we have no means of even guessing. We know only that he was out of Britain at a time when at least one man was canvassing for his appointment as bishop; and even the barest possibility of his becoming bishop can only have arisen after he had put in years and years of study of the Bible and other preparations. No one would have dreamed of proposing for a bishopric the earnest but almost totally ignorant young man who had recently escaped from slavery overseas and whose education was admittedly defective. Patrick's ministry among the Irish may have begun when he was still a mere deacon. It will be worth our while to come back to this possibility.[4]

2. — Education and Language

When the Romans began the conquest of Britain in A.D. 43 the Britons spoke a Celtic language. When the Roman power collapsed in

---

4 See p. 168f. below. *Confession*, §27 (243.24), deacon. In *ibid.*, §26 (243.20) Patrick is *proselito et peregrino propter nomen suum*. The word *proselitus* in Patrick means 'foreigner': Mohrmann, *The Latin*, p. 25. I do not know why Bieler, *The Life and Legend*, p. 135 n. 57, writes, 'Wherever Patrick lived at the time of the British synod mentioned in §32, it was certainly not in Ireland.' In studying Patrick we can rarely talk of certainties, and in this case Bieler has to go on to ascribe (quite gratuitously) a 'patent anachronism' to the saint. It is hardly necessary to add that no British synod is mentioned anywhere in Patrick's writings. The three terms which he uses about the periods of his life are *pueritia*, 'boyhood', *Confession*, §10 (238.1), §27 (244.1), *adolescens*, 'youth', *ibid.*, §2 (235.17), §10 (238.1), and *iuuentus*, 'young manhood', *ibid.*, §15 (239.13), §48 (250.3).

Britain early in the fifth century, most Britons still spoke their native Celtic (which survives to this day in an up-dated form as Welsh). But the language of the Roman administration and army was Latin, and those Britons who collaborated with the invaders, threw in their lot with the conquerors, and prospered under Roman rule, quickly learned to speak Latin, though most of them continued to use their Celtic as well. Latin in due course became fairly widely spoken in the British cities, though most of the city-dwellers were bilingual in British Celtic and Latin. Latin was also spoken in the rich men's villas: as in all the provinces of the Western Empire, so also in Britain, the landed gentry spoke Latin. But Latin was not spoken by the poorer rural classes. They were not bilingual. They spoke Celtic only. That is to say, the bulk of the population, numerically speaking, spoke nothing but Celtic. So the landowners were to some extent separated by language from those whose labour they ruthlessly exploited. In fact, those who gained from the Roman conquest spoke Latin. Those who gained nothing but perhaps lost a great deal from the conquest spoke no Latin.

Patrick, then, a member of the rich or relatively rich landowning class, would have spoken Latin in his home as his normal language when conversing with his equals; and he may have been able to address the workers on his father's estate (if he ever chose to speak to them) in their native British Celtic. A question to which we cannot hope to find an answer is to what extent, if any, he was fluent in British Celtic. It is not out of the question that he could speak very little Celtic before he was carried off to Ireland.

Whatever the oddities of his Latin as he wrote it, we should be wrong to think that he was not completely at home in spoken Latin. To speak of his 'imperfect command of Latin' or to think that Latin was for him an acquired language into which he had to 'translate', would be a mistake. As a matter of fact, to think that his native language was Celtic and that Latin was for him an acquired language is to make him all but unique among the vast multitude of extant Latin authors. How many of the hundreds of Latin books which have come down to us from antiquity were written by men whose native language was neither Latin nor Greek? Even as a child he did not need to go to a schoolmaster to learn his *mensa, mensam*, etc. He grew up speaking Latin. We cannot suppose that all those Romano-Britons who composed the *graffiti* which have been found by archaeologists scrawled on stone or pot or lead or tile in British cities had attended Latin language classes, elementary if not advanced. It was their native language, or one of them; and it was Patrick's native language, or one of them. Even for British Gildas early in the following century Latin was 'our language'. Patrick may have written Latin with difficulty, and he may have included in it an occasional Irishism, but it does not in the least follow that he had any difficulty in speaking it.[5]

Now, the colloquial Latin of the townsmen and the villa-owners was by no means identical with the artificial literary Latin which was written by the famous writers on the Continent in the fifth century and which was still to be written by Gildas later on. This literary, written Latin could only be acquired by three years of study and practice at the school of a teacher called the 'rhetor'. It was often characterised by such a flowery elaboration of style and literary devices and classical references that even educated contemporaries might sometimes find it hard enough to understand. Could anything be more unlike Patrick's plain and stumbling style of writing? Attendance at the school of the rhetor was confined to the sons of the well-to-do classes. It marked them off from the rabble. Patrick's father as a landowner and a city-councillor would certainly have sent his son to a rhetor. So the higher education stamped a man as belonging to the rich classes. To be without it was vulgar. Indeed, as the Western Empire decayed further and further and the great offices of state became meaningless, the large Gallic landowner Sidonius wrote, 'as the grades of office are removed by which the highest used to be distinguished from the lowliest, the only indication of noble birth hereafter will be a knowledge of literature'. So skill in literary Latin and knowledge of Classical Latin literature were not simply a pleasant amateurish accomplishment: they were an essential in the life of a rich landowner and the male members of his family. At this date the Church did not found Church schools. A bishop or priest might

5 For Irish constructions in Patrick's Latin see Greene, 'Some Linguistic Evidence', p. 78, O Raifeartaigh, Review of Hanson and Blanc, p. 220. The basic work on the subjects discussed in this section is, of course, Jackson, *Language and History*, pp. 97−105, but it is important to study Jones, *The Later Roman Empire*, pp. 986−97. I venture to differ from Jackson on one important point. In *Language and History*, p. 103, he infers from the case of Patrick that the villa-owners had to acquire Latin at school and that they did not pick it up from infancy as a truly native language. This is not proved by the case of Patrick. There is a judicious treatment of the topic in Hanson, *St Patrick : His Origins*, pp. 160−70. (Note also Hanson, *St Patrick : A British Missionary*, p. 14f.) I differ from him on two points: (i) the fact that a man cannot write a language fluently by no means proves that he cannot speak it fluently; (ii) he accepts Jackson's view that the Latin spoken in Britain was in some sense archaic. This opinion has been exploded — no milder word will do — by Gratwick, 'Latinitas Britannica', pp. 1−79; but Gratwick himself has come under heavy fire — the subject is an explosive one — from Charles-Edwards, Review of Brooks, *Latin and the Vernacular Languages*, p. 253f.

give basic instruction in doctrine and morals to converts, as Patrick himself did later on to the man who carried his first letter to Coroticus. Education was still based wholly on the pagan classics and was hardly affected by the rise of Christianity. The schools were not concerned with Christian dogma in the time of the Christian Empire. They were concerned with social status and class distinction.[6]

But Patrick was a slave in Ireland during the years when other British landowners' sons of his age were receiving their advanced education, learning to write the complex sentences and studying the classics and the legal texts. So at the time when he was writing the *Confession*, he says, he was trying to achieve in his old age what he had not acquired when he was a young man, that is, the ability to express himself as an educated 'eloquent' man ought to be able to do. But that, he says (quite rightly), was now beyond him. For a long time he refused to write at all for fear of the criticism which his writing would bring down upon him. There is no mock-modesty about what he says. Here is a translation of his words about his potential critics: 'I had not read as the others had, who had imbibed in the best manner civil law and holy scripture in equal measure, and have never changed their spoken language since their infancy but rather always added to its perfection. For my spoken language was changed into a foreign tongue, as can easily be inferred from the savour of my writing, how I was taught and educated in the spoken language', etc. This passage is nonsensical if he is referring to his British Celtic (if it existed). No one could possibly deduce from his written Latin anything about his Celtic. He would certainly not have made a fuss about his Celtic, the language of servants, farm-workers, and of others who had nothing to do with education. Whether or not he was obliged to stop speaking British Celtic would have been in his eyes a matter of no consequence at all. He is guilty of a gross, indeed an impossible, *non sequitur* unless he is talking about his own Latin as contrasted with 'their' Latin. That is to say, we make him talk gibberish unless we interpret him as referring to his change of spoken language from Latin to Irish. His native language was Latin, but for the six years of slavery he had to speak Irish. British Celtic does not come into the matter. On the other hand, the fact that his spoken Latin was replaced by spoken Irish when he became a slave could not possibly be deduced from the 'savour' of his writing. The savour of his writing can throw light only on his Latin. All that his readers could deduce from his Latin (that is, of course, from his written

6 Sidonius' *Epistles*, VIII. 2. 2 (ed. Anderson, W.B., II, p. 405).

Latin) is that it is imperfect by the standards of the educated. But what he says is undoubtedly ambiguous. The reader might infer, for example, that Patrick was not the son of a landowner and that that was why he had never been trained to write literary Latin. That would be a legitimate inference though as a matter of fact a false one. The truth is that he has not been able to express his thought here quite adequately. He means that his written Latin is imperfect, not simply because of the change in his spoken language, but because, while others were attending the classes of the rhetor, he was shepherding sheep on an Irish hillside. And his point is that his education had been broken off at the age of sixteen, and with the ending of his education he could indeed write Latin of a sort but he could not write elegant Latin. This, he rightly says, is plain for all to see. He had not been able to develop his spoken Latin into literary Latin. The fact that what Patrick writes is not far removed from the Latin which he spoke gives his writings, in our eyes though not in his, much of their liveliness and immediacy.[7]

Although Patrick is by no means a resentful man, he does seem to resent strongly his fate in this matter of his higher education and sometimes even to carry over his resentment — that is hardly too strong a word — into his attitude towards the educated landowning class in Britain, or part of it. At one point in the *Confession* where the manuscript tradition of his text is most unfortunately corrupt, he seems almost to become abusive and calls them 'upper class' and 'educated' ('rich highbrows') in a far from flattering tone. He talks endlessly of his own 'rusticity'. True, he had a good excuse, but of what use is that? Who would believe it? He had been carried off when still only a boy, and so he now blushes and deeply dreads to expose his inadequacies because he cannot express briefly what his spirit wishes to explain. At all events, he is sure that he is a 'rustic exile' in Ireland.[8]

I have laboured this matter of Patrick's language and education because it was something which worried him to the end of his days. He could never forget his inadequacy, as he thought it to be. As Hanson says, Patrick is 'acutely, perpetually, embarrassingly conscious of his lack of education'. He calls himself 'most rustic' in the opening words of the *Confession*. He speaks of his 'lack of knowledge'. He is 'rustic and unlearned'. Even in the very first sentence of the *Epistle* he is 'unlearned', an admission which seems

7 *Confession*, 9f. (237.16−19), with O Raifeartaigh, loc. cit.
8 *Confession*, §10 (238.1−5).

remarkably out of place in this context. He says elsewhere, 'And so today I blush and deeply fear to lay bare my ignorance because I am not able to explain to educated men with brevity what my spirit and mind long to explain'. He repeatedly gives us to understand that he felt himself to be at a disadvantage over against the well educated, to be inferior to them. And this feeling of inferiority was one which he did not like. In fact, it would hardly be an exaggeration to say that in this matter he had a chip on his shoulder.[9]

Now, so far as we know, no other person besides Patrick himself ever criticised him on this score. It is of the first importance to grasp this fact, for it has been constantly misstated or ignored. There is not a single passage in his writings from which we can deduce with certainty that this criticism was levelled against him publicly. He had one and only one critic, his own relentless self.[10]

But the most astonishing aspect of all this is that he cared about it at all. The shortcoming (as he thought it) is one which would have been unintelligible to his Irish converts and to the mass of his British contemporaries. It has meaning only in connexion with the esteem in which his fellow-landowners in Britain held him — or failed to hold him, as he thought. He is deploring his loss of a class-characteristic. Secondly, he thinks that he is the odd man out. In this matter he is nothing if not class-conscious. These are the feelings of a landowner's son, Christian or pagan. Why such criticisms, if they were ever made, should have been so important in his eyes even towards the end of his life, when he had long since migrated from Britain and knew that he would never return, is unknown and not easy to understand.

3. — Dreams

Patrick's narrative of the time between the last days of his slavery in Ireland and his first days (or months or years — he does not tell us

9 Hanson, *Patrick : His Origins*, p. 125; cf. *Confession*, §10−13 (238.1−24), §46 (249.18).
10 In *Confession*, §11 (238.8) he is criticised for pushing himself forward, that is, for his arrogance: his ignorance and his hesitant speech made his pushing himself forward seem arrogant. It is sometimes thought that *Confession*, §46 (249.27−9), shows other people accusing him of being 'rustic'. But the passage cannot be translated with anything like certainty. It contains an otherwise unknown construction of *sapio*; and when *sapio* recurs in the next line but one, it has to be translated in a wholly different sense. Patrick appears to say here that people had not understood him because he had been unable to make his position clear. At all events, we must not invent an entire school of critics on the strength of one untranslatable sentence!

which) when he was at home again with his parents is marked by a peculiar characteristic: he reports that at each major turn of his story he dreamed a dream which guided him on his way, told him what to do, or foretold his future. (He never speaks of day-time visions.) In the opening chapters of the *Confession* until he reaches the episode of his slavery in Ireland and how it was coming towards its end, there are no reports of dreams; and that is also true of his description of his career as bishop. It would be a mistake to say that the voice he heard in his dreams was his constant companion in life. It was his companion only during one period of his life. True, he may have experienced dreams and visions and ecstasies throughout his entire life; but, if so, he passes over the others in silence. He certainly claims to have been guided by God at other times, but he does not claim that this guidance came to him in dreams.

But why does he report the dreams only from the one period of his life? It is probable, as we shall see, that he is arguing with his critics. He was obliged to justify himself, it seems, for wishing to return to Ireland, and such visions, sent by God, were his justification. This we can deduce from the nature of the dreams which he describes for us. They all bear on his escape from slavery and then on his decision to return to Ireland. His reply to his critics is that God directed him to go back there: God directed him by means of dreams. He takes no account of the opinion held by many Christians that, while some dreams come from God, others are sent by demons and evil spirits, whose aim is to mislead the dreamer. For Patrick all his dreams come from God. On that point he expresses no doubt or hesitation. Nor did the dreams come from angels, whom he never mentions (except in Biblical quotations), nor from any other holy being but from God in person. At that date men had no hesitation in acting on the instructions which were given to them, as they believed, in dreams. It was even said that Constantine the Great founded his new capital at Constantinople rather than elsewhere because 'God appearing to him during the night bade him seek another place when he had already decided on the ancient site of Troy'. Patrick never claims to have asked for the advice which reached him in his sleep although he calls these utterances 'responses' or even 'divine responses'. Heaven spontaneously sent him his dreams, according to what he tells us, without any request from him. But it is sad to think that although so much advice and guidance was lavished on Patrick, to the prayers of the other British slaves in Ireland, God was deaf.[11]

11 *Confession*, §17 (239.23−5). For Constantine see Sozomen, *Historia Ecclesiastica* II. 3. 2f

The dreams which he describes, or tries to describe, number eight in all. The first group of four dreams relates to his forthcoming flight from Ireland and his separation (or escape) from the ship's crew. The next group of three encouraged him to go back to Ireland, but they gave no hint that a return to Ireland would be something like a return to slavery. That is a modern idea which has been read into the dreams by recent scholars. There is no hint whatever in Patrick's own words that he might have regarded the mission to Ireland as a hardship or a penalty. On the contrary, it was an ambition which he had struggled to realise, something which he 'thrust himself forward' to obtain, something which eminent clerics other than himself had wished to win. The eighth and final vision also relates to the mission to Ireland, and its purpose was apparently to condemn his false friend whose indiscretion (if that is what it was) seems to have prevented him for a while from going to Ireland as bishop, as we shall see.[12]

Patrick makes a general comment on these dreams. He says that God knows all things even before they happen, and God brought it about that many a divine message had warned him in spite of his being a poor, weak, ignorant person. Whether in this remark he is referring to the dreams which he reports or whether he had later on seen others, too, he does not say: but the remark loses its relevance if it alludes to unrecorded dreams. Why does he raise the matter at all? He leaves us in no doubt about the answer to that question. There were people who laughed at him and insulted him on that score — for claiming that God guided him by means of visions. In fact, this seems to have been one of the criticisms which he wrote the *Confession* to answer. He replies, 'Let anyone who wishes to laugh at me and insult me. I shall not be silent or hide the signs and wonders which have been pointed out to me by the Lord many years before they happened, since he knows all things even before the world began.' These words make it certain, I think, that Patrick encountered scoffers and mockers who laughed at his reports of his dreams. They were sceptical of his claim to have direct communication with heaven. Their scepticism reminds us that in the fifth century men

---

(ed. Bidez, p. 51f.). For *responsum* see *Confession*, §17 (239.24), §21 (242.4), §29 (244.14), §35 (246.7). In the last of these, *responsum diuinum*, there is a hint that he did receive dreams during his bishopric, but he specifies none of them. The Irish noblewoman received a *responsum*, and we may guess that the advice given to her came in a dream: *ibid.*, §42 (248.12). Patrick asserts explicitly that his dreams came from God: *ibid.*, §21 (242.4), §24 (243.6f), §25 (243.12), §29 (244.14).

12 *Confession*, §11 (238.8).

were not so gullible as we sometimes believe. Sulpicius Severus, who wrote the *Life* of St Martin of Tours at the beginning of the century, was bluntly accused of lying when he reported face-to-face communication between Martin and various supernatural beings; and he refers to the matter several times. Of course, Martin of Tours and Sulpicius Severus dealt in crudities such as have no parallel in the life and writings of Patrick (though they have all too many parallels in the mediaeval *Lives* of Patrick). For example, we are piously told that Martin once managed to penetrate into the very room in which the Emperor Valentinian I (364—75) was sitting. The Emperor was angry that a complete stranger should make his way unannounced and unattended into his private room. When the holy man came in, he did not stand up — at any rate, at first. But then the seat of the Imperial chair caught fire, and a hot blast blew, as Sulpicius Severus phrases it, 'on that part of his body upon which he was accustomed to sit'. At that point the Emperor did indeed stand up: he lost no time whatever in springing to his feet. Now, Valentinian I was not noted for his sense of fun or for his appreciation of practical jokes. If Martin had been instrumental in inflicting this type of humour upon him, his career as a miracle-man could only have continued by a miracle. Sulpicius tells this story without a smile. He believed it! Fortunately, we find no such laughable farce in the *Confession* of St Patrick.[13]

The point is that although Sulpicius Severus swallowed this nonsense there were men in the fifth century who did not. So, too, with Patrick's critics. The one thing which we can be sure of concerning those who doubted him in the matter of his divinely inspired dreams is that they were Christians. The opinions of pagans in this connexion would have been of no interest whatever to him or to his readers: his readers were exclusively Christian, and it was Christians who doubted his direct communication with heaven.

The first group of dreams, then, concerned his escape from Ireland. When he was still a slave a voice warned him twice in his sleep that his escape from slavery was at hand. It is remarkable that Patrick should think that his escape from slavery calls for justification. Was it sinful for a slave to take flight from his master? Did Patrick feel that he had disregarded St Paul's inexcusable instructions

---

13 *Ibid.*, §35 (246.6), §45 (249.13). For the heating of Valentinian I see Sulpicius Severus, *Dialogue,* I (ii). 5, 7—10. For the scepticism of some of Sulpicius's readers see *Vita*, 25.7; *Dialogue,* ii (iii). 5. 6; ii. 13. 7; ii (iii). 15. 4, cf. i. 26. 3—6 (ed. Halm, pp. 135, 203, 196, 214, 178, respectively).

in Ephesians, vi. 5, 'Be obedient to your masters', etc.? At any rate, God gave Patrick a special and personal dispensation by telling him explicitly to take to his heels and by giving him a helping hand on his way. Again, when the appearance of the herd of pigs and the finding of the wild honey ended the famine among the sailors in Gaul (or Britain) Patrick dreamed one of his most remarkable dreams: 'The same night I was sleeping, and Satan forcefully tempted me, a thing which I shall remember as long as I am in this body, and he fell upon me like a huge stone, and none of my limbs had strength. But whence did it come into my ignorant mind to call upon Elias? And at that moment I saw the sun rise in the sky and while I was shouting 'Elias, Elias' with all my might, look! the splendour of the sun fell upon me and immediately scattered from me all the weight, and I believe that I was helped by Christ my Lord, and his spirit even then was shouting out for me, and I hope it will be so in the day of my tribulation, as he says in the Gospel, "In that day" (the Lord bears witness) "it is not ye that speak but the spirit of your father which speaketh in you" (Matthew, x. 20)'.

In this experience he strangely confused the name of Elijah (*Helias* in Latin) with *Helios*, the Greek name for the sun. The similarity between these two names was noticed more than once in the ancient Christian world, though not perhaps so often as we might have expected. The similarity is attested both in literary and in archaeological evidence. But, as Bieler astutely points out, Patrick does not seem to be fully aware that he is identifying *Helias* with *Helios*: 'there is merely some vague connexion between the two names at the back of his mind'. At any rate, the interpretation of this dream is not easy, and Patrick does not tell us what significance he placed on it. He says simply, of Christ's assistance to him in this dream, that he hopes that it will be so also 'in the day of tribulation' (cf. Psalm, 50. 15). (It will throw light on the character of much Patrician scholarship if I quote the comment on this dream which was made by an eminent, though not impeccable, scholar, R. A. S. Macalister: 'After his long experience of semi-starvation as a slave, his digestion was unequal to a surfeit of pork, with the consequence, normal in such cases, of a terrific nightmare, which made a lasting impression on him'. From this comment we learn something about the digestion of R. A. S. Macalister, but not much about St Patrick's dreams.) Be that as it may, this is the only one of his visions of which he says that he would remember it for the rest of his life, although as a matter of fact he remembered the others, too. When he was mysteriously enslaved for the second time, a divine voice assured him that he would be with his captors for sixty days; and so it turned out. Those are the visions which he saw before and during his escape from slavery in Ireland.[14]

Immediately after telling of his return home, he goes on to give us an account of three more visions, beginning with the one in which Victoricus appeared to him and which we have already studied (p. 37 above). Unfortunately, he does not make it clear whether he dreamed this dream immediately after reaching home or whether he had been home for a longer or shorter period before seeing it. In association with the vision in which Victoricus appeared to him he mentions another in which he could not understand the words which were spoken to him except at the end where the words were, ' "He who gave his life for you, he it is who speaks in you", and so I awoke rejoicing.' Patrick goes on, 'And again I saw him praying within me, and I was, so to speak, inside my own body, and I heard <him> above me, that is, above the inner man, and there he was praying loudly and with groans; and during this time I was amazed and was wondering and thinking who it was who was praying in me; and at the end of the prayer he spoke out that he was the Spirit, and so I awoke.' Both this and the previous vision were designed to assure him that the voice which had been and still was addressing him was that of the Holy Spirit (and by implication that any critics who denied this were in the wrong).[15]

After telling of these dreams he goes straight on to narrate the interview with the 'seniors'. He saw the last of his visions after he had been rejected by the 'seniors', and we shall consider it in a later chapter.

Although Patrick fully and seriously accepted Christianity when he was a slave in Ireland, it was *not* when he was a slave in Ireland that he decided to go back some day and convert the pagan Irish to Christianity. That decision came later, when he was at home in Britain and had seen the vision of Victoricus. The function of the visions was not to prove that he was the legitimate bishop. The question of his legitimacy as bishop does not arise in the descriptions of the dreams; and indeed if Patrick had been called upon to prove that he was a lawfully appointed bishop, he would presumably have had a more telling and conclusive proof to offer than a series of dreams! What the dreams did was to direct him towards Ireland and 'to thrust

14 *Confession*, §17 (dreams in Ireland); §20, §21; Bieler, *Libri*, ii, p. 145; Macalister, *Ancient Ireland*, 166.
15 *Confession*, §24f. (243.4−16).

himself forward', as his critics put it. It was God who encouraged him to escape from Ireland, and it was God who urged him to return there, to go back to the Wood of Voclut. He insists that 'God resists them all, so that I came to the tribes of Ireland to preach the gospel and to endure insults from unbelievers'.[16]

The accounts of the dreams, then, relate to his return to Britain and his departure thence for Ireland, and this part of the *Confession* is followed immediately by the description of his bishopric; and throughout the account of the bishopric there is no further mention of dreams. The purpose of reporting the dreams appears without doubt to have been to justify his escape from Ireland and his return to Ireland. There was certainly speculation about his motives in wishing to go back to the land of his bondage, as we shall see, and this is part of Patrick's reply to that speculation. He had no base motives. It was God's will that he should go there — of that he had no doubt. God had summoned him home when he was in Ireland. When he was at home, God called him to go back.

It is hardly possible to doubt that Patrick's dreams, as he describes them, really *were* dreams, authentic dreams. He did in fact see these visions. If he had invented them he would certainly have made their message far clearer and more explicit than in fact it is. The only purpose of inventing a 'dream' would be to justify clearly a decision which he had already taken and which perhaps had met with some opposition. But consider again that dream in which Patrick seems to confuse Helias with Helios. It is so obscure that it could hardly be used to justify anything. What is the point of Satan's temptation? Indeed, why does he infer that Satan was tempting him? Tempting him to do what? A reporter of fictitious dreams would have to do better than this. He would have to make the lesson of each dream far clearer and more pointed than Patrick does. The obscurity of the dreams is a good reason for thinking that they were genuine.

16 *Ibid.*, §37 (246.17). For Patrick's critics see *ibid.*, §45 (249.13).

CHAPTER FOUR

Palladius

In the year 431 Pope Celestine appointed a man called Palladius as bishop of 'the Irish who believe in Christ'. This is the first certain date in Irish history, and I do not know how many generations we have to wait before we come upon another. But 431 is recorded for us by an exact contemporary and a first-rate authority, Prosper of Aquitaine, writing in an edition of his *Chronicle* which he published in 433, only a couple of years after the event. The date of Palladius's appointment cannot be doubted and in fact never has been doubted by any sane man, so far as I know.

Prosper says more. He says that Palladius was the first bishop to go to the Irish; and that, too, we cannot possibly doubt. And we can also be sure that he was the only bishop in Ireland in 431. If Celestine had sent two bishops to the Irish, Prosper would hardly have fobbed us off by saying that he had sent only one. It would be wrong to argue that while Palladius was sent as bishop to the Irish Christian community or communities, someone else was sent to convert the pagans. The idea of a Catholic missionary bishop did not yet exist in the early fifth century. And it would be equally wrong to imagine that while Palladius was sent to the northern part of Ireland, someone else was labouring in the south, or *vice versa*, or that Leinster and Ulster were Christian while Munster and Connacht were pagan (or was it the other way round? It is hard to remember all the permutations.). Yet another opinion, supported by distinguished scholars, is that Patrick did indeed go to Ireland before Palladius because he was not strictly speaking a bishop at all — he was never consecrated canonically but simply called himself a bishop. I mention all these variations simply in order to illustrate how students of St Patrick have worked over the meagre evidence again and again, over and over, often with an axe to grind, not content with the obvious interpretation, but always hoping to discover even a single grain of wheat from a crop which was efficiently harvested years ago. But all such fantasies alike are mere wisps of smoke which a breath of wind can blow away. We know nothing whatever except what Prosper tells us; but what Prosper tells us we can believe without hesitation. So we have not the faintest idea which part or parts of Ireland Palladius visited. All we know is that he was the first Catholic bishop to go to Ireland, and in 431 he was the only bishop there. So whatever else may be doubtful in the career of St Patrick, one thing is certain: he was *not* the first bishop of the Irish.[1]

1. — *Palladius and Pelagius*

Palladius's appointment to Ireland was not his first appearance in history. He had also been concerned in combating the heresy of Pelagianism. Pelagius was a figure of capital importance in the West in the fifth century. Indeed, Dennis Bethell called him 'the greatest heretic ever produced by the Latin Church'. He was a Briton. Some scholars think that he was in fact Irish, having been born in one of the Irish settlements which seem to have existed in western Britain at this time. But I doubt it. He was a highly educated man, and it is improbable that these Irish settlers had already developed a system of higher education in Latin and that they were willing and able to send their sons to Latin 'rhetors'. If such Irish settlements existed at all, it is very unlikely that they included educated men like Pelagius. Let us say, then, that he was British, and that the hints that he was Irish were attempts by St Jerome (who was not noted for his generosity to his opponents) to smear him as a barbarian as well as a heretic. There is no doubt, then, that for the first and only time in ancient history a Briton created a storm among the educated classes of the Roman

1 Prosper, *Chronicle*, §1307 (Mommsen, *Chronica Minora*, I, p. 473). Macalister, *Ancient Ireland*, p. 169f., believed that Patrick was not a regular bishop, cf. Esposito, 'The Patrician Problem', p. 150f., Powell, 'The Textual Integrity', pp. 403−6, Müller, 'Der heilige Patrick', p. 102; but this view is strongly opposed by Nerney, 'A Study', p. 101f. There is a good page on Palladius in Binchy, 'Patrick and his Biographers', p. 134.

world. And what a storm he caused! 'There has never perhaps been another crisis of equal importance in Church history in which the opponents have expressed the principles at issue so clearly and abstractly.' Pelagius had left his native land before the end of the fourth century and had gone to Rome. About the time when Rome fell to the Goths in 410 this British layman was expressing opinions on the Christian religion which after a while caused intense and bitter controversy throughout the Christian West and to some extent even in the East. But it would be misleading to call Pelagianism 'the British heresy', for although Pelagius himself was a Briton his heresy is not known to have been an outgrowth of the specific conditions of the Church in Britain or of Christian opinion there. We know of no exceptional circumstances or opinions in Britain which would stamp the heresy as distinctively British. And indeed as long as Pelagius himself lived in Britain, he is thought to have been orthodox. It was only when he began to live in Italy that his opinions became heretical.[2]

The controversy centred on questions of Grace, Free Will, and Predestination. To the modern mind Pelagius's opinions seem harmless enough, but they caused St Jerome to experience a paroxysm of frantic rage and to write that Pelagius was a huge, corpulent man crammed with Irish porridge! (Hence the view that he may have been Irish.) Unfortunately the saint forgot to tell us whether there was some connexion between the Briton's taste for Irish porridge and his interest in free will. Pelagius's opinions were attacked year after dreary year by St Augustine, who, without citing much in the way of evidence — what could he cite? — propounded theories concerning the Fall, Original Sin, Predestination, and the undeserving few, upon whom God has conferred 'Grace', and the great bulk of us, equally undeserving, who will be punished for ever — not because of our sins, of course, but because we have inherited 'Original Sin'![3]

Palladius became convinced that the successes of the heresy in Britain were dangerous, and on his first appearance in history he urged Pope Celestine to send a champion of orthodoxy to combat Pelagianism in the island. Celestine was impressed. He acted on Palladius's advice and sent Germanus, bishop of Auxerre, and Lupus, bishop of Troyes, to Britain in 429. This proposal of Palladius's to the pope, that he should send a representative to Britain, now outside the Roman Empire in the remote north, shows that

2 The quotations are from Bethell, 'The Originality', p. 39, and Harnack, *History of Dogma*, V, p. 160, respectively.
3 For a brief account of Pelagius and Augustine see Brown, *Augustine of Hippo*, pp. 340—52.

even before he himself was appointed to Ireland he had a considerable knowledge, perhaps even first-hand experience, of conditions in the far north-west of the Empire and even of conditions outside its frontiers. Undoubtedly, the biography of Palladius, if only we had the materials to write it, would make an unusually interesting story. What had aroused his interest not only in the old lost province of Britain but even in the 'barbarian island' which had never been Roman? Is it possible that he had visited Ireland even before 431? If so, he had done what few Romans other than a handful of traders are known to have done.

It was in 412 that Augustine began the series of his writings against Pelagius. So far as Patrick was concerned, he was wasting his time. Augustine and Pelagius alike might well never have taken up their pens. Patrick, for all that we can tell, never heard of the controversy which gripped educated Christians throughout the outside world, or, if he had heard of it, he wisely decided to put it to one side. His adult life coincided with the period of the Pelagians' greatest activity in Britain, and that is why some scholars have thought that it is 'antecedently likely' that he had heard of it. But he never hints that he had. There is not a phrase in his writings which suggests that he knew anything about it. Whatever else we may say of him, it is certain that he did not see his task in Ireland as aimed at fighting Pelagianism.[4]

How can we account for Patrick's dead silence about a movement which had electrified the highest ecclesiastical circles of Gaul, Italy, and Africa? As we have seen, Patrick was not a speculative theologian. It is in the highest degree unlikely that he studied the new books and tracts as they came out — I mean, the books and tracts which dealt with theological speculations. His interests lay elsewhere, in mission work, a new kind of mission work. But there is a further point. The only other British author who might have been expected to mention Pelagius is equally silent about him. Gildas early in the following century set out to list the evils which Britain had inflicted on the rest of mankind. He is interested in heresy and knows of Arianism (which had never been a threat in Britain). Surely Pelagianism was a wonderful example of what he was looking for,

---

4 Nerney, 'A Study', p. 22, but he puts forward not a single argument to support this theory. See the criticism of Hanson, *Patrick: His Origins*, pp. 173–5. Even Bethell, 'The Originality', p. 40, writes that 'he protests so strongly that he is not Pelagian', without giving his reasons for so thinking. In this matter Nerney has been followed by Malaspina, 'Patrizio', pp. 131–60. That Patrick was not familiar with Augustine's *Confessions* was shown by O'Meara, 'The Confession of St Patrick', pp. 190–7; cf. idem, 'Patrick's *Confessio*', pp. 44–53.

the best imaginable stick to beat the Britons with. Among their other wicked acts (he might have said) the Britons had inflicted a vile heresy upon the Christian world. Pelagianism was tailor-made for his argument. Yet of Pelagius he says not a word, and it would be hard to show that he was being deliberately silent. The inference is that he had never heard of him. My own view (which is incapable of proof) is that the teachings of Pelagius, in so far as they had reached Britain at all, were spread *not* throughout the island as a whole but only in a restricted area, perhaps in the south-east of the island which was the part most open to influences from the Continent. And so, Patrick and Gildas, both of them probably west-countrymen, had never heard of it.[5]

Prosper pays more attention to Pelagianism than to any other heresy — naturally enough, since it was the major heresy in the European provinces in his day. But his chronicle, like all the fifth-century chronicles, is short, and he has space to tell his readers only about the highlights of the history of the Pelagian heresy — its origin, the condemnation by Pope Innocent and by St Augustine, the struggle of a high official called Constantius against it, the condemnation by a council of 214 bishops at Carthage in 418, the rejection of Julian of Eclana by Pope Sixtus. He has no room for the attitude of St Jerome or for the expulsion of the Pelagians first from Italy and then from Gaul, or for the condemnation of the heresy by Pope Boniface and by Pope Zosimus, or for the passing of a law against it which has been described as 'the most depressing edict in the Later Roman Empire'. And yet he has been able to find room to include among the really outstanding events of the struggle Germanus's visit to combat the heresy in Britain. His inclusion of this matter shows of what major importance he thought the British episode to be. It was one of the big events, and yet since the year 409 Britain had lain outside the frontier of the Roman Empire.[6]

2. — *Palladius and Ireland*

When Prosper reports the appointment of Palladius to Ireland, he says nothing of the possible conversion of the pagan Irish to Christianity. No pope before Gregory the Great, who died in 604, is

5 Thompson, *St Germanus*, pp. 50–54.
6 Brown, *op. cit.*, p. 361, commenting on Migne, *Patrologia Latina*, XXXVIII, col. 379–86.

known to have taken the lead in mission-work; and Celestine was no exception. He did not intend Palladius to become a missionary, or at any rate did not intend his main effort to lie in mission-work. He was to minister to the Irish who already believed in Christ. Those whom Prosper calls 'Irish' undoubtedly included a number of British Christians who had either left their homes in Britain voluntarily or as refugees, or had been taken away by force like Patrick himself. It is hardly likely that the new bishop was intended to ignore or neglect these. But Prosper's wording suggests that the Christians in Ireland were mostly Irish. The bulk of them were not Romano-British immigrants but Irish natives. That is hardly a point on which Prosper can have been very well informed — nor would he have taken many pains to clarify it, if he ever thought of it at all. But we cannot ascribe a mistake to him without any evidence to support us. We must take his words literally: the bulk of the Christians in Ireland in 431 were Irish, not immigrants from Britain. So when Palladius was appointed, it was none of his business to go out among the heathen and convert them: he had enough to do among the faithful.

Prosper never mentions events merely because they were quaint or strange or because they took place in a far distant country. He is not writing a book of wonders or oddities. Yet he gives not much less space to the appointment of Palladius as bishop in Ireland than to the death of St Augustine or the Council of Chalcedon (which admittedly was greatly underestimated in the West). It does not follow, of course, that he thought all these events to be equally important, but he certainly thought all these matters to be very much on the same general level of importance. He did not think it absurd to mention them all, as it were, in the same breath. Having decided to chronicle the outstanding events of his time, he included the death of St Augustine and the appointment of Palladius to Ireland. The latter event, too, was an important one. It could not be omitted. His record of the chief events would be incomplete without it. It was one of the highlights. But wherein did its importance lie in the opinion of this Gaul of Aquitaine? It was certainly not important because it took the bishop across an ocean which no bishop had ever crossed before: at best, that was a matter of indifference. Travelling to the end of the earth was not a romantic or exciting thing to do in the eyes of a Roman chronicler at this date. Patrick himself never tires of telling his readers that he went to the very extremity of the world; but that was not intended as a boast. It was a hardship, a dangerous hardship, something which a wise man would avoid if he could. There was nothing romantic about it, nothing inspiring. It was a fulfilment of the scriptures.

We do not know the answer to the question, Where in the judgement of Prosper did the importance of Palladius's appointment to Ireland lie? But it is at first sight tempting to assume that there was a connexion — though nobody has ever been able to prove a connexion — between Palladius's mission to the Irish and the mission, which Palladius himself instigated, of Germanus to Britain. The aim of that mission was to crush the Pelagianism of the Britons (or some of them). In other words, it is tempting to assume that Pelagian ideas had gained a foothold among the Christian communities in Ireland and that it was Palladius's task to combat them. Or perhaps the pope feared that Pelagianism might begin to spread to Ireland in the near future, and it was Palladius's task to anticipate the danger and stamp it out as soon as it made its appearance. This idea is an old one and has often been discussed. The wisest course is to take up the opinion of Bury, who remarked that the theory is 'not impossible, though it is not proven'.[7]

If the fight against heresy had been a major part of Patrick's mission, he would inevitably have let slip a word or two about it either by design or by accident. Indeed, if it had been a major aim of his bishopric to refute the Pelagians, his procedure in writing the *Confession* is unaccountable. My own view is that if the purpose of sending a bishop to Ireland had something to do with heresy, the appointing committee chose the wrong man when they recommended Patrick! Or perhaps the original purpose of the mission had been very decidedly forgotten by the time when Patrick was sent out. The safest course is to think that Prosper admired the initiative of the pope in sending Palladius to Ireland, not because this was a blow against Pelagianism, but because the mission so quickly brought such rich returns for the Catholic Church, or was thought to have done so, as we shall see.

But if that was the case, we must count ourselves lucky enough that Prosper made any reference at all to the mission of Palladius. This entry about Palladius's appointment to Ireland is unique in Prosper's *Chronicle*. There is no other like it. Elsewhere he never records the appointment of its first bishop to any community of converts inside or outside the Roman Empire. Yet throughout the first half of the fifth century the popes must have sent their first bishops to

7 Bieler, *The Life and Legend*, p. 70, accepts the idea that Patrick was appointed to combat Pelagianism; cf. his 'The Mission of Palladius', pp. 3, 23. Contrast Bury, *The Life*, p. 52.

several groups of Christians in several parts of the world. But, if so, they never earned an entry in any of the chronicles for doing so. If Prosper mentioned the appointment of Palladius to the Irish Christians merely because it was an oddity, a bishop working outside the Imperial frontier, then why did he not also mention Ninian (or whoever it may have been) who went to the Picts north of the Firth of Forth at some date which his chronicle certainly covered? That bishop converted them, or some of them, not to the Arian heresy but to Catholic Christianity, and so in Prosper's judgement his importance would have been undeniable — if he had ever heard of him.

Having told how Palladius was sent to Ireland, Prosper in his *Chronicle* says no more about that country and never mentions Patrick. Having told how Germanus of Auxerre went to Britain to combat Pelagianism in 429, the chronicler says no more about Britain. Although his chronicle continues to the year 455 he never mentions Germanus's second visit to the island or the fate of Pelagianism there. To have done so would have been contrary to the normal practice of the fifth-century chroniclers. To give a second entry to either of these two events, the mission of Germanus and that of Palladius, would have been regarded by Prosper as wholly unnecessary, even unthinkable, and as actually devoting excessive space to them. He would have gained nothing by adding that after the death or retirement of Palladius another bishop was appointed. We are lucky enough to have the name of the first bishop and the fact of his being sent to Ireland. It was one thing to date the pope's original initiative in Ireland. It was quite another to write a brief history of the Church in Ireland with a clerical *Who's Who* thrown in.

3. — Christianity among the Northern Barbarians

Palladius went to serve 'the Irish who believe in Christ'. How had Christianity reached Ireland before 431? A mid-fifth-century pamphlet called *The Call of All Nations* — we cannot doubt now that it was written by that same chronicler Prosper of Aquitaine — tells of the ways in which Christianity crossed the Imperial Roman frontiers into the lands of the barbarians. In fact, this was a subject which was of little interest to the Christian writers of the fourth and fifth centuries, and it is difficult to find any extended discussion of it.

But Prosper in this pamphlet does deal with it, though very briefly. He says that barbarian warriors who had enlisted in the Roman army might come to know and accept the religion of many of the inhabitants of the Empire and would then take the new faith back with them to the country of their origin. Since we rarely hear of Irishmen enlisting in the Imperial forces, it would seem that few Christians can have been won in Ireland by ex-soldiers. Secondly, he observes that the Christians, when carried off captive by the barbarians, would sometimes enslave their masters to the gospel of Christ and would win them to the faith. It is worth bearing in mind that the tribal leaders might well be given a disproportionate share of the captives and would certainly be the most likely people to have enough surplus goods to buy imported slaves. It follows that enslaved Christians might well have access to the most influential figures in the land of their captivity.[8]

The mid-fifth-century Greek ecclesiastical historian, Sozomen, also speaks of the spread of Christianity outside the frontier. He appears to think that this second method of conversion was common enough in the East. Writing of the Gothic raids on Asia Minor in the dark years of the mid-third century, when the Roman Empire appeared to be falling apart and breaking up, he remarks that the raiders carried off many of the inhabitants of the raided provinces. Some of these were Christians. The Goths carried them back to their homelands north of the Black Sea into what is now the Ukraine and later into what is now Romania. Sozomen goes on to say that among the prisoners taken away to 'Gothia' were a number of Christian clergy, and these men attracted the attention of their masters by performing cures in the name of Jesus Christ, whom they called the son of God. They attracted further attention by the blameless lives which they led, and their virtues disarmed mockers among the tribesmen. As a result some of the barbarians would try to imitate them. They would receive instruction from them and eventually were baptised. What Sozomen in the East and Prosper in the West report in this connexion would apply, no doubt, not only to the lands north of the Black Sea and the lower Danube but also to regions beyond other frontiers, including Ireland. Neither Sozomen nor Prosper claims that a high percentage of the barbarians was converted by means of the prisoners, but no doubt they won local successes. What no

---

8 The authorship of the *De Vocatione Omnium Gentium*, II, p. 33 (in Migne, *Patrologia Latina*, 51. 712f.) has been settled in my opinion by Cappuyns, 'L'auteur', pp. 198–226 (a reference which I owe to Professor R. Markus of Nottingham).

ancient writer claims is that traders carried the Christian religion with them across the Imperial frontiers, and there is no reason to suppose that traders crossing the Irish Sea were any different in this respect from Continental traders. Probably few of them were Christian; and in any case, as Esposito puts it, 'the picture of wine-merchants as propagators of the gospel is far from convincing: they had wares of stronger immediate appeal to dispose of'.[9]

If we ask, then, how Christianity had reached Ireland before 431, the answer is very obscure. A number of the Christians there may have been converted by some of the prisoners whom they had shipped over from Britain, and especially perhaps by the clergy among those prisoners. It is remarkable, however, that Patrick does not mention that members of the clergy had been taken captive. Perhaps that means that what he saw on the stupifying, stunning day of his own capture was blurred in his memory, or perhaps it means that any such admission would have contradicted his statement that the British victims were carried away because of the sinfulness of their lives. Perhaps it simply was the case that no clergy were taken on that day in his vicinity. The clergy would most likely have been inside the towns, and so did not fall into the raiders' hands. At all events, he never speaks of any successes that such clergy may have won. This may be due to lack of information. He was separated from his fellow-prisoners when he was sold away to Co Mayo, and even if others were sold to the same neighbourhood he was isolated from them by his lonely work as a shepherd. But Patrick's silence concerning the work and even the existence of his Christian predecessors in Ireland is all too well known, and is not the most attractive feature of his writings.

Of course, there were many ways in which British Christians could have reached Ireland besides going there as kidnapped slaves. Britons might have fled there to escape the Imperial tax-gatherers, as men fled to other barbarians from other parts of the Empire. Some of the fugitives might have been army deserters, and so on. The essential point is that a proportion of them must have been Christian and free; and we must never forget Patrick's statement that 'as for those of our race who were born there [in Ireland] we do not know their number.' The pope would hardly have sent a bishop so far away if the new

---

9 Sozomen, *Historia Ecclesiastica*, II. 6, 2 (ed. Bidez, p. 58). For a specific case note the bishop's daughter in Augustine, *Epistle*, CXI. 7 (*CSEL* XXXIV, ii, p. 654), but she is not said to have converted the barbarians. The quotation is from Esposito, 'The Patrician Problem', p. 145.

bishop was to minister only to a handful or a few dozen converts. Now, it was a rule formulated by Pope Celestine himself that a bishop must not be sent to a community of Christians which did not want to have a bishop. So, although the Irish Christians may have been few in 431, they must have had some sort of organisation which the pope or his advisers could consult on the question of appointing a bishop. And the existence of such an organisation shows in itself that the Christian communities included others besides slaves. For clerics to come from outside Ireland and arrange a Christian organisation among the slave-population would have been to invite merciless punishment. There was some means, then, of sounding out opinion among the Christian communities in Ireland and of deciding that a bishop would be welcome; and this could only be done among freemen.[10]

There is no great difficulty in seeing how Christian slaves came to exist in Ireland in some numbers. The problem is to account for the existence of numbers of Christian freemen and free-women and especially of free British Christians there. The fact that their opinion could be sounded out implies the existence of at least one free community. How did it come into being, and how was it replenished? These are questions to which we cannot even guess the answers. But although we cannot account for the existence of such a community or communities, it or they must have existed.[11]

4. — Christian Missions

What neither Sozomen nor Prosper nor anyone else mentions in the early fifth century is the conversion of the barbarians by organised Catholic missions. And for a very good reason: there were none. It is

10 For Romans among the barbarians see e.g. Orosius, *Hist.* VII. 41, 7; Priscus of Panium, *Hist.* fragment 8 (in Müller, *Fragmenta*, IV, pp. 86−8), Sulpicius Severus, *Dialogue*, I. 3, 6; Prudentius, *Hamartigenia*, 455−61 (ed. & transl., Lavarenne, II, p. 57). Various linguistic arguments used to be brought forward to prove the existence of Christianity in Ireland in the fourth century, e.g. by O'Rahilly, *The Two Patricks*, pp. 42−5, Binchy, 'Patrick and His Biographers', pp. 165f., Greene, 'Some linguistic Evidence', pp. 78−81. But these have been criticised by Jackson, 'Some Questions in Dispute', pp. 18−32. Note also Binchy's review of Jackson, *Language and History*, p. 289, and Shaw, 'The Linguistic Argument', pp. 315−22. But McManus, 'A Chronology of the Latin Loan-Words', pp. 21−71, sees no grounds for supposing that there was any break between early and late groups of such words: the adoption of Latin words was continuous. In fact, there is no direct evidence for Christianity in Ireland in the fourth century.

11 Celestine, *Epistle*, iv 'nullus inuitis detur episcopus' (in Migne, *Patrologia Latina*, 50 p. 434).

of the utmost importance for understanding St Patrick's place in history to know that in the fourth and fifth centuries the Catholic Church was not interested in diffusing Christianity outside the frontiers of the Roman Empire. It is significant that in the whole range of West Roman Christian literature only one writer — Prosper in *The Call of All Nations* — troubles to tell us specific ways in which Christianity managed to cross the frontier, and even he does so in a very few lines of the modern printed text. Augustine has one or two remarks on the subject. He says that there were countless barbarian tribes in Africa among which Christianity had not yet been preached. He had learned this from some of the tribesmen who had been brought into the Empire as slaves. Within the past few years, he says, the Imperial government had imposed Roman prefects in place of their native chieftains on some of these tribes; and in such cases, which were very few, the people had adopted the religion of their new ruler. But the tribes living in the interior, away from Roman influence, remained pagan. Augustine, while noting this situation, shows no uncontrollable eagerness to change it. To all the other writers of that period the question was of no interest whatever, and hardly one of them refers to it, still less discusses it. And even Prosper treats it as a very minor topic indeed.[12]

And yet the Arians sent out missions to the Germanic barbarians; and very successful they were. The Catholic writers hardly ever comment on these Arian successes. It does not seem to occur to them to ask how Arianism had won its victories or who had propagated the heresy or to suggest that these victories could and should (from the Catholic point of view) be countered by Catholic missions. The concept of an organised mission to convert the pagan or heretical barbarians is apparently beyond their grasp. Such an idea lies on the other side of the horizon. Condemn the heresy at Councils of the Church, and you have done all that can be done. In fact, leaving the case of Ireland aside for the moment, the first occasion on which we hear of the conversion of a barbarian people to Catholicism in the West is when we hear that Clovis and the Franks had been won over at the end of the fifth century. Then at the beginning of the sixth century an African chronicler tells of the conversion, not of a Western people, but of a Saracen chief far away on the eastern border of the Empire in 512. (It is noteworthy that this chronicler had apparently never heard of Clovis and the Franks in the remote north.) But no

12 Augustine, *Epistle*, CXCIX, 46 (*CSEL*, LVII, p. 284f.).

fifth-century Catholic, so far as we know, asked why the Arians found it worth while to propagate their beliefs among the Germanic barbarians, or what methods they used, and whether the Catholic Church could or ought to imitate them.[13]

But in all this the chroniclers are only imitating the attitude of the Church itself. The Catholic Church is not reported to have sent any bishop or lesser clergy to minister to the Catholic prisoners held in Gothia during the later third century or the first decades of the fourth; and even the Arians did not consecrate Ulfila as bishop until 341. In other words, for two generations after the prisoners had been carried off from their homes in Asia Minor and elsewhere they were neglected by the churches. Then in 341 Ulfila was appointed not to act as bishop of the Goths in general but to serve as bishop of those Christians who were already living in Gothia in 341 and who were probably for the most part not Visigoths at all but Roman prisoners or their descendants. That is to say, it was not the aim of those who appointed Ulfila as bishop that he should win the pagan Goths to Christianity but simply that he should serve and organise those Romans and others in Gothia who had already been converted. The conversion of the barbarians was outside his terms of reference. The parallel with Palladius is exact.

Moreover, the conversion of the Vandals, Ostrogoths, and the others who became Arians may well have been due to the work not of Roman but of Visigothic missionaries. At all events, there is little evidence that Roman Arians went to work among them. The only Arian Roman author who has anything to say about the conversion of the barbarians has no more sympathy with them than the Catholics had felt. He admits that God is prepared to call barbarians as well as civilised men, but he castigates the priests who propagate the word of God among 'unlearned, undisciplined, and barbarian peoples, who neither seek nor hear it with judgement, and who have the name of Christians but the manners of pagans.' If that was the normal attitude of Roman Arians towards the barbarians, it is hardly surprising if the attempts to convert them were the work of Arian Gothic missionaries and not of Romans at all.[14]

One reason for the backwardness of the Church in trying to convert the barbarians was presumably the view held by a number of churchmen that the barbarians were not fully human. According to

13 Victor Tonnennensis, *Chronicle*, §512 (Mommsen, *Chronica Minora*, II, p. 195.).
14 *Opus Imperfectum In Matthaeum*, Homily XXXV (Migne, *Patrologia Graeca*, 56. 824, cf. 864).

the devout Spanish hymn-writer Prudentius, 'Roman and barbarian are as far apart as the quadruped is distant from the biped, or the dumb from that which can speak.' Another bishop speaks of the Huns as being 'almost human', 'quasi men'. Roman clerics treated barbarians accordingly. So pious a Christian as St Ambrose, for example, advocated a policy of exporting wine to the barbarians so that they might become addicted to it and then might be conquered by their own inebriety, as he charmingly puts it. Indeed, even within the Imperial frontiers distant peoples might seem to those in the centres of civilisation to be none too human. St Isidore of Seville quotes the view, for example, that the inhabitants of Britain are called 'British' in Latin because they are 'brutish' (an etymology which has found few supporters in Britain). St Jerome describes as 'British' a mysterious people called the *Attacotti* (though whether from inside Hadrian's Wall or outside, he does not say). Like the Irish, he tells us, they held their wives in common. They also raided Gaul, and when he himself was a lad, he had watched some Attacotti eating human flesh — they were cannibals as well as British — and although they did not abstain from pigs, cattle, and sheep, their favourite titbits (if I may phrase it so) were women's breasts and shepherds' buttocks. Incidentally, if Jerome was standing there watching them, we might wonder why they did not eat *him*, too. If a non-cannibal may have an opinion, I suggest they knew such a scholarly ascetic would not make an appetising dinner.[15]

It is no surprise, then, to find that when Prosper reports the appointment of Palladius to Ireland, he says nothing of the possible conversion of the pagan Irish to Christianity. That was not what Pope Celestine had in mind. Palladius was to minister to the Irish who already believed in Christ. The reason why the Irish were singled out for special treatment *may* have been the fear of the pope and his advisers that heresy might win a footing in Ireland if no action was taken to counter it. But whether such a possibility is worth discussing is open to doubt. At any rate, those whom Prosper calls 'Irish' undoubtedly included a number of Christians who had been taken from their homes in Britain or else had migrated voluntarily. It is hardly likely that the new bishop was intended to ignore and neglect these. But Prosper's wording suggests that in his opinion (if he ever thought about the matter) the Christians in Ireland were

15 Prudentius, *Contra Symmachum*, II, 816–9 (ed. & transl., Lavarenne, III, p. 186); Jordanes, *Getica*, 122 (ed. T. Mommsen, p. 89); Isidore, *Origines* (ed. Lindsay); St Jerome, *Adversus Iouinianum*, ii, 7 (Migne, *Patrologia Latina*, 23, 308f.).

predominantly Irish, not British. What is of the first importance to understand is that there was no question of sending a mission to convert the pagans. We may be sure that such a proposal was never put forward at the councils of the pope. It was none of Palladius's business to go out among the heathen and try to convert them. The pagan Irish were of as little interest to the authorities in Rome in 431 as the pagan Visigoths had been to the authorities in Constantinople in 341.

It is not a matter for surprise that we know so little about the ways in which Christianity reached the barbarians outside the Roman Empire. We know astonishingly little about the methods which Christians used to diffuse it *inside* the Empire. The ways in which the new religion travelled from city to city along the great roads is an obscure and tantalising chapter in Roman history.[16]

16 On the diffusion of Christianity inside the Roman Empire see the brilliant book by Macmullen, *Christianizing the Roman Empire*.

CHAPTER FIVE

Patrick Appointed Bishop

Before Patrick could become bishop in Ireland he seems to have suffered a major defeat, a reverse of such a size that he can speak of himself as 'trampled underfoot' by it. But the part of the *Confession* which deals with the incident is extraordinarily hard to understand even by Patrick's standards. Each word he writes here is simple enough in itself (though one or two are ambiguous); but the meaning of the passage as a whole is almost unfathomable. To some extent this is because he assumes his readers to be familiar with the general outline of what happened, so that he can be content with filling in the details. But he does not expect his readers to know everything about what happened. It seems to have been only in part a public event, and to say it happened at a 'synod' is only less absurd than to say that it took place at 'a large clerical gathering at Auxerre'! Scholars are divided on other issues in Patrick's life, but on this they are separated by a bottomless chasm. And yet he has more to say about this incident than about any other single event apart from his escape from Ireland. To him it is of crucial importance. It is an event on which he has the deepest feelings. Even towards the end of his life, when writing the *Confession*, he is as anxious as ever that his readers should understand and accept his point of view. Let us hope that they grasped it more easily than we can![1]

1 For Bieler's revised judgement on this episode see his 'Patriciology', pp. 25–9, repeated in his 'St Patrick and the British Church', cf. MacNeill, *St Patrick*, p. 63f., etc. In general, I accept their interpretation of the incident rather than that supported by Bury, Binchy,

1. — Patrick's Narrative

Here is a translation of what he says:

And when I was tested by some of my seniors, who came and <urged> my sins against my laborious episcopate, on that day I was pushed forcefully that I might fall here and for ever; but the Lord kindly spared a stranger and sojourner for his name's sake and helped me powerfully when I was thus trampled underfoot. What a blessing that I did not fall into ruin and disgrace! I pray God that it should not be accounted to them as a sin.

They found an opportunity against me after thirty years in a word which I had confessed before I was a deacon. Because of my anxiety I sorrowfully made known to my closest friend what I had done in one day, or rather in a single hour, in my boyhood because I was not yet strong. I do not know (God knows) if I was then fifteen years old, and I did not believe in the living God and had not done so from my infancy, but I remained in death and in unbelief until I was severely punished and in truth was humiliated by hunger and nakedness, and that every day.

No, I did not go to Ireland of my own free will until I was almost at the end of my strength, but this rather was good for me seeing that I was corrected by the Lord thereby, and he fitted me so that I might be today what once was far from me, that I might have compassion and might busy myself for the salvation of others, when at that time I used not to think even of my own self.

So on that day on which I was rejected by the aforementioned and aforesaid, in that night I saw in a vision of the night there was a writing without honour opposite my face, and then I heard a divine response telling me: 'We have seen with displeasure the face of . . .' — the person mentioned, and his name laid bare; and it did not begin thus, 'You have seen with displeasure', but, 'We have seen with displeasure', as though including himself with <me>, as he said, 'He who touches you is as if touching the pupil of my eye'.

So I give thanks to him who comforted me in all things because he did not prevent me from setting out on the journey which I had decided upon nor from the work which I had learned from Christ the Lord, but rather from him I felt in myself no small strength, and my faith was approved before God and man.

That is why I say boldly that my conscience does not blame me here

---

Carney, Hanson, and others, in spite of the eminence of the latter group. But I cannot accept the view of Bieler, 'Patriciology', p. 28, that *responsum* in *Confession*, §32 (244.27) refers back to the *responsum diuinum* in *ibid.*, §29 (244.14). The passage which follows in translation is *Confession*, §26−32 (243.17−245−6).

and in the future, God is my witness that I did not lie in the talks which I have reported to you.

But I grieve more for my closest friend <as to> why we deserved to hear such a message. To him I entrusted even my soul! And before that defence of mine I learned from some of the brethren — since I was not present nor was I in Britain, nor did the initiative arise from me — that he struggled for me in my absence; and he even said to me with his own lips, 'Look, you ought to be [or, you are going to be] raised to the rank of bishop', of which I was not worthy. But what came over him afterwards that he should dishonour me in front of all, good and bad, and publicly, in a matter in which he had indulged me previously of his own accord and gladly — and the Lord, who is greater than all.

2. — *The Meaning of the Narrative*

From this rigmarole a few things seem to be clear enough. Patrick was interviewed or examined by persons whom he calls 'seniors' but whom (most unfortunately) he does not define further. In their estimation his boyhood sin counted against him: they had been told about it by the friend to whom he had confided it thirty years previously. Accordingly, the seniors formed an unfavourable view of him. All this happened when he was not in Britain: presumably, he was already living in Ireland. At any rate, God kept his morale high and did not prevent him from setting out on the journey which he had planned. The upshot was that he did not go to Ireland as bishop until he was old.

The main problem is to decide whether this event took place *before* Patrick became a bishop, or at a time when he had been bishop for many years — for thirty years, according to one theory. If the former, Patrick is telling here how he was interviewed for the post of bishop and was not appointed. If the latter, he is talking about criticisms which were made of him after he had been bishop in Ireland for many years. Scholars are fairly evenly divided on the question. For my part, I am convinced that the former view of the passage is correct. If we adopt it, we are admittedly faced with one difficulty, but only one, of any great consequence. If we accept the second interpretation — that he is talking about criticisms made of him long after he became bishop — we are confronted not with one but with a whole army of crises and problems, marching down upon us, four abreast, in a most menacing way.

Patrick discusses this incident immediately after describing the visions which called him back to Ireland — that in which Victoricus appeared to him and the two subsequent dreams in which he was encouraged to return there (pp. 37, 40 above). And immediately after telling of this episode he begins to describe his aims and his work as bishop in Ireland. So if this incident occurred after he decided to go to Ireland but before his mission actually started, all is well. He is narrating the events in chronological order — his youth, the interview with the seniors (whoever they may have been), his eventual career as bishop. But on the theory that he was a bishop of several years' standing when the interview took place, his narrative of events is not chronological. It is chaotic. The plan of the *Confession* would show neither rhyme nor reason, and Patrick would be open to the accusation of skipping to and fro in a most unbishop-like manner and of jumping backwards and forwards in time quite arbitrarily. That would certainly not be beyond him: as a writer, it is an understatement to say that he leaves much to be desired. But there is no just cause for us to confound the confusion still further. In fact, he gives no hint that the interview was a recent event. It might have stopped him from setting out on the journey which he had decided on, that is, no doubt, his journey back to Ireland; and he is grateful to God for not so stopping him. His gratitude on this score would have been pointless if in fact he had set out on his mission years ago whereas it is very much in place if the interview was held before he became bishop. So the order in which he narrates the events favours dating this episode to the time before he became bishop. But since he is so disorganised a writer, it would be unwise to lay much stress on this fact.

Our second argument is a stronger one. The inference that Patrick had been a bishop for some years is not easy to reconcile with his friend's assurance that 'You ought to be raised to the rank of bishop'. It is not easy to imagine any circumstances in which a man would say these words to someone who had been a bishop for years. And Patrick also says that *before* his defence at the meeting of the seniors his old friend had struggled for him — perhaps we might say, had 'canvassed' for him. Why should he struggle or canvass for him if he had already been consecrated years before? That would be a ludicrous case of labour lost! If the friend made these efforts when Patrick was already a bishop, our difficulties are insurmountable. We cannot even begin to overcome them. Here, then, is a formidable argument: it is decidedly unusual for a sober man to say to a bishop,

'You ought to be raised to the rank of bishop'.[2]

Again, if Patrick was a bishop at the time of the incident, who were his 'seniors'? To say that 'they were the group of ecclesiastics in Britain who in the beginning, though far from unanimous, endorsed his mission', men who 'continued to exercise a right of advice and criticism, and when Patrick had been a bishop in Ireland for thirty years, censured and possibly made an effort to recall him', is to write historical fiction. And not very good fiction, for such a type of adviser and controller would be hard to parallel in the rest of Western church-organisation. Who then are a bishop's superiors? Patrick does not for one moment question the right of the seniors, as he calls them, to interview and reject him. He takes it for granted that they had indeed such a right. If their business was to appoint a new bishop, or to advise on such an appointment, his attitude is clear enough. But otherwise, what did they hope to gain by taxing an established bishop with a sin which he had committed, or rather had confessed to, *thirty years* earlier? What was their motive? Suppose that they did indeed establish the point that Patrick was a bad missionary and that thirty years ago he had disgraced himself, what would they have gained? His recall, admittedly somewhat late in the day? But who had authority to recall a bishop from Ireland? Who can have had authority even to rebuke a bishop there on such a charge? The absence of any clear motive on the part of the seniors is in itself a strong argument against the theory that they criticised Patrick when he was bishop. On this theory it would not be too much to say that the incident is meaningless, had no cause and no effect other than the inflicting of pain on the missionary. On this theory, the whole affair is inconsequential, like a scene from *Alice in Wonderland*. Did the seniors travel over to Ireland simply to tell the hard-working bishop there that he was a failure? But most ecclesiastics in Britain, if they knew of Patrick at all, must have been delighted with the results of his labours in Ireland, or, if they thought little of the conversion of mere barbarians, at least they can hardly have been purple-faced with rage and determined to go over there and give him a piece of their mind. In fact, the very vagueness of the incident is in itself almost decisive against any such interpretation.

But another, and no less strong, argument is Patrick's own vagueness in narrating the matter. If he does not explain to his readers the identity of the critics (other than by calling them 'seniors'), their

2 For the friend's words see *Confession*, §32 (245.2f.). Bieler, *The Life and Legend*, p. 68, and Carney, *The Problem*, p. 86, believe that the friend was one of the seniors.

motives in criticising him, the nature of their criticisms, and the results of their action, what is the point of speaking of the matter at all? On this theory his readers might be forgiven for wondering what it was that they were reading about — unless in fact they knew the answers to these questions already, in which case it was hardly worth Patrick's while to discuss the incident at all. What Patrick does tell us is what the critical seniors did *not* achieve: they did not stop him from setting out on the journey which he was determined to make or from achieving that work which he had learned from Christ. But that in itself might be taken to mean that the interview with the seniors took place *before* Patrick set out for Ireland as bishop. Our third and fourth arguments, then, are that if Patrick is telling how he was censured after being for many years a bishop, his narrative comes close to being gibberish.[3]

Carney supports the view that Patrick was censured when already a bishop, and he depicts the scene as follows: 'As historians we shall have to face the fact that a council of Patrick's contemporaries, high-ranking ecclesiastics, sat in judgement of his thirty years' work and saw fit to censure him!' It is true, as Carney says, that although we have the speech for the defence, the prosecution's case is missing. But if these high-ranking ecclesiastics really censured a man who had braved death and slavery on endless occasions and who was in a position to say without fear of contradiction that he had baptised 'thousands' of the Irish, they were (we might think) a shade heavy-handed, a trifle ham-fisted, and inclined in addition to be more than a little flat-footed, while he himself was unwise to be troubled over-much by their crass opinion. Yet he was a man for whom the risk of enslavement and of murder was all in the day's work throughout the time when he was a bishop. Is it likely that he would have lost much sleep because of the impertinent criticisms of a handful of nameless, faceless stay-at-home nonentities? Perhaps. Perhaps not. The unlikely *gaucherie* of the seniors if they were dealing with an established bishop is another argument. But if the incident occurred when he was not yet a bishop, we can understand why he was deeply wounded by the criticism: this was something like a vote of no confidence.[4]

Again, we must ask in what sense a bishop can be said to be rejected — the Latin word could hardly mean 'deposed'. There is no

3 See Bieler, *The Life and Legend*, p. 135 n. 36. Note also Binchy, 'St Patrick and his Biographers', p. 93–5. The quotation is from Carney, *The Problem*, p. 95.
4 Carney, *op. cit.*, p. 97.

reason to think that the seniors were backed by the authority of a synod; and indeed it is not clear that a British synod could have exercised any legitimate power over a bishop living and working in Ireland. When the Church tried to crush the Pelagian heretics in Britain in 429, it was not a synod of the Gallic bishops who sent Germanus of Auxerre across the sea (although Constantius of Lyons in his *Life of St Germanus* would have us believe that it was and himself believed that it was). It was Pope Celestine himself who sent Germanus to Britain. Is it likely that the pope of the day sent out Patrick's seniors (whoever they may have been) to resurrect and criticise a boyhood sin, a sin of which they knew only by hearsay? Of course not. Heresy is one thing, a personal sin committed at the age of fifteen is quite another.

The fact is that if we accept the theory that the seniors criticised Patrick when he had been a successful bishop for many years, we lie buried under a mountain of problems like the giant who is said to lie buried under Mount Etna; but whereas the giant under Etna is able to rumble and belch out a cloud of smoke from time to time, there are no such luxuries for us. We must lie there belchless, unrumbling. But on the other theory there is indeed a problem, a very difficult problem (it has to be confessed). What are we to make of that phrase at the beginning of the passage which I have just translated — that they balanced 'my sins against my laborious episcopate'. That phrase about his 'laborious episcopate' is the main argument, the only argument, at the disposal of those who assume that this entire incident took place when Patrick had been a bishop for years. I am tempted to agree with Bieler's opinion that Patrick is looking here at his bishopric retrospectively. He is looking back at it from the time when he was writing. He is not speaking of it from the point of view which was his at the moment of the event. He says that his sins prevented him from obtaining that episcopate which in the end, when he was eventually appointed to it, had turned out to be so laborious. In writing this phrase he anticipates the bishopric. Powell states the argument succinctly: the bishopric 'can hardly have been laborious if it had not yet started. But the objection is hardly conclusive: by the time that Patrick was writing, the episcopate had proved very laborious indeed, and the word points the irony of the original objections to it.' The translation 'laborious, as it turned out to be' gives the sense. It must be admitted that this explanation is not wholly satisfactory, and in a more sophisticated writer than Patrick it would hardly be tolerable. But it is the best that we can do, and it is a small hurdle compared with the obstacles which we should have to jump over if we accepted the alternative theory.[5]

On either interpretation, why did Patrick deal at such length with what was probably the greatest failure of his life, the failure to be appointed on this occasion, or (if we take the other view) the failure to win the approval of the seniors? Whichever interpretation we accept, it is odd that he lingers over the matter at all and especially that he does so at such length. We have here one of the occasions when Patrick turns aside to assure his readers that he is not lying: 'So I assert boldly my conscience does not blame me on this occasion and for the future: I have God as my witness that I have not lied in the talks which I have reported to you'. We shall see reason later on to think that Patrick uses this phrase when he is contradicting some version of events with which he disagreed. If that is what he is doing here, the implication would perhaps be that the meeting with the seniors had not been a public one and different accounts had circulated about what had been said and done. The matter was controversial, and Patrick is now giving his version of what had taken place. We have no idea, of course, what was the report which he was trying to refute.[6]

I conclude, then, that the seniors interviewed him when he was not yet a bishop and that the only reason why they turned him down (so far as we can make out from such an obscure narrative) was the 'sin' which he had confided to his friend thirty years earlier and which his friend now disclosed to all and sundry. At the critical moment, it seems, just before the interview the friend broke faith and told Patrick's secret to everyone in general, 'to all, both good and bad, and defamed me publicly in a matter in which previously, of his own accord and joyously, he had held me pardoned, and the Lord, too, had done so, who is greater than all'. Even after so long a time this sin was held to disqualify Patrick, although his sufferings as a slave in Ireland had changed him into a very different person from the unbeliever who had committed the sin at the age of fifteen. It was merely a sin of his boyhood which counted against him, but scholars have not been content with it: they have felt that the charge-sheet should be touched up, expanded, made more colourful. And so they have added quite a list of wholly fictitious charges against him — his lack of education, his tendency to take unnecessary risks, his

5 Bieler, 'Patriciology', pp. 25–9; Powell, 'The Textual Integrity', p. 406. This translation is that of Hitchcock, 'The Confession', p. 92.
6 Confession, §31 (244.23–5). On Patrick's assertions that he is not lying see p. 107f. below.

spending of too much money, his aiming at financial gain for his own pocket, and even heterodoxy! According to one scholar, the seniors led against him 'a campaign of extreme bitterness, secret intrigue, and even treachery'! In fact, Patrick says and implies nothing whatever about bitterness, intrigue, treachery, or extremes of any kind! There is no authority for any of these grisly but ghostly accusations at this time. After all his lamentations about his 'rusticity', his lack of education, it is something of a surprise to find that the seniors made no reference whatever to his lack of education or of literary Latin. Why should they make any such reference? Of what importance would literary Latin be among the pagan or newly converted Irish, who knew not a syllable of Latin, literary or non-literary?[7]

It is remarkable that Patrick makes no comment on the person who was preferred to him. He does not even allude to his existence. But then, he does not allude directly even to Palladius, who beyond any doubt preceded him as bishop in Ireland. Still less does he hint that the successful rival was unworthy of preference or that his appointment was a mistake or an injustice or due to outside influence or to the crossing of palms with silver. Nor does Patrick express anger against the seniors or suggest that they preferred another to himself because they were unwise, wrong-headed, corrupt, hallucinated, fuddled with drink, or anything of the sort. But he does pray that God may not reckon their rejection of himself as a sin!

I said that God, in Patrick's opinion, came to his aid and kept his morale high. The way in which God did so was the familiar one: Patrick saw a vision in the night following on the interview with the seniors, the last of the eight dreams recorded by him. The account of this vision is exceptionally obscure even by the standard of Patrick's other dreams. There is a translation of the passage — or what may pass for a translation — on p. 67 above. The dream's purport seems to be that God took Patrick's side, and that the name which Patrick has suppressed in his account of the dream is the name of the false friend, though the name was not suppressed in the dream itself — that is one reason for the obscurity of his description of this dream.[8]

In his account of the dream Patrick takes pains to hide the friend's name, but it is not clear why he does so. The friend had tried to discredit Patrick 'in front of everyone, good and bad'. So would not

---

7 *Confession*, §32 (245.4−6).
8 The sense of this passage would be impossible to establish, I think, if with Bieler, *The Life and Legend*, p. 69, we suppose that Patrick saw *his own* face with his name written against it.

everyone, good and bad, recognise the reference in the *Confession* and be able to identify the friend easily? In fact, we know no more of him than that he was a Briton who was already a trusted friend before Patrick became a deacon. We do not know what his office may have been — if he held any office. If Patrick and he were approximately of the same age, they had known each other since at least their twenties and during the intervening years Patrick had continued to trust him. He speaks of him with deep sorrow and cannot understand how he came to betray his secret. Yet he never utters a work of bitterness or of criticism or of blame. He is never angry with him. He speaks of him sadly but tenderly, though he cannot hide how deeply the friend had hurt him. What is clear is that vindictiveness was no part of Patrick's nature, nor was it his way to harbour grudges or to allow his resentment to smoulder for years on end. But that is not to say that he forgot his wrongs or that he was able to put them out of his mind. That would have been inhuman. We must bear in mind, of course, that we do not have the friend's version of what he did or why he did it. Was he merely indiscreet, or did he act from malice or envy, or had he some other more high-minded motive which misfired and which is totally unknown to us and may not have been known, or may not have been completely known, even to Patrick? It certainly seems odd behaviour on the friend's part to keep the secret for no less than *thirty years* and then to blurt it out to all and sundry at a moment which could not have been more embarrassing for the man who had trusted him. At all events, Patrick always refers to him, not as a 'false friend' or 'my former friend', but as his 'closest friend'.

In another matter, too, we cannot be certain that Patrick was wholly right. Was he right in his conviction that it was the divulging of his boyhood sin that had wrecked his standing with the seniors? The deliberations of the seniors are unlikely to have been public, or at any rate wholly public. Can we be certain that other factors, too, in addition to the boyhood sin did not weigh with them? Patrick held his own opinion of the matter genuinely and sincerely, but the seniors may have had other reasons of which he heard nothing and knew nothing and so could report nothing. The seniors were not obliged to tell him every detail of the considerations which had convinced them that Patrick was open to criticism. We cannot be sure that we know the whole truth about the affair. It may be that Patrick, too, did not know the whole truth about it.

One important inference from this episode in his life is that the first bishop or bishops who succeeded Palladius in the Irish see (though not Palladius himself) were appointed by British bishops. After the appointment of Palladius there was no question of the pope's making the appointment. (There had never been any question of the Gallic bishops' making it.) And there is no hint that the seniors consulted the laity about the appointment which they proposed to make, though such consultation would have been normal inside the Empire. But Patrick does not mention the point, and presumably he had no fault to find in this direction. No one can tell who the successful candidate may have been, or how long he occupied the see, or whether he was called (as later and worthless sources tell us) Secundinus or Auxilius or Iserninus. We have seen that Patrick refrains from any word of criticism of this shadowy, nameless figure. But it is also true that he has no word of praise for him, no admission that he made good use of his appointment, no generous concession that 'the best man won', a sentiment which is rare among defeated competitors in the ancient world and rarer still nowadays.

Did the seniors announce their final decision about the appointment when they were in Ireland or did they wait until they returned home to Britain? We do not know. But some time before the appointment was finally made, the close friend had told Patrick by word of mouth that he was going to be elevated to the bishopric. Does this mean that the friend had been in Ireland or that Patrick had recently visited Britain? And several of the brethren — these were Britons who were on friendly terms with Patrick — let Patrick know before the interview, at a time when he was not in Britain, that his close friend was supporting his cause in the hope of winning him the appointment. Presumably more than one letter or more than one traveller crossed the Irish Sea in this connexion. There seems to have been no great difficulty at this stage of Patrick's career, or at this stage of the history of Britain, in travelling from Britain to Ireland and back again.[9]

3. — Bishop at last

Eventually Patrick was appointed and took up the post of sole bishop to the Irish, of which post, as he remarks three times, he felt that he

9   *Confession*, §32 (244.28).

was not worthy. In the *Confession* he is so engrossed in giving his version of what had happened when he was *not* appointed that he omits to mention (except by implication) that in the long run he *was* appointed. Although he describes himself as bishop he never tells us why and when the seniors came to change their minds. He says nothing of the details of his consecration. Perhaps, as MacNeil suggests, he 'supposed the facts to be well known'. That may be so. If his critics had questioned the manner of his consecration or if they had said that it was irregular or uncanonical or that he was not a legitimate bishop at all, we may be sure that he would have spoken of it at length. His silence on the details of his appointment has suggested that there was something odd and irregular about it. In fact, it suggests the opposite. If Patrick had not been regularly appointed, his critics would have had a devastating weapon to use against him, but since he says nothing, we may infer that they were silent.[10]

When he returned home from slavery his parents had begged him never to leave them again. Presumably they only did so after he told them of his dreams and of how God was directing him to go back to Ireland. Before they knew of the dreams and the decision to which the dreams led him, the parents would hardly have had occasion to beg him to stay at home, for they could scarcely have imagined that he would ever wish of his own free will to go back to the land of his slavery. Many gifts were offered to him (perhaps by family and friends) 'with weeping and tears' that he might stay at home; but he disregarded them all, and in so doing gave offence and acted against the wishes of some of his 'seniors'. The 'seniors' of this incident are clearly Britons of his own locality and were no doubt older men higher up in the hierarchy than he was at the time. They are not the 'seniors' who interviewed him on a later occasion.[11]

When Patrick had been rejected as bishop he felt his self-confidence strengthened: 'From this moment I felt no small virtue in myself, and my faith was proved before God and man'. But when eventually he was appointed he seems to have suffered momentarily a failure of nerve: 'I did not quickly find comfort in what had been shown to me', and 'I was not quick to recognise the grace which was then in me'. It is the one moment of self-doubt which he ever mentions. But it is a gross exaggeration to say that at this time he felt

---

10 MacNeill, *St Patrick*, p. 66. For his view that he was not worthy to be bishop see *Confession*, §15 (239.10), §32 (245.2), §55 (251.20). Wilson, 'Romano-British', p. 15, makes the extraordinary suggestion that 'in the interval the friend had switched his allegiance from the Catholic to the Pelagian party in the British Church'!

11 *Confession*, §23 (242.13), §37 (246.12f.).

himself unworthy to be a bishop, that he wavered seriously in his vocation for the Irish mission, and that 'almost up to the moment of departure for Ireland he had hesitations and self-questionings on the propriety of his going'. In fact, this is the sort of reckless exaggeration which has too often bedevilled the study of Patrick. He admits to a moment of doubt, and we infer a spiritual crisis of elephantine proportions! The truth is that any doubts which he may have felt were soon put aside, and he does not report that they ever troubled him again. His eventual success left him in a state of exultation. He never to the end of his life ceased to be impressed by the strangeness of his fate in being abysmally obscure in his boyhood and yet God's chosen instrument in the end. 'Before I was humiliated', he says, referring to his enslavement, 'I was like the stone which lies in deep mud; and there came one who is powerful, and in his mercy he raised me up and lifted me on high, and he placed me on the top of the wall'. Indeed, there is a note of triumph in one or two passages of the *Confession* which some readers may have found less than attractive, especially where he exults over the educated men to whom he had eventually been preferred. The lesson which he learned from his unexpected promotion above the heads of these men was that he must 'without fear and in confidence spread the name of God everywhere, so that even after my death I may leave as an inheritance to our brethren and sons <in Christ> so many thousands of persons whom I baptised in the Lord: and I was not yet worthy, nor was I such that the Lord should grant this to his poor slave, and that after troubles and such great difficulties, after captivity, after many years he should give so much grace to me in respect of that nation, which I never hoped for or thought of when I was a young man'.[12]

At any rate, with his appointment as bishop we can give no further narrative of any of the events in Patrick's life (except perhaps for the calamitous raid of the soldiers of Coroticus). We have no further stories such as that of the escape or the interview with the seniors. It looks as though Patrick expected that from this point of his career onwards the external events of his life would be familiar to his readers. He spent the rest of his days in Ireland as sole bishop there. He carried out all the routine duties of a bishop, baptising, confirming, ordaining, and so on. But his greatest work lay among those who were not Christian at all.

---

12 *ibid.*, §30 (244.20f.), §46 (249.28), §12 (238.17−9), §14f. (239.7−13) respectively. The quotation is from O Raifeartaigh, 'St Patrick's Twenty-Eight Days', p. 411 n. 18, whose opinions are usually so sound.

CHAPTER SIX

The Mission to the Irish

Nothing could give more pleasure to the student of St Patrick than a description of what happened when he entered for the first time a pagan, or an almost wholly pagan, Irish village. What sort of person did he first seek out? What kind of thing did he say to them? How did he set about expounding the new religion and undermining their faith in the gods which had satisfied them and their ancestors hitherto? The answers to these and countless similar questions are utterly beyond us. We cannot ever hope to find them. But we can form some impression of what it was that he set out to achieve, and we can form a very vague idea of what he succeeded in achieving. It will be worth our while, too, to tackle the important but desperately obscure problem of the finances of his mission: how did he pay his way?

1. — The Aims of the New Bishop

When Patrick set off at last for Ireland as bishop, 'many' were opposed to his mission, and it is important to see the grounds for their opposition. The critics did not say now that he was an unsuitable candidate for the post owing to his boyhood sin (as the seniors appear to have thought on another occasion) or because of his lack of education (though Patrick himself seems to have thought this) or because 'he thrust himself forward' in order to obtain the appointment. Not all the critics were motivated by malice: Patrick explicitly assures us of that. In fact, there would have been little point in hurling criticisms of his personal qualities either publicly or behind his back *after* he had been appointed. The time for criticism of his personal qualities was then past. And no Catholic at this date would criticise a bishop for going to such an outlandish place as Ireland: had not the pope himself sent Palladius there? To go to the Christian community or communities in Ireland in the mid-fifth century cannot in itself have been a controversial action. Far from it. Many important and influential men had competed with Patrick for the bishopric. And yet there were 'many' people who tried to prevent this mission, as Patrick candidly tells us. Why? What was their objection?[1]

The fact is that the critics did not object to Patrick's mission as such, but rather to the kind of mission which he proposed. His best claim to originality was his aim to use his bishopric in Ireland not simply so as to serve 'the Irish who believed in Christ' but rather to convert the heathen barbarians there to Catholic Christianity. At the beginning of his account of it he writes that God brought it about 'that I came to the Irish tribes to preach the gospel and to endure insults from unbelievers, that I should hear abuse for being a foreigner, that I should endure many persecutions even unto imprisonment, and that I should give up my freedom for the benefit of others, and, if I were worthy, I am ready even to expend my life for his name, without hesitation and most gladly, and I desire to spend it there even unto death, if the Lord should indulge me because I am very much a debtor to God, who gave me so much grace that many peoples were born again into God because of me and were afterwards confirmed, and that clergy were ordained for them everywhere, for a people lately coming to believe, a people which the Lord took from the ends of the earth'. In a word, his aim was to convert the heathen. His bishopric was to be of a wholly new kind in the West. He would do what no Catholic bishop had ever done before. He would go out among the heathen barbarians outside the Empire to convert them to Catholic Christianity.[2]

This is very different from the type of conventional Catholic

---

1 *Confession*, §46 (249.26). That others competed for the bishopric I infer from *ibid.*, §11 (238.8), §13 (238.25−239.3).

2 The translation is of *ibid.*, §37f. (246.16−27). Charles-Edwards, 'The Social Background', renders *peregrinationis* in this passage in a technical Irish sense indicating that this Briton in Ireland did not have the status even of a freeman, that he was a complete outsider. If Patrick was addressing Irish Christians or Britons familiar with Irish conditions, this may well be right. It would hardly be clear to Britons living in Britain.

ministry which Pope Celestine ordered for Palladius. Palladius was simply to serve as bishop for 'the Irish who believed in Christ'. Patrick says nothing about the Irish who already believed in Christ even before he first reached Ireland as bishop. Presumably he takes them for granted. No doubt they were at the back of his mind. At the front of his mind are the heathen Irish. It is these whom he looks forward to reaching. His aim is not service to believers, but conversion, the conversion of the pagan Irish as far as the western sea. He is aware of the dangers involved in his programme. He needs no well-wishers in Britain to point these out to him. He knows very clearly that imprisonment and murder may well be his lot. But he is not dismayed by any such prospect. Indeed, he would welcome it, if the need arose.

On this topic of conversion, the conversion of the heathen Irish, he goes on for pages. He is almost obsessed by it. No reader could doubt that this work is to be nothing less than his life. Indeed, that is what he himself says at the beginning of the *Epistle*, where he writes, 'I live for God, so as to teach the pagans'. And that is where he is unique, and that is why his critics objected to what he was doing.

They objected to the use which Patrick proposed to make, or was already making, of his bishopric. He quotes the question which 'many' kept asking behind his back:. 'That man, why is he pushing himself into danger among enemies who have not known God?' That question must have been asked first after his appointment but at an early stage of his mission: there would be little point in raising it for the first time if he had been living in danger for years. But it was still being asked near the end of his career, when he was writing the *Confession*. After some years he was still living in danger. Clearly, this is not a criticism of his appointment as such. It has nothing to do with his lack of education or with his going to Ireland. It is a criticism of his going of his own free will into conditions of danger in Ireland. His bishopric would be dangerous, so dangerous that men feared for his life. The objectors were concerned for him. The critics had not spoken in malice, as Patrick explicitly assures us. They were anxious for his safety. They were afraid that he would come to harm. They found fault, not with his appointment, but with the use which he made of it. The clergy in his part of Britain will cut a rather better figure when we realise that they felt concern for Patrick than if we accuse them, as scholars have normally accused them, of sneering and sniping behind his back. But why did they express their fears behind his back rather than remonstrate with him face to face? No one can tell. Patrick gives no reason. He merely says that they did not speak from malice. He adds a sentence which most unfortunately cannot be translated with anything like certainty. It may mean that the opponents of his mission could not understand his point of view because of his inability to explain it to them persuasively. But is it certain that these men who wished him to come to no harm were in Britain? Perhaps not. When he says that they spoke 'behind his back' he perhaps implies that they could have addressed him to his face if they had chosen to do so. Was he, then, in Britain or in Ireland at the time in question? At the time when he wrote this comment on the criticism he was certainly in Ireland, but, as we have seen, the criticism may not have been made recently: we only know that the words which the critics spoke came to his knowledge in due course. But it is not out of the question that the critics were British clergy living in Ireland and familiar with the conditions there. That is a possibility to which we shall have to return.[3]

At all events, Patrick's purpose was 'to benefit that nation to which the love of Christ transferred me and presented me in my lifetime', that is, the Irish. He expresses this intention several times. He justifies the decision at great length in the Confession and includes a virtual mosaic of biblical passages in support of his project. (He omits to quote Matthew, xv. 24, however, where Jesus states that he was sent to Jews alone, or the same gospel, x. 5f., where Jesus instructs his twelve apostles not to proclaim the gospel to Gentiles or Samaritans. But Patrick is not the only Christian missionary to turn a blind eye to these embarrassing instructions!) To this purpose of Patrick's there is no parallel in any earlier Western Catholic bishop. Not one of them had planned to go across the Imperial Roman frontier into the lands of the barbarians for the specific purpose of winning over the heathen who were living there. His mission was something dramatically new. In Gaul and Italy we have to scour the literature of the fifth century before we can find two or three short and incidental sentences about the conversion of the barbarians outside the old Imperial frontier. And when we do find them we see that they do not relate to plans and projects for organising foreign missions: they are exclamations of pleasure and surprise that someone else has unexpectedly taken on this work. We shall see later on that they are comments apparently on a single mission which some

---

3 Patrick's aims in Ireland: Confession, §14 (239.5−9), §37ff. (246.16−247.7), Epistle, §1 (254.7). He reports the critics who spoke behind his back in Confession, §46 (249.25), where the last sentence cannot be translated with certainty.

anonymous labourer had already launched (probably in Ireland) with success (p. 171f. below). The difference between the comments of these continental writers and the *Confession* of Patrick is that the Gauls will write a thousand, or even ten thousand, lines about Pelagius and his heresy to every one line about the conversion of the barbarians, whereas Patrick has no interest whatever in the heresy and says nothing directly or indirectly about Pelagius, but he speaks at length about converting barbarians. In Gaul there is no theoretical or programmatic discussion of the spreading of Christianity outside the frontiers of the Empire, no plan to extend the success which had already been won or to reinforce the workers in the field or to begin the work again in a new field. There is hardly a hint that such work has even been taken in hand. There is only a brief comment or two in Prosper of Aquitaine on what had already happened. In itself the subject was of minimal interest even to Prosper and of no interest at all to others. The victory in a land which Roman arms had never conquered but which the Roman Church had now subjugated gives a neat but shallow and common antithesis, a minor stylistic ornament, one which most authors ignored.

This, then, is where we should place the originality of St Patrick. When we turn to his *Confession* we find not simply an occasional comment on the conversion of the barbarians but paragraph after paragraph, page after page, on that topic — not merely an incidental exclamation of surprise and passive pleasure, but endless comments and plans and buzzing swarms of scriptural quotations in support. In this matter Patrick is absolutely original. He had no forerunners, at any rate among the Catholic Romans who could write. No one had used a Catholic bishopric as he did.

What a striking contrast to St Severinus, for example, who was living in the second half of the fifth century in the riverside towns of what is now Austria! Severinus used to hobnob with the leaders of the barbarian Rugi who lived north of the Danube. They were Arians, and Severinus, when conversing with their kings and queens, would touch on the sectarian differences which separated them from himself. But he is never said to have tried to convert them or to show them the error of their ways. It never seems to occur to his splendid biographer to explain why this was so.

It is hard, too, to refrain from contrasting Patrick's attitude of hope, confidence, and optimism as he set out for Ireland with the terrors of Augustine as he and his numerous companions started the long journey to Britain in 597. Ireland in the fifth century was an even more frightening place than Britain in 597. Ireland had never been a Roman province. Practically nothing was known of it. There was certainly no Christian queen there as there was in Canterbury in 597. Yet here is what Bede tells us of the ignominious start of the mission of Augustine: 'When the missionaries began to carry out the aforesaid work in obedience to the Pope's orders and had already completed some little distance of the journey, they were struck with paralysing fear, they planned to return home rather than to approach a people which was barbarous, wild, and heathen, whose very language they did not know; and they decided by common consent that this was the safer course'.[4]

To return home to Bannaventa would have been the safer course for Patrick, but he did not take it.

2. — Patrick's Achievement

In some parts of the *Confession* Patrick does not understate what he had achieved during his mission to the Irish. True, in a passage of the *Epistle* where, according to some scholars, he claims to have converted 'an uncountable number' of the Irish, the Latin text is corrupt, and in all probability Patrick makes no such claim. But in a highly emotional part of the *Epistle* he cries out (paying as little attention as ever to his grammar): 'O fairest and most loving brethren and sons whom I begot in Christ I am not able to count'. After his death, he says, he will leave a legacy to 'my brethren and sons whom I baptised in the Lord, so many thousands of men'. That is a claim which he makes repeatedly. The Lord took pity on me 'in respect of thousands and thousands'; 'Many peoples were re-born in God through me'; 'I baptised so many thousands of persons'. But we have already seen that when he uses the word 'thousands' he is hardly expounding mathematics or statistics to his readers: that phrase about the 'many thousands of persons' with whom he was carried off into slavery in Ireland cannot be taken literally. But in another passage he is not content even with 'thousands'. 'Hence those peoples in Ireland who never had knowledge of God and until now always worshipped idols and unclean things, how have they lately been made the people of the Lord and called the sons of God?' He actually

4 Bede, *Hist. Eccles.*, I.23 (ed. Plummer, I, p. 42).

appears to be claiming here that he converted the pagans of Ireland *en masse*, every man-jack of them. If that is what he has in mind, it is a wild overstatement, as we shall see. But there is no reason to doubt that he did indeed convert hundreds, if not 'thousands', of the Irish.[5]

He is certainly not exaggerating when he says several times that he preached in a region beyond which no man lives, that is, a region bordering on the western sea, and that he ordained clergy in those wild and distant places. But we must not read too much into that claim. It does not follow that he had evangelised the entire west coast from Donegal to Kerry. It *could* mean that he had reached on one occasion, and perhaps not more than one, a place from which he could catch a glimpse of the Atlantic as it attacked the giant cliffs of Clare or Connemara. We have no means of deciding whether he means this or more. But in general, if we may trust a statement in the *Epistle*, he was well enough pleased with the achievement of his mission, for he says of the 'flock of the Lord' that it was 'increasing excellently under his very devoted attention'.[6]

When he begins his account of his bishopric he tells at length how God overcame all obstacles which might have prevented him from going to Ireland and how Patrick as a result made many converts, an achievement which he supports by a cloud of Biblical quotations. He then goes on, remarkably enough, to tell how the sons and daughters of the Irish chieftains are seen to be not simply Christians but nuns and monks. (He gives no hint here or elsewhere that the chieftains themselves were affected by his teachings.) As a generalisation, that would appear to be improbable, and having made this remark he goes straight on to cite one single specific example. This is the case of a nobly born Irishwoman (and a very beautiful one, as he adds unnecessarily and uncharacteristically), whom he had baptised and who came to him a few days after her baptism wishing to become a nun, a 'virgin of Christ', as he puts it. Now, this is the only instance of an individual conversion which he mentions in the whole body of his work. Why does he give this specific example when he has just told us that the sons and daughters of the Irish chieftains in general, or at any rate a substantial number of them, are now seen to be monks and nuns? Apart from his father and grandfather, the only individuals specified in the whole of the *Confession* are Victoricus,

5 For Patrick's claims see *Confession*, §41 (248.6−9), §38 (246.24), §46 (249.21), §50 (250.19), and for the passage quoted last see *ibid.*, §41 (248.6−9). Note also *Epistle*, §2 (254.15) *in numero* (where the text is unsatisfactory), §16 (258.1f.).

6 *Epistle*, §12 (256.28f.). For his penetration to the distant west see *ibid.*, §6 (255.9), §9 (256.5), *Confession*, §11 (238.11), §34 (245.28), §38 (246.26f.), §51 (250.26f.).

whom he saw in a dream, the surly captain of his escape-ship, and the very close friend who, he believed, in the end had let him down. He mentions these individuals — only one of them by name — because, if he did not do so, his narrative would hardly be intelligible. Why then does he mention another individual here, the beautiful noblewoman? Is she essential to his narrative? It is not out of the question, in my opinion, that this remark about the sons and daughters of the chieftains who had now become monks and nuns does not describe something which has already happened but that it is rather a prediction: this is what is going to happen. The specific case of the beautiful Irish noblewoman shows that the nobility is on the verge of coming over to Christianity and monasticism. The struggle to win the nobility, he seems to say, is as good as won. He is on the brink of success. Patrick is anticipating (we might think), not stating an accomplished fact. He is in fact counting his chickens prematurely. If we reject this or some similar interpretation, we must assume that he specifies the beautiful woman who a few days after her baptism asked to become a nun and became one only six days after making her request because her transition from paganism to Christianity and then to a nun's life was such a high-speed affair. But can we really think that Patrick, who is usually so reluctant to mention individuals, has told us of this lady for so banal a reason? In the eyes of a man reviewing the Irish mission as a whole, did it matter whether she waited six days or six weeks or six years? I think that it is easier to hold that he cites this specific case in order to justify the generalisation which he has just ventured to make. In the *Epistle* he goes very much further. He admits there that 'I am not able to count the number of the sons and daughters of the Irish chieftains who are monks and virgins of Christ'. That, I fancy, is something like propaganda for Coroticus's consumption. If it were literally true, Patrick's life and the lives of his converts would have been very much less dangerous than in fact they were. With this interpretation of his mention of the noblewoman we accuse him of wishful thinking and of generalising from a single instance. Now, to predict the future from a single case is not a procedure which logicians or mathematicians would normally recommend, but Patrick is not trying here to teach his readers logic or mathematics.[7]

There is a parallel to this kind of 'anticipatory' generalisation. In fact, as we know, the nobility did not come over to Christianity, still

7 *Ibid.*, 41f. (248.6—15), where note the repetition of *Epistle*, §12 (256.29f.).

less to monkery; and when Patrick speaks elsewhere about the sons of the 'kings' he implies that they were pagan. In order to travel through the country he had to pay the kings, and he also had to make payments to their sons who then travelled with him but were treacherous and even dangerous. It may be that, when he tells us this, he is once again speaking not of the general experience but of a specific instance. He begins a sentence by telling us of how he 'used to' pay the kings and their sons; but he goes on in that very same sentence to mention one definite occasion when they seized him, stole his goods — or, as he puts it in his own individual way, 'everything which they found with us they took it' — and enslaved him for a fortnight. Once again, his generalisation even as he is in the act of narrating it becomes one specific case. Can we be sure that the kings and their sons were not particularly treacherous except on this one occasion when they became decidedly unpleasant? And can we be sure that Patrick is not generalising from this one incident and describing them as normally treacherous when they were only once treacherous? The passage may be a parallel to that in which he speaks of the conversion of the nobility when all he really means, one might think, is that one of their number had come over.[8]

But even if he speaks of the 'treachery' of the kings, may he not be describing extreme conditions? May he not mean that some parts of Ireland were hostile in this way and to this extent but that other parts were less so? When he says at the beginning of the Confession that the captives taken from Britain at the same time as himself were dispersed 'among many nations even to the end of the earth, where now my insignificant self is seen to live among aliens', he could be taken to mean that, at the time when he was writing the Confession, he was living not simply in Ireland but in a remote part of Ireland, even at the end of the earth. If he does indeed mean that he was writing the Confession in some remote place like Co Mayo, then we could suppose that in less remote parts of Ireland the chieftains were less hostile and the dangers less menacing. But it is not easy to see why this should have been so. Why should a kinglet living in eastern Ireland be less hostile than one living in the west? There is little evidence that Roman influences had made much more impression on the south-east of Ireland than in the far west. Indeed, the archaeological evidence suggests that throughout the whole period of the Roman Empire Roman influence on Ireland was not extensive or

8 Confession, §52f. (250.30−251,13).

deep. The number of traders who visited any part of Ireland in the fifth century must have been moderate, and their civilising influence no greater than that of any other wine-merchants or slave-dealers. And it is certain that in some parts at least of Patrick's work the phrase 'the utmost places of the earth' means Ireland as a whole, not the more remote parts of Ireland. I conclude that Patrick says at the beginning of the *Confession* that the Lord scattered us among many nations 'even as far as Ireland', *not* 'even as far as a remote part of Ireland', and hence that he is speaking in these passages about Ireland as a whole. The whole of it was remote, and the whole of it was dangerous.[9]

In spite of his alleged 'thousands' of converts and in spite of his ordinations and his monks and his nuns Patrick leaves us in no doubt that the society in which he was living and working at the time when he was composing the *Confession* was a hostile one, a very hostile one. It is folly to suppose that the Ireland to which he first came was largely Christian already and that he had merely to busy himself with outlying districts which the new religion happened not yet to have reached. Bieler was right to conclude that towards the end of his life 'Patrick describes a country almost entirely pagan'. The evidence, he rightly says, 'does not give the impression of a more than sporadic penetration of Christianity into Ireland at the beginning of Patrick's mission.' Even towards the end of his mission the country was very dangerous. Patrick repeatedly speaks of the perils which threatened him, frequent enslavement, imprisonment, threats of death, the likelihood that if he were murdered his body would lie unburied for the dogs and birds to eat, limb by limb, the ultimate horror for the inhabitants of the Greco-Roman world. He has to take the utmost care to avoid arousing a persecution. Whatever claims he may make about converting 'thousands' of the Irish, yet towards the end of his life he every day expected death or slavery. Far from being daunted he prayed that he might one day be martyred! He writes, 'I ask God that he should grant me to pour out my blood for his name in company with those strangers and captives', that is, with a group which we shall try to define later on (p. 122f. below). When we study Patrick, we must never forget that even towards the end of his career

---

9 At *ibid.* §51 (250.26f.) *usque ad exteras partes* means 'more remote parts' of Ireland, not the whole of Ireland. The meaning is not quite certain *ibid.*, §11 (238.11), §38 (246.26f.), both of them Scriptural quotations, but I conclude that *ibid.*, §1 (235.13) *ad ultimum terrae* simply means that the Lord scattered us among many nations 'even as far as Ireland', not 'to a remote part of Ireland'. The archaeological evidence for Roman influence on Ireland is relatively slight: Bateson, 'Roman Material', and 'Further Finds'.

he was living in a grimly hostile environment. Even at that date he was far from confident that his Christian communities would survive. 'Wherefore may it not befall me from my God that I should never [he means 'ever'] lose his people which he has acquired at the end of the earth'. No one could argue that Patrick, when he was writing the *Confession*, was over-optimistic or confident about the future. He reserves judgement. Whether or not his mission would survive at all seems to have been still in the balance. The Apostle of Ireland certainly did not convert Ireland.[10]

What we cannot describe are the methods which he used when setting to work in these perilous conditions. In later times Christian missionaries and propagandists who went among the barbarian tribes found that if they could convert the king or the tribal chief the tribesmen would usually (though not always) follow his lead and become Christian, too. Even in earlier times Gregory the Illuminator, as he is called, managed to convert the king of his native Armenia, who then imposed Christianity on his subjects. It was said, too, that a woman prisoner called Nino converted the king of the Iberians (who lived in the neighbourhood of the modern Georgia in the Caucasus). The Iberians then followed suit. Both these events took place about the year 300 (even before the conversion of Constantine the Great), and there is no reason to think that Patrick had ever heard of either of them. But he thought out the procedure for himself. He gives us clear evidence that he mixed with the tribal nobility of Ireland to a considerable extent. He mentions his conversion of the 'very beautiful Irish noblewoman'. He had access to the 'kings' whose sons he paid to accompany him on his travels. He twice boasts that many of 'the sons and daughters of the Irish chieftains' are seen to be monks and nuns. Although he never formulates the theory explicitly, it looks as though he, too, tried to begin at the top: if he could convert the tribal leaders the tribesmen would probably follow their lead.

It is hard to imagine how he set about convincing the Irish to abandon their familiar gods and accept a new one about whom they knew nothing except what he chose to tell them. What would be the advantages to them of making so radical a change? If the old gods and the old ways had served reasonably well in the past, why should the people turn to new ways and a new god of which they knew little or nothing? Why should they take such an enormous risk of offending

10 Bieler, *The Life and Legend*, p. 73. On Patrick's dangers see respectively *Confession*, §35 (246.3), §37 (246.18), §52 (251.2), §59 (252.15). The quotation is from *ibid.*, §59 (252.14).

their traditional deities merely because a British stranger had landed on their shores and was urging them to do so? It must have seemed to the pagans to be an exceedingly dangerous step to take. From his silence on all these matters we may at least infer that Patrick's methods, whatever they may have been, were not criticised by his Christian opponents who had obliged him to write the *Confession*. He merely says that 'today among the nations I constantly exalt and magnify your name in whatever place I am'. That is, he speaks only of preaching the gospel. Since the barbarians could not read, they could only judge Christianity by what they saw and heard of it from its practitioners. Missionaries, therefore, in other parts of the world would take care to exhibit an impressive picture of the faith. So Patrick probably anticipated the methods of Augustine of Canterbury (who, so far as we know, had never heard of him). Augustine with his followers made a sustained and ostentatious display of holy living. They gave themselves up to unbroken prayer, watching, and fasting. They preached to all whom they could button-hole. They rejected all the things of this world as being alien to them. They accepted from those to whom they preached only those things which were seen to be necessary for their sustenance, and made it plain to all that they were prepared to suffer and even die for what they were preaching. It all resembles what Sozomen told us of the Roman prisoners beyond the frontier. As in the case of the Goths, a number of the Saxons then believed. When Augustine and his men had converted the king of Kent and his followers, they confirmed their belief by a display of miracles. It is most unfortunate that we are not told how they engineered these miracles. Some, no doubt, were due to nothing more than the medical knowledge of the Romans which was superior to that of the barbarians. But it is difficult to resist the conclusion that others were rigged. Even inside the Roman Empire 'miracles' played a crucial part in spreading Christianity among the uneducated. But there is no reason for thinking that Patrick tried his hand at this style of persuasion. Also, two courses of action were recommended by Pope Gregory the Great to his missionaries in England — preaching and coercion. It is certain that no such choice was open to Patrick in Ireland. The pagans were far too powerful and menacing to allow him to try anything which looked like coercion even if he had felt inclined to the use of force (and it is hard to imagine that a man of his character felt any such inclination). And he was doubtless aware that if he gave any sign of trying to impose his views on the Irish pagans against their will, his mission would come to an abrupt and bloody end.[11]

As for the converts, he made some inroads among the younger generation of the Irish people, especially among the tribal nobility — to the intense annoyance of their parents. The children suffered severely in some cases at the hands of their outraged parents; but it would be a mistake to think that the number of those who came over to the Christians was vast. Patrick also managed to convert some of the slaves. He mentions in particular the female slaves; and those whom he has in mind appear to have been Irish, for he has just mentioned (by way of contrast, it seems) 'those of our race', that is, the Britons. It would be of exceptional interest to know how he managed to make contact with the slaves and to expound his dogmas to them without their owners' permission. It was they, and especially the women among them, who suffered most for becoming Christians: their owners did not spare them. Yet Patrick still makes no criticism of slavery as an institution.[12]

Interesting too, would be information on how he managed to provide services for persons who did not know Latin. He had come to Ireland under the disadvantage of being a foreigner outside the native tribal system. But by the end of his six years of slavery he must have been a fluent speaker of Irish. True, Bieler thought that there was 'no reason for assuming that Patrick's Irish was much better than his Latin: both were for him acquired languages, and he was not the person to learn a foreign language easily'. But, as we have seen, Latin was not an acquired language for Patrick. If it had been an acquired language and if his Irish was also acquired, and if, like other land-owners of Late Roman Britain, he spoke British Celtic only to servants, then we should be close to describing him as hardly able to speak at all! It would not have been impossible, of course, for him to win converts even when addressing them through interpreters; but after his six years in Ireland such a procedure was doubtless unnecessary. From his own point of view the simpler his message, the better and the more readily the natives would understand it. But, as the late Dennis Bethell wrote, 'The whole Irish people could not learn Latin. This provided a problem with regard to religious teaching and liturgy which had not previously occurred. In the East, where whole new peoples were converted, Bible and liturgies were translated into Syriac, Armenian, Coptic, Ethiopian. In the West in Gaul, the

---

11 The quotation is from *ibid.*, §34 (245.18). On Augustine see Bede, *Hist. Eccles.*, I, 26 (ed. Plummer, I, 47), and for Gregory's strategy see Markus, 'Gregory the Great', pp. 29–38.
12 *Confession*, §42 (248.17), on which see p. 110 below.

Gaulish speaking peasantry learned Latin and thus became French . . . But no work in Latin could be popular in Ireland. What the previous situation was in Welsh-speaking Britain, we do not know. In Ireland, quite simply, the congregation was not going to understand the service. What was to be done?' What indeed? We simply do not know.[13]

We must not think that in his work of conversion Patrick was helped by the enormous reputation of the Roman Empire among the barbarians who crowded on its frontiers. It is sometimes thought that when Constantine the Great accepted Christianity he gave his new religion a prestige and an authority commensurate with the prestige and authority of the Empire which he governed: the religion of a higher civilisation must be superior to the religion of a lower civilisation. This prestige would have helped Patrick in his work of impressing and converting the Irish. But is this likely? In the scattered farmsteads of Ireland, how many persons had ever heard of Constantine? How many had heard at the time of the event or in the time of Patrick that Constantine had adopted a new religion? How many would have cared an iota if the news had been broken to them or would have even understood what was meant? Indeed, how many had heard of the Roman Empire or could form any idea of its vast size and wealth? News cannot travel in a primitive society unless there are men moving around for the purposes of trade or plunder or the like who will spread it; and if indeed they did arrive on an Irish doorstep, they would probably have other things to talk about than the size and wealth and even the name of the Roman Empire. In any case, such traders and raiders must have been few, and the tribal frontiers, which might put a stop to their journey, were many. As for raiders who plundered western Britain, they can hardly have consisted of more than a tiny percentage of the manhood of Ireland, and when engaged on their forays they were less than interested in thinking of the emperor's personal religion or the dimensions of his empire. Had the men who plundered Bannaventa ever heard of London or Chester? Had they heard of Rome? Did they even know the name 'Bannaventa'? It is in the last degree unlikely.

It is important not to overload that word 'conversion'. It by no means follows that Patrick's converts, as soon as they had been baptised, instantly adopted a pure and unadulterated Christianity purged of all traces of paganism. They often continued to observe

13 Bieler, 'A Linguist's View', p. 151; Bethell, 'The Originality', p. 42.

pagan practices and to hold pagan beliefs long after their official conversion. In this case the Irish were far from unique: the Germanic
peoples, too, combined Christianity with paganism long after their
official 'conversion', even though not all of them went so far as
Redwald, king of the East Angles, who was openly a Christian and a
pagan at the same time! And pagan practices can be found in Ireland
long after the days of St Patrick.[14]

Whatever Patrick's personal ambitions he was obliged to carry out
the routine duties of a bishop. As sole bishop he had pastoral responsibility for all the clergy in his vast diocese. For all those whom he
converted he was obliged to ordain clergy: there was no other bishop
in the land who could supply them. He remarks that 'clergy were
ordained everywhere for people lately come to belief'. He spread his
net so that 'there might be everywhere clergy to baptise and exhort
the people who needed and desired it'. Indeed, he must have
ordained a considerable number of clergy because the Christians in
Ireland beyond doubt were exceptionally scattered — by sale, for
example, when they were slaves. The task of providing clergy and
places of worship for this scattered population cannot have been
easy. He ordained clergy 'everywhere'. On three of the four occasions when he mentions his ordination of clergy, he says explicitly
that he ordained them 'everywhere'. He never hints that any clergy
had been ordained by Palladius or any other predecessor, and yet it is
inconceivable that his predecessors had ordained none and that the
Christian communities to which Palladius had been sent could not
boast of a single deacon or priest. But he implies the existence of
clergy before his own arrival. He says that he visited places which no
bishop had visited before so that there were no clergy there until he
arrived and provided some. The implication is that there were other
places where others had indeed ordained priests.

As for the character of his ordinands he tells us nothing. It is
hardly credible that he usually ordained Britons except perhaps for
those communities which were wholly or almost wholly made up of
captive or other Britons. No doubt he had Britons on his staff when
he first arrived in Ireland, but the new clergy in the main will have
been Irish Christians, whether converted by Patrick himself or by
one of his predecessors. But how did men who knew no Latin read
the Bible or understand the liturgy? How did Palladius communicate
with his Irish followers? We do not know.

14 Bede, *Hist. Eccles.*, II, 15 (ed. Plummer, I, p. 116).

Did Patrick try to establish a parochial system such as he had known in Britain? Certainly. How could he have imagined any other system? No other was known throughout Western Christendom. Over a hundred years after his time documents still show a Church governed by bishops with territorial dioceses surrounded by pagans. But how did he define a diocese in the townless conditions of Ireland? He never refers to a diocese in his day — for the good reason that the whole island was his diocese. There is no reason to think that he established his headquarters at Armagh or that he founded a see there, still less that he gave it pre-eminence over the other churches of Ireland, or even that he had ever been to Armagh or had ever even heard of Armagh.[15]

He must also have acted as supervisor of the monks and nuns who existed in Ireland in his day. He certainly added to their number. Unfortunately, he does not let us know what he meant by the monastic life or what it entailed for its devotees. It would be rash to assume the existence of communities of monks and nuns. His words suggest celibate women living in the world and exposed to all its trials and dangers and persecutions rather than in communities. The monks were probably hermits. There is no reason, of course, to suppose that it was Patrick himself who introduced monasticism into Ireland, still less to think that he himself ever became a monk. But we never catch a glimpse of him as he advised his monks or visited his churches. Nor do we know how he settled the disputes which must inevitably have broken out among his clergy or how he encouraged those whom he had ordained — perhaps years previously — to maintain the impetus of the mission. Were they, too, expected to convert the heathen, to venture out among threatening and hostile tribesmen among whom death or slavery would never be far away? Or was their task simply to consolidate the position won by Patrick himself and to confirm the converted in their faith? What steps did he take to tend the poor and the sick or to redeem prisoners or to comfort the enslaved? He says not a word to enlighten us. How did he obtain land on which to build churches — if he did build churches? What was his attitude towards pagan holy places? On all such matters he is silent. He mentions baptism, confirmation, and ordination, but he never hints at the existence of administrative problems. But his unending problem was the hostility and threatening attitude of the inhabitants of Ireland.[15a]

15 On Patrick and Armagh see Sharpe, 'St Patrick and the See of Armagh'.
15a On Patrick and monasticism see the full discussion in Hanson, *St Patrick : His Origins*, pp. 140–58, who is inclined to think (*ibid.*, pp. 154–8) that Patrick was probably himself a monk.

3. — *Finances*

Here is a somewhat shortened translation of Patrick's remarks on the subject of his expenditure:

> For even though I am inexperienced in all things yet I tried also to preserve myself from my Christian brethren and the virgins of Christ and from religious women, who used to give me spontaneous gifts and used to throw some of their ornaments on to the altar, and I used to give them back again to them, and they were offended with me because I used to do this; but I <used to do it> in the hope of the permanent success <of my mission>, so as to preserve myself without risk in all things in the same hope <of success> so that they might not catch me out on some pretext of dishonesty and so that I might not give room to unbelievers to defame or belittle me even in the smallest matter.
>
> When I baptised so many thousands of persons did I chance to hope for even half a ha'penny from any of them? 'Tell me and I shall give it back to you' [i Kings, xii. 3]. Or when the Lord ordained clergy everywhere by means of my insignificant self and I conferred the ministry on them free of charge, if I demanded from any of them even the price of a mere shoe of mine, tell it against me and I shall give it back to you.
>
> Rather, I spent for your sakes in order that they might receive me, and I used to go among you and everywhere for your sake in many dangers even into outlying parts beyond which there was no one, and which no one had ever reached to baptise and to ordain clergy or to confirm the people. By the gift of the Lord I did everything diligently and most gladly for your sake [*or* your salvation].
>
> In the course of my work I used to give presents to the kings in addition to giving pay to their sons who walk with me, and nonetheless they seized me with my companions and on that day they used most greedily to long to kill me, but my time had not yet come. And all the things that they found with us they seized it, and myself they bound with iron, and on the fourteenth day the Lord freed me from their power and whatever was ours was given back to us because of God and necessary friends whom we had provided beforehand.
>
> But you have experienced how much I spent on those who used to act as judges throughout all the regions which I used to visit often. I estimate that no less than the price of fifteen men was distributed to them in order that you might enjoy me and I might always enjoy you in God. I do not regret it: it is not enough for me. I am still paying and shall pay more. The Lord is powerful so that he may grant to me hereafter that I may expend myself for your souls.

Look, on my soul I invoke God as witness that I am not lying; nor would I write to you that there might be any opportunity for flattery or greed or because I am hoping for honour from any of you . . .

But I see now in the present age that I am exalted by the Lord beyond measure, and I was not worthy nor was I such a man that he should bestow this upon me, since I know most assuredly that poverty and calamity suit me better than riches and luxuries (but Christ the Lord, too, was poor for our sake, but I, miserable and unfortunate as I am, even if I should wish for riches, do not have them now, and I judge not my own self) because every day I expect either destruction or to be defrauded or to be reduced to slavery or some hazard, but I am afraid of none of these things owing to the promises of heaven, because I have cast myself into the hands of the all-powerful God, who is lord everywhere . . .

Wherefore may it not befall me from my God that I should never [he means 'ever'] lose his people whom he acquired at the ends of the earth. I ask God that he should give me perseverance and deign that I should render him true witness to the day of my death because of my God.

And if I have ever accomplished any good for my God whom I love, I ask him that he should grant to me that along with those sojourners and captives I should pour out my blood for his name's sake, even if I should lack burial itself or if my corpse should most miserably be torn limb from limb by the dogs or wild beasts or that the birds of heaven should eat it. I most assuredly think, if this had happened to me, I had gained life with my body because, without any doubt, on that day we shall rise again in the brightness of the sun, that is, in the glory of Jesus Christ our saviour, . . .

For the sun itself which we see rises every day for our sake at his bidding, but its splendour will never reign or abide, but all who worship it will come miserably and unhappily to punishment. We, on the other hand, who believe in and worship the true sun, Christ, who will never perish, nor will he who does his will but he will remain for ever even as Christ, too, remains for ever, who reigns with God the Father almighty and with the Holy Spirit before the ages and now and eternally. Amen.[16]

Patrick stresses that he spent heavily, and he denies hotly that he used any opportunity for making a personal gain in Ireland. His main point here is that so far from making a profit out of his mission to Ireland he had to spend and spend again. He charged no fee for his 'thousands' of baptisms or for ordaining clergy. He had accepted

16 The translation is of *Confession*, §49−60 (251.10−253.4).

none of the trinkets which women converts placed on the altar for him. The argument that he had not gone to Ireland for personal gain is the argument to which he gives the longest exposition of all those criticisms of him which he sets out in the *Confession*. This is the subject which he keeps to the end, 'the position of greatest emphasis', as Carney calls it; and presumably this was the subject about which he had the deepest feelings and which was perhaps the main charge lodged against him.[17]

In recent years it has been agreed universally, I think, that Patrick's mission was financed from Britain. As O Raifeartaigh says, 'His enterprise was supplied, financed, and supervised from Britain — this is generally accepted'. (The old opinion that he was financed from Gaul is hardly heard nowadays.) But those who accept that his finances came from Britain never tell us which British diocese was in a position to supply him with funds. Nor would it be fair to expect any student of the subject to do so: our evidence for the British Church and its various parts at this date is exceedingly slender, and our knowledge of the relative wealth of its dioceses is slenderer still. But it is fair to ask in what form these funds, if they existed, reached Patrick in Ireland. Certainly, he was not paid in cash. Supplies of coin had continued to reach Britain until about the year 402, but thereafter few coins arrived as the Western Empire broke down. The people then went on using the stocks of coins which were already in the island for about thirty years, but after that they were obliged to fall back on barter exclusively. The use of coined money came to a complete stop in Britain about the year 430. In what form, then, can the British Church have supplied Patrick, if it supplied him at all? Are we to imagine shiploads of grain and cattle crossing the Irish Sea for his benefit? It seems improbable. Any such exports would not have increased the popularity of the Church in Britain as the faithful, and still more the pagans, watched their meagre food-supplies sailing off westwards across the greedy sea. It is true that the Caesar Julian ordered very considerable quantities of grain to be exported from Britain to the Continent in the year 359; and this is often taken as a sign that Britain was sufficiently prosperous to spare grain for the use of others. Unfortunately, it more probably means that in 359, in the interests of Julian's defence of the Rhine frontier, the British consumers were squeezed even more fiercely than was normal in Late Roman times. But to transfer considerable quantities of grain for

17 Carney, *The Problem*, p. 100.

ecclesiastical purposes, and especially to transport it outside the Imperial frontiers, would be wholly unparalleled in the Western provinces. And it is not immediately obvious that the Church in Britain had sufficient funds at its disposal to buy up grain with a view to financing the conversion of outsiders — and we have seen that the conversion of barbarians was not a main or even a secondary objective of the churches in the West. Would any British diocese grasp with delight the chance to convert at high expense people who were normally known mainly as pirates and kidnappers? The idea of a mission to convert murderous barbarians — or even barbarians who were not murderous — was not widely accepted anywhere in the fifth century, at any rate by Catholics; and Britons in the area subject to heavy Irish raiding may well have been unenthusiastic at the sight of their foodstuffs being shipped away — if they were shipped away — to feed the barbaric raiders who had done them so much harm.[18]

On the other hand, it is not easy to see how Patrick could have financed the entire mission out of his current earnings (if he had any). Did he use the income of the estate outside Bannaventa? Any such theory would give rise to the same problems: in what form did he export the income of the estate? What were the feelings of those who worked the estate when they saw the fruits of their labour being exported for the benefit of persons who had outraged them so cruelly? Patrick insists that he did not extort funds from his converts in Ireland. But none of the suggestions which have been put forward to solve the problem is persuasive — such as that Patrick inherited wealth from his father, or that he had private backers in Britain, or that he had patrons among the Irish landowners, and so on. None of these suggestions is supported by a shred of evidence, and it is not easy to see how funds could be transferred regularly from Britain to Ireland, and a large capital sum exported, in the absence of coins. A trader could operate by means of barter; but how could a British landowner finance a spiritual enterprise in Ireland over a period of years by means of barter? By shipping slaves, bullion, and cattle across the Irish Sea?[19]

The sums involved were considerable, to judge by the figure which Patrick actually gives us for part of them. For he does give us a figure as clearly as he can. To the judges of the regions of Ireland which he

18 Kent, 'From Roman Britain'; O Raifeartaigh, Review of Hanson and Blanc, p. 122. For Julian's grain extractions see Ammianus Marcellinus, *Hist.*, XVIII. 2, 3 (I p. 406, ed. Rolfe), Zosimus, III. 5, 2 (p. 117, ed. Mendelssohn).
19 See e.g. Bury, *The Life of St Patrick*, p. 173.

visited often he gave the price of fifteen men. Unfortunately, he does not make clear whether he refers to the price of fifteen slaves. (He is certainly not speaking of slave-women, who were to become a unit of value later on in Ireland.) We have no information which would enable us to estimate the market-value of a slave in Ireland in the fifth century. Prices could no longer be reckoned in terms of the Roman coinage even in Britain in the mid-century, and we do not know what unit of value took the place of the coins there. Still less do we know what unit was used in Ireland. And if Patrick is speaking of the price of fifteen slaves, he does not make clear whether he has in mind the price of fifteen unskilled adult male slaves or of some other kind of slave. Nor does he tell us whether he has in mind Irish or British slaves, if they differed in exchange-value. Why should he? There can be no doubt that throughout the whole of this part (at least) of the *Confession* he is addressing Christians living in Ireland. It would seem to follow that he had Irish conditions and prices in mind, not British ones. But in fact he speaks of 'men', not of slaves. Perhaps, then, he is thinking not of the price of slaves but of the number of cattle or the like which would be required to ransom a captured warrior or a kidnapped relative. Whether he has slaves in mind or freemen, the sum which he mentions is a large one. An adult unskilled male slave on the Continent might cost some twenty *solidi*. (Bear in mind that a man could live, or at any rate exist, for a year on two *solidi* or even less.) Patrick, then, may be talking of the equivalent of some three hundred *solidi* on this reckoning; and that is a huge sum even when spread over several years — and this on judicial arrangements alone! But if the saint has in mind the price of ransoming from an enemy fifteen freemen who had been taken prisoner, the price might be much higher. Presumably such sums could be raised in Ireland only in terms of cattle, a substantial number of cattle.[20]

It is remarkable that the item of expenditure which he specifies and which he therefore presumably thought to be the heaviest burden is payment to the local judges. We might have expected that the relief of poverty and above all the ransoming of Christians, especially British Christians, or the freeing of them from slavery would have been a heavy, perhaps the heaviest, financial burden to Patrick. When St Martin of Tours (to cite only one example) received a windfall of 200 lb. of silver from a Christian nobleman, he instantly devoted it to the ransoming of captives; and later on in Ireland

20 Fifteen men: *Confession*, §53 (251.9).

collections for the redemption of captives were a regular charitable practice. Does not St Patrick himself admire the Gallic Christians who send 'thousands' of *solidi* to the Franks and the other barbarians in order to ransom Christian prisoners? But in fact he says nothing about any such expenditure in Ireland. Nor does he mention smaller but not negligible items of expenditure: presumably he had to import oil, for instance, for baptism, wine for the mass, and so on. And according to Bethell, 'you may have to slaughter as many as 400 cows [read 'sheep'] to write a whole Bible' on parchment. How Patrick collected sheephides for this purpose, if he did collect them, nobody knows. His congregation will hardly have contributed many on the collection plate on Sundays.[21]

Again, if he was really receiving subsidies or an income from one or more of the churches in Britain, he is guilty in this passage of something like a concealment of relevant information. He makes a merit of never having taken gifts from the Christians in Ireland, and he also prides himself on having spent considerable sums for the Christians' benefit. But if the means of making these payments were put at his disposal by Britons in Britain, he would have done well to say so, to acknowledge the generosity of his benefactors, and above all to add that he had spent the total amount of what he had received without holding anything back to line his own pocket: was not this precisely the crime of which he had been accused? But in fact he says nothing of the sort, and so we might infer that no criticism on this score had been aimed at him by his opponents. Indeed, embezzlement of the Church funds would be hard to reconcile with the character which the *Confession* reveals to us. And for what purpose would he engage in embezzlement? High living? The idea is grotesque. But since his opponents would not have overlooked so simple a charge if it had been available to them, we may deduce that payments of this kind were not reaching him. But in that case where did his funds come from?

If we insist that an answer *must* be found to so fundamental a question as the source of his mission's income, we are not wholly at a loss. There is a passage in the *Epistle*, repeated less explicitly in the *Confession*, where Patrick asserts that he was well born, the son of a

21 Sulpicius Severus, *Dialogue*, ii (iii). 14. 3−6 (I, p. 212, ed. Halm); Bethell, 'The Originality', p. 43. For Patrick on the Gauls see *Epistle*, §14 (257.10−12). The fact that the Gauls were ransoming prisoners from the Franks does not necessarily imply that there had recently been a war with these barbarians (as e.g. Grosjean, 'S. Patrice à Auxerre', p. 163, and others). The prisoners may have been kidnapped. So there is no dating evidence to be found here. I owe the correction of Bethell to Dr R. S. Smith.

city councillor. 'For', he goes on, 'I sold my noble status — I do not blush nor do I regret it — for the benefit of others.' That is a strange metaphor: how does a man sell his noble birth or status? But in fact it is no more a metaphor in Latin than it is in English. You can hardly 'sell' something metaphorically. Suppose, then, that he means that he sold that which made him a local nobleman, a member of the local gentry in the district where he had been born, that is to say, that he had sold his land. He sold the land on which his social status depended. We could then declare that the sale of the estate at Bannaventa supplied him with his funds and that this was the ultimate source of his mission's income. We are still faced, of course, with the problem of how he transported the market price of his land from Britain to Ireland. There were laws prohibiting the sale of land by city councillors, but at the time which concerns us Britain was no longer a part of the Roman Empire, and the Imperial laws would no longer apply there. But when Patrick says those words about selling his noble status, he writes in a defensive tone. The sale may not have been illegal, but it looks as though other members of the gentry thought it regrettable, perhaps even shocking. And if it was known to have been sold to benefit the souls of murderous barbarians, it must have seemed very shocking indeed, at any rate to those to whom he addressed the *Epistle*.[22]

Let us suppose — since nothing better suggests itself — that Patrick sold the estate which, if he were in Britain, would have given him the status of a city councillor. How much land would he need to sell in order to acquire the 300 *solidi* (if that is the approximate sum) which he says, or seems to say, that he spent on the judges? We have only one document from the whole of the Roman Empire which states the price of land outside Egypt in Late Roman times. This relates to Italy and dates from a century after Patrick's time. It seems to suggest that land would cost four or five *solidi* for a Roman acre, that is, for five-eighths of an English acre. But since the figure of 300 *solidi* paid out by Patrick is nothing more than a guess, and since land-prices in Britain are wholly unknown even when the island was still part of the Roman Empire, and doubly unknown (if that is possible) after the fall of Roman power there, this calculation is as near to being worthless as it could possibly be. Several other highly relevant factors are

22 *Epistle*, §10 (256.12), *Confession*, §37 (246.19), interpreted by Nerney, 'A Study', p. 274, Bieler, 'The Christianization', p. 119, Thomas, *Christianity*, pp. 332, 335, 338. It was the view of Macalister, *Ancient Ireland*, p. 171, that Patrick drew from the revenues of his estate enough for his needs; but this does not account for *uendidi*. For *ingenuitas* = 'well born status', 'nobility', see Thesaurus, VII. 1542. 36ff.

completely unknown. For example, we do not know at what rate, if any, land was taxed at Bannaventa in post-Roman times; and the rate of tax could affect the market-value of a piece of land. But for what they are worth, the available figures suggest (at any rate, to the imaginative mind) that Patrick could have obtained 300 *solidi* by selling between 40 and 50 acres of land. That a British city councillor should have owned this amount of land, and indeed much more than this, is in no way unlikely. But since this concerns only one source of Patrick's expenditure, he might be assumed to have sold a much larger area than 40—50 acres. For example, Patrick further remarks that he paid sums to the Irish kings (as he calls them) and to their sons who travelled with him and who were often treacherous and dangerous. But we cannot even begin to guess what these sums may have amounted to.[23]

We shall see before long that this matter of his finances and the charges which had been made against him in connexion with them were of crucial importance in his eyes.

23 See Jones, *The Later Roman Empire*, II, p. 822.

CHAPTER SEVEN

The Confession

The *Confession* falls into a small number of clearly defined parts:

1—3: Patrick introduces himself, tells of his enslavement by Irish raiders and of his conversion while a slave to a most earnest form of biblical Christianity

4: His formula of faith

5—8: An undertaking to reveal the works of God and to do so truthfully. The emphatic statement that his assertions will be truthful suggests that other versions existed and were regarded by him as false

1—15: His defective education and his hesitation about writing in spite of which defects God chose him in preference to men better educated than himself to go to the Irish bishopric

16—25: Escape from Ireland and return home

26—34: Failure to be appointed as bishop, though this is disputed

35—55: His aims in Ireland and reflections on his work there

56—62: Conclusion, with a final and most emphatic statement on why he went to Ireland

So it is possible to set out the contents of the book in clearcut parts, but that is misleading. Patrick digresses, turns aside to reflect, professes his faith, and so on: we must not expect a logical exposition. In each of the sections there are what we should call irrelevancies and digressions and unnecessary appeals to the deity and clouds of quotations from the Scriptures and echoes of the Scriptures.

We do not move from point to point as though developing a logical argument. But it is clear that on the whole the first half of the *Confession* tells why he wanted to become bishop in Ireland, why he thought that God had chosen him for this work, and after what dangers and disappointments he obtained the post, while the rest of the book deals with the period of his bishopric, his aims and achievements, and tries to justify them. So in studying the earlier part of Patrick's life we can construct a narrative, a discontinuous narrative, of various separate episodes — his childhood, enslavement, escape, unsuccessful interview with the seniors — but after his appointment as bishop this becomes impossible. We can now deal only with themes — his aims as bishop, his finances, and so on — but we can never narrate, never tell a story. MacNeill thought that this change in the character of the *Confession* was due to the fact — if it is a fact — that after his appointment as bishop his personal history was known well enough to those by whom he expected his book to be read. And so he deals with later events not so much by telling what happened as by commenting on the events and, where necessary, explaining and justifying them. If that opinion is right, it would be an argument — not a very powerful argument, perhaps, but an argument all the same — for thinking that Patrick wrote the *Confession* for men who were familiar with his life since he came back to Ireland as a missionary but were not familiar with his early days before he became a missionary.

However that may be, there is no reason to doubt that the whole lay-out of the work is due to Patrick himself. The opinion that an 'editor' put it together as a hotch-potch from a variety of works by Patrick is fanciful — and we do not know that he wrote a variety of other works. Nor is it true to say that the *Confession* is 'a very muddled account'. Even the notorious paragraph describing his second enslavement is not out of place chronologically, according to the interpretation put upon it above. But we shall see shortly that beneath all the divisions and sub-divisions and digressions there is one underlying purpose of fundamental importance.[1]

---

1 MacNeill, *St Patrick*, p. 59; 'editor', Powell, 'The Textual Integrity', p. 402, whose theory is regarded with some favour by Wilson, 'St Patrick', p. 365. See p. 108f., below.

1. — *The Character of the* Confession

It is easy to say what the *Confession* is *not*. It is not an auto-biography. It is not intended to supply the materials for a biography. It is not aimed at describing a random selection of 'events and situations bearing on his spiritual life and his apostolate'. There is nothing random about it. The book does not contain an estimate of the value of Patrick's life's work as a whole — for example, there is no reference in it to Coroticus and his men's brutal action. Least of all is the *Confession* a comment on the world in general in the writer's day. What are we to call it, then? At the beginning of the little book Patrick gives more than one reason for writing. In the first place, he must publicise the benefits and the grace which the Lord has given to him. As a measure of thanks he will exalt and confess God's wonders to every nation under heaven. God has advanced him in the world, and so he 'must shout out loudly so as to give some return to God for his great benefits here and for ever, benefits of which the mind of men cannot assess the value'. To Patrick this is a major reason for writing. He mentions it again and again. He also says that, although he is imperfect in many ways, he wishes his relatives to know his quality. To this reason for writing he (fortunately) does not return. We shall see that he had a reason for writing which was more precise than the first of these, and more edifying than the second. But by what criteria did he decide to include this event and exclude that?[2]

Patrick wrote in a given situation. One feature of that situation (so far as we can see) was that he had been criticised, and he thought that the criticisms called for an answer. As John Gwynn put it, the *Confession* 'is a work of one who feels that he has been treated with misrepresentation and contumely, and smarts under the wrong'. His readers knew exactly what these criticisms consisted of and who the critics were and what their motives had been in putting forward their criticisms. Well then (we ask), who were the critics and what did the criticisms amount to? That is where our problems begin. Patrick was addressing his critics and there was no need to tell them who they were: they knew that already. Nor did he need to define their criticisms: they had done that themselves (and had done it all too well for his liking). So we have to try to infer from his answers both the identity of the critics and the nature of their accusations. We have

---

2 *Confession*, §3 (236.6), cf. §57 (252.3). As Mohrmann, *The Latin*, p. 39, points out, *retributio* means 'what we give to God in acknowledgement of his graces'; for the word see *Confession*, §3 (236.5), §11 (238.7), §12 (238.20), §57 (252.3), and in general for his giving of thanks to God, *ibid.*, §34 (245.13), §46 (249.17).

to reconstruct from what he says the entire context in which he says it. All too often we have his comments on a situation but cannot visualise the situation itself or else we can visualise it only with difficulty or only in part. The criticisms must have been loud or widespread or else aimed at him by people whom he considered to be important, for otherwise he would hardly have answered them at all and certainly not with such earnestness — indeed, such vehemence — as he shows in every line of the *Confession*.[3]

There are great tracts of his life on which he says nothing at all or practically nothing. These presumably are the periods which the critics had passed over. Patrick says little or nothing, for example, about the years, or rather decades, which elapsed immediately after his escape from slavery and his return home, years when he was preparing himself for his life's work in Ireland. He mentions incidentally that he became a deacon in that period, but he says nothing about becoming a priest. Evidently, his earlier years after his escape from slavery in Ireland were not the object of criticism or discussion, and so the nature of the *Confession* does not call for any reference to them. Patrick simply wishes to explain and justify parts of his career to groups of people some of whom were critical of him. What future generations would think is an idea which never occurred to him. That the *Confession* would be preserved at first perhaps by accident but then deliberately, that it would be copied and re-copied, that for hundreds of years men would study it, and study it again and again, in the hope of gleaning fresh details about his life and thoughts, did not and could not have occurred to him, for he believed that he was living 'in the last days'. The world would soon end. The gospel had been preached to the very end of the earth. There was no future in this world. So his book was not consciously written, like the *History* of Thucydides, to be 'a possession for ever'. It was written to answer the criticisms of the moment.[4]

It was written nearly at the end of his career, later than the *Epistle*. When he speaks of episodes in his past, he says that this is what 'used to' happen and that that is what he 'used to' do, and so on. The last words in the book are: 'This is my confession before I die.' It is the work of a man who thinks that his life's work is over, or nearly over. He is no longer active as he used to be. But although what he

3 Gwynn, *Liber Ardmachanus*, p. LXXXI.
4 *Confession*, §34 (245.28), *Epistle*, §5 (255.4f.), §11 (256.23). It is a most uncharacteristic error of judgement on the part of O Raifeartaigh, 'St Patrick's Twenty Eight Days', p. 399, to suppose that Patrick means to leave his *Confession* as a legacy to his successors: *Confession*, §14 (239.8).

reports had happened in the past, some of it in the remote past, he remembers it vividly. Even if the day of his capture by the slavers had become blurred in his memory, yet on the whole he writes as though his entire life had all happened yesterday. He can write a lively account of his escape from Ireland and tell of his emotions and of his visions at that time, although that time lay half a century behind him. When he writes of how he was passed over for the post of bishop in Ireland, his words picture vividly for us the feelings of stress and profound disappointment which he felt at the time. But they do not reproduce any feelings of malice, bitterness, or vindictiveness. The reason is that he felt none. Those are attitudes to which he was a stranger. And he was equally a stranger to self-pity, of which there is not a trace in either of his writings. Pity for others, yes; for himself, never. But every word in this part of his *Confession* shows how deeply the criticisms of the seniors had wounded him years before. I say 'years before': as we have seen, they appear to have criticised him before he became bishop, many years earlier.

In the third of the subdivisions of the *Confession* noticed above Patrick stresses the penalty of not telling the truth. Elsewhere in his book he comes back to this point: he turns aside to declare that he is not lying. Where he does this he often seems to be rebutting specific and important critics. There were evidently other versions of these particular matters, and Patrick is emphasising that what he says is the true account. Why otherwise should he take the trouble to state so forcefully that he is not lying? Why not take it for granted that the readers would assume without any protestations from him that he, the bishop, is giving a truthful account of matters which had become controversial? Evidently, the critics were loud and persistent.

The first of these assertions that he is telling the truth is to be found in the introductory passage near the beginning of the *Confession* where he is speaking about his work in general. He fortifies his words with echoes of half-a-dozen biblical passages. He inserts another claim to be telling the truth in the middle of his account of how he was not appointed to the Irish bishopric (if that is indeed what he is describing). His long description of this event is certainly intended, I think, to be a reply to criticism; but the form which the criticism took is anything but clear. He means no more, I suppose, than that his account of the interview with the seniors, which he has just concluded, is the true one. He stresses in it with great emphasis as the cause of his rejection the sin which he had committed as a boy and his friend's unfortunate publication of this sin. He says nothing of the nature of the sin, presumably because his readers knew already what it was: the friend had proclaimed it indiscriminately. Patrick stresses the sin in this passage to such an extent that it is tempting to think that this was the point at issue: the critics had alleged some other reason for his rejection, and Patrick denies their allegation. But of course there can be no certainty that this was the point which he was trying to make.[5]

Next, Patrick remarks 'I am not lying' in a passage where he goes on to say that he had been mocked because of the signs and wonders in which God foretold the future to him in some cases 'many years' before the events in question happened. It was these visions which urged him, not only to escape from slavery in Ireland, but also — and this was perhaps the biggest decision of his life — to go back there. Evidently, Patrick had the reputation in some circles of being a man who justified his actions rather too often by claiming to have had direct and personal advice and instruction from the deity whenever his critics called him in question. At the beginning of his description of his bishopric in Ireland he repeats emphatically that God often sent him personal messages. Later on he calls God to witness that he is not lying when he says that he is writing *not* so as to win flattery or honour from any of his audience.

It seems fairly clear that all these matters were controversial, and Patrick is trying to correct the false opinions of others. But one of these subjects was of vastly greater importance than the rest. This is the charge that he had gone to Ireland in order to enrich himself by means of his mission. He is more than ordinarily emphatic that he is not lying in this connection. In the second last paragraph of the *Confession* before he (so to speak) signs his name, Patrick writes even more earnestly and more solemnly, if that is possible, than he does elsewhere: 'Look, I shall yet again set out briefly the words of my confession. I bear witness in truth and in joy of heart before God and his holy angels that I have never had any reason except the gospel and its promises for ever coming back to that nation from which in earlier times I escaped with difficulty.'[6]

This is illuminating. He says clearly that this is a brief summary of the whole book. This is in one sentence the content of the *Confession* — not of part of the *Confession* but of the whole of it. The *Confession* in its entirety is concerned with his motives in coming back to

5 *Confession*, §7f. (237.5—12), §31 (244.24).
6 *Ibid.*, 44f. (249.10), §61 (253.5—9); and note §35 (246.7), *creber admonere* or whatever the right reading may be.

Ireland. It is a reply to the criticism that he had returned to Ireland for other reasons than religious ones. At first sight we might think that this sentence is a summary of that part of the *Confession* in which he vigorously rejects the charge that he was in Ireland for the sake of personal gain. But that is not what he says. He does not say that he is summarising that one section of his book. He says that he is summarising the *Confession* as a whole. If we ask whether one theme runs through the entire book making all the others subordinate, the answer is that this is indeed the case; and that one theme is stated to us here. It had been alleged against Patrick that he went to Ireland for contemptible motives, such as to make a financial profit out of his mission; and the purpose of the *Confession,* as he tells us here, is to make clear that this is not true: he went for one reason only — to spread the gospel. This is also what he set out plainly at the beginning of the book. In return for God's kindnesses to him and God's grace shown to him during his captivity in Ireland, he will give thanks; and he will do so by exalting God and confessing his miracles before every nation under heaven. He repeatedly makes this point. He comes back to it again and again. Even if he had been well educated, he would not have been silent in giving thanks to God for his benefits. In fact, he went to Ireland, he says, in gratitude to God. That is the message which he wishes to tell to his critics. He had no other motive for going there; and he stresses the punishment which awaits liars on the day of judgement.[7]

Patrick says in the *Confession*, then, that God arranged the whole course of his life in order that he should go to Ireland to preach the gospel there. But who were the critics who denied this and maintained that he went there for very different motives?

2. — *Patrick and Nationalism*

We might begin by asking whether these critics were British or Irish. But to answer that question we must first look at his attitude towards national differences. If we ask, Does he address British Christians or Irish Christians? the answer is that to Patrick the question would have been all but meaningless. He is hardly ever interested in differences of nationality although he is aware of them. In one passage he

7 See n. 2 above.

mentions explicitly a difference of nationality among the Christians in Ireland. He writes of monks and nuns in his ungrammatical way, 'Of those who were born there [in Ireland] of our nationality we do not know their number.' The fact that he speaks of 'our' nationality here seems in itself to show that he and his readers are of the one nationality: they are all alike Britons, or at any rate Romans. (The view that he means here 'of Christian race' rather than 'of British race' is not convincing.) Incidentally, he never mentions pagan Britons living in Ireland. Yet a number of the Britons in Ireland, in fact a majority of them, must have arrived there after being kidnapped from the open countryside of Britain and would therefore have been pagans, for we have seen that Christianity at this date had not made much headway among the rural poor in the Western Empire (outside Africa). On the other hand, Patrick is very interested indeed in the difference between Christian and pagan. His book is addressed neither to Britons nor to Irish but to Christians irrespective of whether they were British or Irish. At the end of the *Confession* he addresses his readers or rather, as he calls them, 'those who believe in and fear God, whosoever will deign to receive and look into this writing which Patrick . . . wrote in Ireland.' For him there is no distinction between British Christians and Irish Christians. He would never have used such phrases. His readers were simply Christians.[8]

But in this he is not exceptional. He is following the outlook of his times. In the period of the Later Roman Empire men did not feel themselves to be Britons or Gauls or Spaniards or the like. In the West they felt themselves to be Romans or freemen or Christians or Catholics or the like as distinct from barbarians or slaves or pagans or heretics, and so on. There was little or no national feeling in the various Western provinces. At that date no one had ever yet cried out, 'Your true Briton (or Gaul or Spaniard) is a match for any three foreigners'. (Indeed, it would not be easy to find a single Latin word which would translate 'foreigners' in this sense — an inhabitant of any part of the Roman Empire exclusive of the speaker's province or group of provinces.) The idea of nationality did not exist, at any rate at a provincial level. The most that we find in the literature of the period is some good-natured bantering of Gauls on the size of their meals and their well developed taste for wine (though an Irish writer

---

8 *Confession*, §42 (248.17), mentions 'those of our race'. Hanson, *St Patrick : His Origins*, 56, writes that the phrase 'could, indeed probably does, refer to British Christians domiciled in Ireland', cf. his p. 138f. But others take the phrase to mean 'Christians', e.g. Bieler, *Libri*, II, p. 173, O Raifeartaigh, 'The Life', p. 137 n. 7, Dumville, 'Some British Aspects', p. 17f.

of the seventh century lists France at the head of the beer-drinking countries of the world!). Men in those days were spared the nationalism and patriotism and racialism which has plagued Europe and other continents in more recent times. There was no sense of provincial loyalty or unity. A man was not committed emotionally to his province. The provincial boundaries had been imposed on the natives from above. And they did not exist to serve the interests of the natives. They existed solely for the convenience of the government and its administration. On the other hand, a man might feel committed to his city-state, especially if that city-state had once been the territory of a free barbarian tribe before the Romans had conquered the area, and after hundreds of years in some cases the old tribal feeling still survived. And of course a man might feel affection for the district where he had been born and bred and where his relatives lived. St Jerome counts a man's native soil (his *patria*) as sweeter than anything else. For St Ambrose love of country was next only to love of God! But neither of these two men tell us what they meant by 'country', though we may be sure that they did not mean the provincial system of the Later Empire. At that time, when Britain had been carved up into several fundamental divisions, a man would scarcely have called himself a 'Briton'. And it would be a mistake to think that Patrick equates his 'native land' with the four or five British provinces. Whenever he uses the term, he normally combines it with the words 'and my parents'. He means simply his 'home and family'. There is no reason to think that the word *patria* meant to him the four or five Imperial provinces which used to make up the (political) diocese known as the 'Britains' (*Britanniae*). The 'Britains', as he speaks of them, are simply a geographical and administrative term, of much use to the Imperial government.[9]

On the other hand, by these standards the difference between Britain and Ireland in Patrick's time was not negligible. A Briton was a Roman: an Irishman was not. A Briton would use the term 'Roman' of himself as a word in which he might (at any rate, if he was a rich and educated landowner) take some small degree of pride, supposing that he ever thought of the matter at all. If he was not a rich landowner well versed in history, he would be unlikely to pride himself on being a Roman. In normal daily life there was no term to which 'Roman' stood in opposition. A modern patriot may contrast himself

---

9 Gallic appetites: Sulpicius Severus, *Dialogue*, i.4.5; 8.5; 9.2. Beer-drinking France: Ionas, *Vita St. Columbani*, I. 16 (ed. Krusch, p. 179). See also Jerome, *Aduersus Iouinianum*, II. 31 (CSEL, 59, p. 94); Ambrose, *De Officiis*, I. 27 (Migne, *Patrologia Latina*, xvi. 65).

with numerous kinds of foreigners; but with whom could a Roman contrast himself? The free barbarians were so far away and normally impinged so little upon his daily life as to be negligible. But if there is no contrast, the original term loses much of its emotional force. If a British landowner, then, thought of himself as a 'Roman', the thought did not cause him to glow with militant pride, nor did it bring hysterical tears to his eyes. But an Irishman could not call himself a Roman in any circumstances, and there was no reason why he should ever wish to do so. In the eyes of a Briton, an Irishman was a barbarian, that is to say, a non-Roman. So while the difference between a Briton and a Gaul or a Spaniard was as nothing, the difference between an Irishman and a Briton or Gaul or Spaniard might be felt to be in some degree significant. But, as we have seen, the distinction between British and Irish may not have meant much to a far-off Mediterranean man, for whom both alike were so distant and remote that the difference between them was more than a little blurred.[10]

But what may or may not have been of significance for other men was certainly not a matter of much importance for Patrick. He does once describe the Irish as 'barbarous tribes', that is to say, 'non-Roman tribes', but he sees no distinction between a British Christian and an Irish Christian. Both alike are simply Christians. Of course, Patrick is not so limited as to be unaware that there is a difference between Britons born in Ireland and Britons born in Britain (p. 110 above); but it was unimportant. There is an interesting parallel in the British author Gildas, writing early in the sixth century. When speaking of Vortiporix, king of Dyfed in his own day, he mentions that the king was old, that his hair was turning white, that he was guilty of various murders and adulteries, that after the honourable death of his wife, he had raped his own daughter (who was not up to much good in any case). What Gildas does not throw in the teeth of this deplorable sinner is that he was an Irishman. That is a fact which Gildas never mentions and which would be unknown to us if the old villain's tombstone had not chanced to survive. Is Gildas's omission due to the fact that murder and rape were worse crimes than that of being Irish? Or is it due to Gildas's belief that Irishness was not among his crimes at all and indeed was an irrelevant detail? The answer to both these questions is in all probability 'yes'. After all, the father of Vortiporix is the only good king in Gildas's pages.[11]

---

10 Jones, *The Later Roman Empire*, II, p. 1021f. See p. 64 above.
11 *Epistle*, §1 (254.3), Gildas, *De Excidio*, §31 (ed. Winterbottom, p. 101). Vortiporix's tombstone: Nash-Williams, *Early Christian Monuments*, p. 107, No. 138.

But when we in the modern world try to study St Patrick we cannot be content with such a detached attitude. Feelings now are different (and by no means better). We want to know more. The fact is that our conception of history or biography is very different from anything which Patrick or Gildas were trying to write. We want to give a systematic account of Patrick's life. We want to define his aims precisely. For us the difference between Briton and Irishman is, rightly or wrongly, of importance. For our historical purpose we must divide the Christians of the British Isles (as we inaccurately call them, though the Romans sometimes made the same mistake) into three groups, as Patrick would have done only incidentally. We must distinguish, first, the British Christians living in Britain, from, secondly, the British Christians living in Ireland from, thirdly, the Irish Christians. I must stress once again that this threefold division, although it would not have been meaningless to Patrick, would have been regarded by him as largely irrelevant. He would not have been greatly interested in it. These people were all alike Christians, not pagans. That was the one and only fact which vitally concerned him. [12]

3. — *What Readers is Patrick Addressing?*

No Briton living in fifth-century Ireland, who wished to make contact with Irish people, would dream of doing so by writing to them. The only written language in Ireland at that time (if we may disregard the ogham inscriptions) was Latin, and so he would have no choice but to write to them in Latin. And since they could not read Irish — it was not yet a written language — let alone Latin, his work would have been singularly pointless. As a means of communication in those circumstances writing would have been unsuccessful. The old view that there were Christian communities in Ireland even in the fourth century and that these had implanted Latin words in the Irish language long before St Patrick's time has turned out to be untenable. The Christian communities in Ireland were new in the days of Palladius and not old in the time of St Patrick, no matter how we date him, so that a knowledge of Latin can have been anything but widespread among the natives. And even towards the

12 The 'British' Isles: see the references in Hanson, *St Patrick: His Origins*, p. 38 n. 2, where add Apuleius, *De Mundo*, 7, 'The two Britains, both Albion and Hibernia'.

end of Patrick's career the number of Irish persons who could speak Latin and were Christian was minute. The number of those who were sufficiently educated to read Latin must have been microscopic. True, there must have been Irish priests in the country to serve the Christians who lived there before Palladius arrived in the island in 431, and others were presumably ordained by Palladius himself. These would certainly have known some Latin and might perhaps have been able to read the *Confession*. But even when other Irishmen had been trained up and ordained by Patrick, the number able to read Latin was so small, I fancy, that a bishop who wished to address them would not have done so in writing. No doubt the Christians in Ireland were scattered over many parts of the island; but Patrick travelled extensively and, although his journeys were dangerous, he never says that he was prevented from reaching his various destinations. So if he wished to defend himself against Irish critics, he would have been far more likely to do so by word of mouth than by writing in a language which only a tiny half-handful of them could read or understand. Yet Patrick speaks of his 'readers', not his listeners. The book was not intended to be read out aloud to open-mouthed and wondering Irishmen. It was intended for literates. At the end of the *Epistle*, on the other hand, Patrick asks that that letter should be read out aloud 'before all the people'. It is aimed in part at illiterates. Coroticus's soldiers may or may not have been able to read. The persons to whom the *Confession* is addressed were expected to read it for themselves.[13]

There is another fatal objection to supposing that the *Confession* was addressed to Irishmen. Is it likely that any Irish Christians, newly come to the faith and still aglow with innocent Christian fervour, would be so grossly inept as to throw doubt on the personal honesty of the bishop who had converted them? Is it likely that any of them, fired with enthusiasm for the new religion, would accuse the bishop bluntly of having come to Ireland not to spread the faith so much as to line his own pocket with the proceeds of the visit? And would brazen Irish Christian malcontents have maintained such a barrage of criticism against their bishop as to oblige him, after many years in their country, to compose the *Confession*? It is inconceivable. If by some unlikely chance a few of the Irish were so

13 For the view of the linguistic evidence which used to be taken to show that Christianity existed in Ireland even in the fourth century see Zimmer, *The Celtic Church*, pp. 24−7, O'Rahilly, *The Two Patricks*, pp. 42−4, Greene, 'Some Linguistic Evidence', pp. 75−86, esp. 81. But this opinion has been criticised by Jackson, 'Some Questions in Dispute', pp. 18−32, McManus, 'A Chronology of the Latin Loan-Words', pp. 21−71.

unpleasant as to do all this, Patrick's best course of action would obviously have been to visit them and to discuss and refute their arguments verbally; and he would certainly have done so in Irish, not in Latin. To write a Latin document about such criticisms might well have given the criticisms publicity in Britain but would have left nearly all his critics untouched.

I take it, then, that the *Confession* was not addressed to Irish readers, and indeed it does not contain a single sentence of which we can say with confidence that this *must* be addressed to Irishmen. We can go further: there is not a single sentence in the *Confession* of which we can be sure that it is addressed to new converts. Patrick mentions Irish converts, but only in the third person. So far as we can see, he never speaks to them directly. In fact, there is no doubt whatever about the destination of the first half of the little book. This tells of Patrick's family, his enslavement, his escape and his journey across the sea and the desert, and his examination by the seniors. All this is beyond doubt addressed to Britons. There would be no point in speaking to Irishmen about Bannaventa and its villa, or in discussing his fear of being criticised on literary grounds, or in mentioning his lack of instruction in Roman law and letters, or in setting out his difficulties in expressing himself elegantly in the Latin language. To Irish readers he would not repeatedly lament his lack of a higher education in Latin language and literature. To them, all this would have been unintelligible. The idea that this part of his book had any Irish readers at all, apart from rare exceptions, is very hard to accept.

So he is writing to Britons. Can we define who these Britons were? Near the beginning of the *Confession* he remarks that he had thought of writing long ago but had hesitated hitherto in case he should be criticised by men who, unlike himself, had 'excellently imbibed law and sacred letters alike in equal measure'. A few pages later he writes a notorious passage — it is notorious because of a corruption of the Latin text which no one has ever been able to correct satisfactorily — in which he says, 'So be astonished, you great and small, you who fear God, and you rich and educated clerics [or the like], listen and examine. He who raised me up, stupid as I am, from the midst of those who appear to be wise and skilled in the law and powerful in speech and in everything, and inspired me beyond all others . . . to benefit that nation to whom the love of Christ transferred me and presented me in my lifetime in order that, if I was worthy, I should serve them with humility and with truth.' Are we to suppose that both these groups of possible critics are identical? They certainly seem to be similar persons, rich and well educated, and both alike are living in Britain, both are Christian, and both inspired in Patrick no small sense of inferiority with regard to his education. They would read his Latin critically and knowledgeably. They were men of literary taste in Latin. In fact, to try to distinguish the two groups would be to split hairs. The conclusion is irresistible that Patrick in these two passages is addressing educated and Christian landowners living in Britain. He is by no means writing these words to all Britons indiscriminately. He is addressing here a very limited class, the class of relatively rich and cultivated landowners from which he himself was sprung. Whatever Patrick's date, civilisation had not broken down completely in Britain or at any rate in his part of Britain at the time when his mission was coming to a close. (Incidentally, it is unfortunate that he does not tell us what it was that had now led him to change his mind and to write in spite of all, or how long the interval had been between his fearing to write because of these men's possible criticisms and the present moment when he is in fact writing at last. He does not say why in the end he had decided to write even though such persons would still presumably speak of him critically.)[14]

Surely we have proof here, then, that Patrick addressed the *Confession* to British landowners and clergy living in Britain? No. The interpretation of these passages, in my view, is not so simple. Patrick is taunting these persons. He has scored over them by being appointed to the Irish bishopric, an appointment which some of them would evidently have been glad to obtain. But in spite of all their worldly advantages God has in the end preferred him to them. Patrick addresses them tauntingly and gleefully as though their opinion was one which he would not value very highly (though we may suspect that in his heart of hearts he would value it very much more highly than he was prepared to admit). On the other hand, he writes the *Confession* as a whole with intense earnestness to persons whose opinions he takes very seriously indeed. It is hard to think that he is addressing the whole of the *Confession* to those educated and (as he saw them) arrogant Britons whose possible condemnation of him he affects to despise. I prefer to think that the second of these passages is a rhetorical address, an 'apostrophe', as the grammarians put it, of people whom he is not addressing directly. He turns aside from his audience to speak to a group of absent persons to whom he has not

14 Patrick's apostrophe: *Confession*, §13 (238.23).

addressed his words hitherto. This figure of speech recurs in Patrick's works. It is one of his few rhetorical devices. The apostrophe of Coroticus in one passage of the *Epistle* does not prove that the *Epistle* is addressed to Coroticus in person: in fact, it is addressed to his followers, not to him. Still less does the moving apostrophe towards the end of the *Epistle* — the apostrophe of the murdered Christians who are now, he says, in heaven — prove that the *Epistle* was posted to an address in Paradise. In other words, the passage of the *Confession* in which he mocks the educated Britons is, I think, a literary flourish and cannot safely be taken to throw a direct light on our question, To whom has Patrick addressed the *Confession*? This passage does not prove that the *Confession* as a whole, or indeed any part of it, is directly addressed to rich, contemporary Britons living in Britain.[15]

But, as I have mentioned, we must certainly agree that Patrick sent the first half of the *Confession* to Britons, whether present or absent. He sent it to educated Britons, not to all Britons. That appears to be unquestionable. He begins the second half by saying that a complete narrative of his bishopric or even a partial account would bore his readers. (Oh, if only he had decided to bore them!) He speaks of his decision to go 'to the Irish clans to preach the gospel and to endure insults from unbelievers'. He often mentions his converts among the Irish people, but he never refers to them as 'you'. His converts are always 'them'. He mentions 'those of our race who were born there', that is, Britons born in Ireland; and one implication of these words is that his readers and he are of the same race or nationality: they are Britons. Some of his readers may be expected to 'mock and insult' him; but I imagine that new converts are the least likely of all people to have been so audacious. The critics are Britons.[16]

But immediately after speaking of these critics Patrick begins to use the second person quite freely. He has used the second person earlier in the passage where he is apostrophising the rich and educated Britons to whom he was eventually preferred. But otherwise he has addressed his readers as 'you' on only one occasion — when he asserts that his account of the interview with the seniors is a true one. But after he mentions those who would prohibit his mission he goes on to use the second person freely. In a passage of profound

---

15 The apostrophe of Coroticus: *Epistle*, §14 (257.12−7), and of the murdered Christians, *ibid.*, §18 (258.16f.).
16 Spare his readers: *Confession*, §35 (246.2−5); his conversion of the Irish, *ibid.*, §37 (246.15−22), §40f. (247.11−248.9), §40 (247.21).

obscurity and of capital importance, a passage which we must examine with the closest attention, he says, 'So now I have made known in a simple way to my brothers and fellow-servants, who believed me, the reason why I have preached and am preaching so as to strengthen and confirm your faith. Would that you, too, should have higher ideals and greater achievements! This will be my glory, for a wise man is his father's glory.' There is a distinction here between two groups of people. Patrick has made something known to persons whom he calls 'my brothers and fellow-servants'. We can only guess at their identity. To his original readers, of course, the point would have been perfectly clear, but it is far from that to us. This group sounds like the men who are working closely with him, his immediate staff perhaps: who else are his 'fellow-servants' likely to be? As for the other group, it is of crucial importance to identify them, for it is these who appear in the second person: it is these who have apparently been criticising him for years, and it is these whom he is addressing directly throughout the whole *Confession*. But the calamitous truth appears to be that the identification can hardly be made. Although the men to whom he speaks in the *Confession* had been criticising him persistently, he seems to regard them as to some extent his children who may bring glory to him. But they are not his converts, at any rate his Irish converts, for Irish converts, as we have seen, would hardly be willing to criticise him or able to read his Latin. Nor does he make any claim here to have converted them. He claims only to have tried to strengthen and confirm their faith. They have the distinction of being the only persons in the whole *Confession* of whom he is directly and explicitly critical. He expresses the wish — and it is most uncharacteristic of him — that they would do better than they have been doing. Elsewhere he refers to his successors and followers as his 'brothers and sons'. It is they who will lead his mission when he himself is dead. They are more akin to the 'brothers and fellow-servants' of the passage which we are discussing. They are certainly distinct from those whom he is here criticising. The latter, those whom he addresses as 'you', are more numerous and extensive than his 'brothers and fellow-servants', but it is exasperatingly hard to see who they can have been. Unfortunately, he gives no indication of the ways in which he felt their efforts to have been deficient. And why should he have told his immediate staff (if that is who they are) that he had strengthened and confirmed 'your' faith? Would not his immediate staff know already of the more important of his activities without being formally notified of them?[17]

But let us see how he goes on. He writes, 'You know and God knows how I behaved among you from the time when I was a young man with loyalty to the truth and with sincerity of heart.' In these words he is addressing, it seems, Christians in Ireland among whom he had been working from the time when he was a young man. (This is all the more probable if we accept the theory, put forward earlier in this book, that he had spent some time in Ireland even when he was a deacon, or at any rate before he went there as bishop.) He certainly could not say that he had been active from his young manhood, or that he was still continuing to work, among Britons living in Britain. On any theory he had left Britain years ago. So here we appear to be on relatively firm ground. Patrick is now addressing Britons living, not in Britain, but in Ireland. We may suppose that these Britons living in Ireland are distinct from the persons whom we have guessed to be Patrick's immediate staff. The critics are British though living in Ireland; and not unnaturally, since they have been so critical of him, Patrick is somewhat critical of them.

He goes on, 'With regard to these tribes, too, among whom I am living, with them I have kept faith and shall keep it. God knows I tricked none of them, nor am I thinking of it, because of God and his Church, in case I should stir up a persecution against them and against us all and in case the name of the Lord should be blasphemed because of me; for it is written, "Woe to the man through whom the name of the Lord is blasphemed" '. In this passage we are back again among our difficulties, and they are as dark and impenetrable as ever. Had he been accused of cheating the pagan Irish in some way? His emphatic denial suggests that he had indeed been accused so. But by whom? Who would bring such a charge? And in what way was he supposed to have cheated the Irish? Again, when he writes about 'a persecution of them and of us all', that word 'them' is a puzzle in itself. What is the distinction between 'them' and 'us all'? In fact, he seems to be talking about several groups of people in this passage as a whole: (i) 'my brothers and fellow-servants', whom we have guessed without much confidence to be his closest associates; (ii) those whose faith he has been strengthening and confirming and with whose performance he is not altogether satisfied; these are the people (Britons, as we believe) whom he is addressing directly and who had been his critics for many years; (iii) the 'tribes' among whom he is living,

17 Second person: *Confession*, §13 (238.23), §31 (244.25), esp. §47 (249.32). His successors as 'brethren and sons', *ibid.*, §14 (239.8). See p. 38f. above.

that is, without any doubt the heathen Irish. And now we have (iv) that puzzling term 'them' as contrasted with 'us all'. It ought in strict grammar to mean the pagan Irish among whom he is living. But that would make nonsense. How could he be said to run the risk of arousing a persecution against *them*? The pagan Irish are not likely to be persecuted. They are likely to be the persecutors. His reason for keeping faith with the pagan Irish tribes is that he does not want to provoke a 'persecution against them and against us all'. It is only too obvious that this is one of the passages of the *Confession* where Patrick has not been able to make his meaning clear, and it would be interesting to know whether it was clear even to his first readers. At any rate, the identity of 'them' in this passage is unknown. We can only be sure that they are Christians living in Ireland and that they are or could be exposed to the unpleasant attentions of the pagan Irish. They do not seem to be Patrick's closest collaborators, and they are not identical with the persons whom he is addressing directly. The latter would seem to be British Christians living in circumstances of less danger than those of the third group. But at least one thing is clear: they could not possibly be British Christians living in Britain, for it would be farcical to suggest that Britons living in their homeland might be liable to persecution at the hands of Irish pagans. Patrick is now speaking to persons who live in Ireland. But does that mean that the readers are now different persons from those to whom the first half of the *Confession* was addressed?[18]

We have seen Patrick's defence against accusations of financial misdeeds which had been brought against him. In the course of it he more than once addresses 'you'; and these passages give us some further information about the persons to whom he is writing, though they do not make it possible for us to identify them. He says that he paid out for 'you' in order that 'they' would receive him, and that he went everywhere for 'your' sake amid many dangers to the most distant places where no bishop had gone before. And he did everything for 'your' safety or salvation. So the people whom he is addressing in the *Confession* live scattered over the whole of Ireland, or at any rate over the whole of that part of Ireland with which Patrick concerned

---

18 The passage under discussion is *ibid.*, §47f. (249.30−250.9). In *Epistle*, §1 (254.6) he says that he abandoned his country (*patria*) for love of *proximorum atque filiorum*. These would be different from the *fratribus et conservis* of *Confession*, §47 (248.30), as *filii* seems to indicate 'converts'. In *Epistle*, §16 (258.1), *fratres et filii* are converts. The discussion in the text goes on to centre on *Confession*, §51 (250.25−9), and §53f. (251.7−18). The possibility that Patrick may have been accused of cheating the pagans was raised by Nerney, 'A Study', p. 273.

himself: they can be found even in the far west of the island. Once again, there is no question here of his addressing Christians living in Britain. But what Christians would benefit from Patrick's making his way to the furthest districts amid dangers? Presumably, Christian prisoners and others — but what others? — living in the far-off parts to which they had in some cases been sold as slaves: Patrick travelled at some expense into remote regions so as to comfort those who were already Christians. They lived at a great distance from wherever he was staying at the time of writing and perhaps from the bulk of his Christian followers. But in what sense would he pay these visits 'for your sake', that is, for the sake of the readers of the *Confession*? Is it likely that copies of the *Confession* circulated among these remote Christians, especially among British captives living near the western seaboard? Slave-owners, not least illiterate slave-owners, do not often welcome strangers who distribute literature among their slaves. And if the bulk of the British slaves in Ireland had been agricultural workers before they were caught and enslaved, it is hardly likely that many of them were either Christian or literate. Yet Patrick never hints that his intended readers will have the slightest difficulty in laying hands on a copy of his work or in reading it when they do lay hands on it. Why then are some readers of the *Confession* expected to be living as freemen in outlying parts of western Ireland?[19]

Towards the end of the passage concerning Patrick's finances, as we have seen, Patrick prays to be allowed to lay down his life for his God's sake along with the 'strangers and captives'. Who are these? Some scholars think that the first of these terms refers to the Irish, the second (the captives) to the Britons among Patrick's Christians in Ireland. But the Irish could not reasonably be called 'strangers' in Ireland; and we have seen good reason for thinking that he is not addressing Irishmen. In Patrick's writings the Latin word often translated as 'proselytes' means strangers, aliens, visitors, and so on, and in this context can only refer to Britons. In other words, when Patrick is bringing his *Confession* to its solemn close he mentions two groups of Britons. One of these groups consists of captives, that is, no doubt, enslaved Britons such as he himself had been years before (though that does not include all the British captives), and another group who could be called 'visitors' in Ireland. He appears to address this long and exceptionally earnest passage about his finances to British 'strangers and captives' in Ireland, not to critics or anyone else

19 See p. 61 above.

in Britain and certainly not to the native Irish. Whatever we are to think about the 'captives', the others are literate and therefore were once well-to-do and may well be clergy. The evidence would fall into place if we could suppose that Patrick was addressing these two groups of Christian Britons throughout the whole of the *Confession*. The difficulty is to account for the presence in Ireland of a substantial number of free and literate Britons.

There are four possibilities, then:—

(i) Patrick is addressing the *Confession* to the Irish Christians. Since these in the main did not know Latin and are unlikely to have kept up a barrage of criticism of their bishop, they may be excluded without ado.

(ii) British Christians living in Britain. One passage seems beyond doubt to be addressed to these, but in my view the passage is, or may be, a rhetorical address or 'apostrophe'. The rest of the evidence is not consistent with this theory — for one thing, the persons whom Patrick is addressing live in constant danger of persecution.

(iii) All the Christians in Ireland, British and Irish alike. But Patrick clearly excludes from those whom he is addressing 'my brethren and fellow-servants', that is, as I have guessed — and it is only a guess — his closest helpers. But if everyone else in Ireland apart from his closest assistants were critical of him, he must have had a remarkable talent for antagonising those whose souls he had come to save; and he must have been a very prickly, unpleasant person indeed. Let us discard this possibility, if it is a possibility.

(iv) Some of the British Christians living in various parts of Ireland, including out-of-the-way places in the far west. I say 'some' of the British Christians living in Ireland: it can only have been addressed to those who could read it, that is, to the literate. The passages in which he laments that while others had a complete education he had been deprived of one by his captivity can only have been addressed to Britons who had not been deprived of an education. To have written such lamentations to British slaves or escaped slaves who had never had any hope whatever of receiving an education, higher or lower, would have been a gross lapse. Even the thickest-skinned dolt would regard such a lament addressed to such an audience as verging on the indelicate. If the *Confession*, then, is addressed to Britons living in Ireland, it is addressed to educated Britons. The problem is to define who such Britons in Ireland can have been, and this is hard to do. Perhaps they were a group of his clergy. There is no evidence in the historical sources or in the archaeological record or in the place-names for a substantial influx of Britons into Ireland at or a little before this date. Patrick does mention 'those of our race who were born there', but their numbers were a mystery even to him, and their reasons for being born there rather than in Britain are an equally profound mystery to us.

I would accept the last of these four hypotheses. It does not contradict any evidence given by Patrick, though it is clear that there can be no certainty. It is never wise to overlook Bury's opinion. Bury thought that some of Patrick's British fellow-workers who had laboured with him in Ireland felt themselves aggrieved, returned in disgust to Britain and spread evil reports about Patrick's conduct of the Irish mission. Patrick then wrote the *Confession* for the communities in Britain where such reports circulated in order to refute them. It is not easy to accept this location of the public to which the *Confession* was addressed. There are two reasons: (i) Patrick could not claim to have been working in any British community since he had become a grown-up man, and (ii) no community of Christians in Britain was in danger of being subjected to persecution. To me it seems unavoidable to think that Patrick addressed his book to disgruntled Britons living not in Britain but in Ireland.

What we cannot accept, in my opinion, is the view that as Patrick went on writing the *Confession* he began without warning to address his words to a different group of readers from those whom he had had in mind when he first took up his pen. We cannot believe, for example, that Patrick began to write to an audience of bishops and other clergy in Britain but that towards the end of the work he found himself (absent-mindedly?) addressing not only bishops and other clergy in Britain but also his friends, converts, and supporters in Ireland, whom he had not had in mind when he first began to write. When a man sits down to write a letter, he may not be very clear about what he is going to say, but he certainly knows *to whom* he is going to say it.[20]

I have spent a good deal of space in discussing the persons whom Patrick addresses as 'you'. The discussion has been inconclusive, but it suggests a comment on the character of Patrician studies. A mountain of literature, a mountain of Himalayan proportions, has grown up about the *Confession*. But for the most part it deals with a

20 It was MacNeill, *St Patrick*, p. 59, I think, who originated the view that Patrick in the *Confession* addresses two distinct groups of reader. Bury, *The Life of St Patrick*, p. 201f. Wilson, 'Romano-British and Welsh Christianity', p. 13, goes so far as to wonder in connexion with the accusations of financial misdeeds 'if it was not his British critics who instigated the Irish to prefer these particular charges'.

surprisingly small number of questions — the chronology of Patrick's life, the site of Bannaventa and of the desert which the ship's company took twenty-eight days to cross, the nature of the interview with the seniors. These are important problems; but the passages which we have been discussing in this chapter are crucial. They could perhaps be made to tell us what persons Patrick is writing to and so could to some extent place him in his social context; yet they have been passed over in relative silence. At any rate, I have not found a single study of the passages addressed to 'you'. If these persons were identified we might be better able to understand the mission as a whole and the character of Irish Christianity in St Patrick's day.[21]

21 There is a discussion of the problem, however, in Grosjean, 'Notes 10', p. 108, but in my opinion his conclusions are incorrect. For O Raifeartaigh's opinion see his 'The Life', p. 131f.: Patrick's writings 'were intended for British ears'. True, but where were those British ears?

CHAPTER EIGHT

Coroticus

The earlier of Patrick's two surviving writings is known as the *Epistle to the Soldiers of Coroticus*. The circumstances in which he wrote it are all too clear. He had just baptised a large group of persons, men and women, apparently Irish converts. They had been anointed with baptismal chrism — it still perfumed their foreheads — and they were still wearing the white clothes which were a symbol of innocence, when a group of British thugs rushed upon them, murdered some, and carried off others of both sexes to sell them away as slaves. Patrick must have been close to the scene of the crime although he was not actually present when it happened and was not an eye-witness. On the very next day after the massacre he sent a letter to the criminals in the hands of a priest, a man whom he had himself educated from infancy, accompanied by other clergy. In this letter, which has not survived, he demanded the return of the booty and of the baptised prisoners; but the murderers spurned his envoys with coarse guffaws. What we possess is a second letter which Patrick then wrote with his own hand. Its purpose is to excommunicate the criminals, who were Christians, and to instruct their neighbours to boycott them until they should repent in tears, give satisfaction to God, and set free the baptised men and women.[1]

Patrick mentions that the cause of the outrage was a certain Coroticus, who had established a 'tyranny', a man who does not fear

---

1 *Epistle*, §3 (254.16−20). That they were new converts is shown *ibid.*, §9 (256.5).

God or his bishops. Coroticus had not conducted the raid in person, but he it was who had given the order for the outrage and who then made over Christians into the hands of Irish and Picts. The survivors of the massacre had been sent to a foreign nation which does not know God. The Church weeps for its sons and daughters whom the sword has not yet killed: they have been sent a great distance away and sold, free persons reduced to slavery, worst of all to slavery among the vile apostate Picts. Patrick speaks in words of anger and then of heartbroken grief at the fate of the murdered Christians until, before the end of the letter, his grief turns to joy as he thinks of the victims' life in Paradise, which he contrasts with the very different fate of Coroticus, whose earthly rule will pass in a moment. Patrick's words are very moving, and the whole of this passage extraordinarily touching.[2]

1. — Who Was Coroticus?

Our first problem is to identify, if we can, this tyrant Coroticus; and the identification has been the subject of prolonged discussion. He was unquestionably a Briton, the first (so far as we know) but not the last British butcher to perpetrate a massacre in Ireland. Patrick makes it quite clear that he was a Briton. Patrick's seventh-century biographer, Muirchu, took the point from Patrick; and since he knew only what Patrick had said, Muirchu does not attach Coroticus to any specific part of Britain. But someone else, not Muirchu himself, added a 'Table of Contents' to Muirchu's biography; and this unknown writer made Coroticus 'King of the Rock' of the River Clyde, that is, of Dumbarton, a description which was unknown to, or at any rate is unmentioned by, both Patrick and Muirchu. Is this description true or false?

Let us follow up this clue; and we do so by merrily jumping ahead a century or two. St Columba died in 597, and Adomnan wrote his *Life of Columba* somewhat less than a hundred years later. Soon after the beginning of his narrative Adomnan reports that in answer to an enquiry Columba predicted that 'king Roderc, son of Tóthal, who reigned on the Rock of Clyde' (Dumbarton) would die in his

2 'Tyranny', *ibid.*, §6 (255.9); 'Irish and Picts', *ibid.*, §12 (256.27), §14 (257.13); 'apostate Picts', *ibid.*, §15 (257.26). For the evidence, such as it is, concerning Coroticus see Hanson, *St Patrick : His Origins*, pp. 21–5.

bed. Sure enough, the prophecy turned out to be true: Roderc died with his boots off soon after 600. Now, this Roderc is thought to appear elsewhere in our records, though not elsewhere in Adomnan himself. The editors of Adomnan suppose that Roderc was identical with the Riderch who fought against the Saxon Bernicians about the beginning of the seventh century. If that is correct, we may date Roderc, son of Tóthal, about the year 600. But there is a third Riderch: he occurs in a Welsh genealogy as the son of Tutagual (Tóthal in another guise?), sixth in descent from a certain Ceretic. We are getting warm, you may think. This Ceretic — can you doubt it? — is none other than Patrick's enemy Coroticus.[3]

To the innocent, the chain of argument seems cast-iron. The Ceretic of the Welsh genealogy was presumably king of Dumbarton like his descendant, Roderc, and being six generations earlier than Roderc or Riderch he must have lived in the fifth century. (It is a convention among historians to allow thirty years to a generation.) But if he was a contemporary of St Patrick, he cannot fail to have been the same man as Patrick's Coroticus, who — does not Muirchu's Table of Contents say so? — was also ruler of Dumbarton. All the pieces of the jigsaw fit together, and the problem of identifying Patrick's Coroticus is solved.

So we are told. The fact is somewhat different. There are so many ifs and maybes in the argument as to daunt all but the most credulous. The truth is that each one of the arguments in this chain of ramshackle reasoning is nothing more than a flimsy guess. The chain has all the strength of a cobweb and must be rejected from beginning to end. The unknown writer who at an unknown date added the Table of Contents to Muirchu's work and who located Coroticus at Dumbarton is assumed to have had access to valid information about the fifth century, information which was not derived from Patrick's works and was not available to Muirchu himself. This is itself out of the question. There was at that date — perhaps early in the eight century — no reliable information whatever in existence about Patrick and his life or about Coroticus except what could be inferred from Patrick's own writings; and Patrick says nothing and implies nothing about Dumbarton. Those who believe otherwise and think that there was a further source of information about the saint and his enemy

3 For the entry in Muirchu's 'Table of Contents' see Bieler, *The Patrician Texts*, p. 66, cf. pp. 9 – 12. See also *idem*, 'Muirchu's Life of St Patrick', pp. 225 – 8. Adomnan, *Vita S. Columbani*, I, 15 (ed. Anderson, p. 238); *Historia Britonum*, §63 (Mommsen, *Chronica Minora*, III, p. 206).

Coroticus in addition to his own writings must let the rest of the world into their startling secret and tell us what this source may have been.

But that is not all. The genealogy according to which Roderc or Riderch was descended from Ceretic is worthless for the historian. Unless we know a great deal about those who drew up any given genealogy of this period and about the conditions in which they worked, genealogies cannot safely be used, this one no more than the others. In early mediaeval times genealogies were put to all sorts of uses. They could be used as a legal title to a throne or as a political argument. They could be a consequence of ignorance or of bribery or of a personal whim, straightforward propaganda, a justification of the existing state of affairs whether political or social — and as the existing state of affairs changed, the genealogies, too, might have to change so as to justify and sanction the innovations — and so on. In fact, 'without the minutest examination, acceptance of any genealogical record is extremely rash'. Moreover, genealogies are so liable to be 'cooked' or doctored that it is naive to assume that in them a generation is thirty years or twenty years. In the turmoil of the Celtic Dark Ages, when rulers were woefully exposed to the assassin's knife, to death in battle, and to uncontrolled diseases, plagues, and epidemics, not many of them could hope to avoid a premature departure from this life and a premature arrival in the next. So a generation for the historian is x years, where x is a wholly unknown and highly variable number. We may notice, by the way, that between 1760 and 1936 Britain was ruled by six monarchs, thus 'proving' that a generation of monarchs lasts for about thirty years. The proof is not quite rigorous, however, for between 1820 and 1937 Britain was again ruled by six monarchs, in which case a generation lasted not for thirty years but for less than twenty years — years in which the knife of the assassin and death in battle were not an obvious threat.[4]

The upshot for our purpose is that we do not know that the Ceretic in question was really perched six places above Riderch in the family tree; and, if he was, we do not know even approximately when he lived or indeed whether he lived at all. Nor can we assume that, if Riderch was ruler of Dumbarton, therefore Ceretic had also been ruler of Dumbarton. Not every Dark Age dynasty was able to maintain itself in the one capital or stronghold for six generations. To

4   See especially Dumville, 'Kingship, Genealogies', p. 88.

suppose, then, that the Coroticus who opposed Patrick was king of Dumbarton is to go careering wildly beyond the evidence, quite out of control. It is wholly uncertain that he was the great-great-great-grandfather of Roderc, or that he lived in the middle of the fifth century, or that he was the ruler of Dumbarton. All three of these assumptions are equally baseless. The only impressive quality which they possess is their power to gull students of St Patrick.

But if we reject the Dumbarton theory, we must face an argument put forward by Binchy: how did the author of Muirchu's Table of Contents know about the Ceretic — he calls him Coirthech — of Dumbarton (who elsewhere survives only as a name in the Old Welsh genealogies) unless there was a written or oral tradition linking him with Patrick? There is less strength in this argument than might appear, for, as we have seen, there is no reason for identifying the Ceretic of Dumbarton (if he was 'of Dumbarton' and if he lived at the appropriate time) with the man of the same name who figures in the Old Welsh genealogies. The question, if properly stated, would be: why did the mysterious author of the Table of Contents locate Patrick's Coroticus in Dumbarton? And to that question O'Rahilly gave an adequate answer: 'the British chieftain, Coroticus, was a neighbour of the Picts to whom he sold his captives, and consequently was king of the Britons of Dumbarton', the best known and perhaps the only well known British site in the relevant locality. So there is no need to make the unlikely assumption of the existence in the eighth century of an independent written or oral tradition about Coroticus, the enemy of St Patrick — I have said more than once that in the later seventh century and after it nothing whatever was known about Patrick except what could be deduced from his writings. To plant Coroticus in Dumbarton was simply a none-too-astute guess on the writer's part designed to explain why some of the Irish captives were sold to the Picts. The truth is that even if Muirchu himself had placed Coroticus in Dumbarton, we should still have no right to follow suit and locate him there.[5]

As a matter of fact, still other persons of this name lurk obscurely in the pages of our shadowy sources. There was Ceredig, son of Cunedda, who either gave his name to Cardigan or else took his name from Cardigan. A famous Welsh tradition told how Cunedda and his sons migrated from near the Firth of Forth to north Wales, where they ousted Irish settlers. The date of this improbable journey

---

5 Binchy, 'Patrick and his Biographers', p. 108; O'Rahilly, *The Two Patricks*, p. 39.

is unknown. A number of scholars identified this Ceredig with Patrick's Coroticus; but Bury rightly remarked long ago about this theory that 'It is hardly necessary to mention it.' And indeed the theory would be considerably more acceptable if we could be sure that this Ceredig really existed in a more tangible form than that of eponym of Cardiganshire. And then again, we are told that an interpreter of the legendary Briton Vortigern, present at a legendary banquet given by the legendary Saxon Hengist, was called Ceretic; and we need not doubt that he was even more legendary than his two superiors. So the name is a common enough one in the dawn-twilight period of the Celtic world; and our only hope of identifying Patrick's opponent is to study Patrick's words and to ignore all that we find in the other sources of information, if 'sources' is the right word to apply to these odds and ends of traditions and inventions, whimsies and fancies. When we discuss Coroticus, then, our first action must be to rid our minds of all the robber chiefs and Rob Roys and hillbillies who ever cut a throat in Caledonia.[6]

But there is nothing whimsical or fanciful about Patrick's evidence. He was living in a treacherous and angry world where there was little room for whimsy (which he is not given to, in any case). He leaves us in no doubt that Coroticus was a Briton. Near the beginning of the *Epistle* he mentions the 'soldiers of Coroticus', and goes on, 'I do not say my fellow-citizens or fellow-citizens of the holy Romans but fellow-citizens of devils'. As Bury rightly remarked, 'the sting of this reproach is that they professed to be Romans'; and H. M. Chadwick agreed that these words mean 'that the recipients of the letter regarded themselves as Romans and were expected to take some pride in the name.' And since the letter is to be read out to all the people, it would seem that the people in question understood Latin and were therefore immigrants in Ireland from the Roman Empire or from what had once been the Roman Empire. That in itself rules out Dumbarton as the dwelling-place of Coroticus, for in no sense whatever could an inhabitant of Dumbarton regard himself as a Roman citizen. That place had been incorporated in the Empire for a very few years in the middle of the second century, that is, some three hundred years earlier than the time of Patrick. Indeed, experts tell us now that the Romans held the Antonine Wall in central Scotland, thus including Dumbarton in their dominions, for barely more than

6 Bury, *The Life of St Patrick*, p. 315; but O'Rahilly, *The Two Patricks*, p. 38f., and Bieler, *The Life and Legend*, p. 37, keep Coroticus in Cardiganshire, accepting *Historia Britonum*, §37 (Mommsen, *Chronica Minora*, III, p. 177).

twenty years. And O'Rahilly does not overstate the truth when he observes that 'it is, to say the least, exceedingly doubtful whether Patrick would, in defiance of history, have regarded the subjects of the king of Dumbarton as Roman citizens'. But indeed, it is not exceedingly doubtful: it is impossible. Patrick was himself a Roman citizen, and he would no sooner have called Dumbarton 'Roman' than he would have called any other barbarian fort 'Roman'. It is not very flattering to assume that he was a geographical ignoramus. And it is inconceivable that after the lapse of such a vast period of time as three hundred years any native of the place could regard himself as a Roman or that he would want to do so. To meet this difficulty some scholars have supposed that as Roman power declined in the Lowland Zone of Britain there spread a veneer of romanisation over the Highland Zone and even that the Roman government towards the end of its history in the West acquired a great extension of territory beyond Hadrian's Wall. I should regard such an extension of Roman rule at this date as impossible. The Western Emperors had their backs to the wall and could not even protect, or begin to protect, the vitally important province of Africa against the Vandals who landed there in 429. And even if such a veneer as these scholars have in mind spread over what is now southern Scotland, it does not follow that Dumbarton specifically was affected by any such latinisation. There is no evidence at all to show that the rulers of Caledonia south of the Clyde-Forth isthmus were in any degree romanised now or earlier, except perhaps momentarily when the Romans were in the heyday of their power and were in physical occupation of the region.[7]

I conclude, then, that Coroticus was a Roman Briton or at any rate that he felt himself to be a Roman Briton and that he was regarded as such by St Patrick. I conclude, too, that there is no reason for identifying him with Coroticus of Dumbarton, still less with the eponym of Cardigan, and far, far less (if that is possible) with any of the other shadowy persons of that name who prowl feebly through our sources. So far as we can tell, the Coroticus who outraged the Christians of St Patrick was a person in his own right and was not identical with anyone except himself. He was a Briton and a Roman citizen in the full sense of the word Roman. That means that he was born in the Roman Empire or in what had once been part of the Roman Empire.

7 Bury, *The Life of St Patrick*, p. 314f.; Chadwick, *Early Scotland*, p. 150. On the Roman occupation of southern Scotland see Breeze & Dobson, *Hadrian's Wall*, p. 124. Cf. O'Rahilly, *The Two Patricks*, p. 39.

But if he did not live in Dumbarton or in Cardigan, where must we locate him? Whatever may have been the nature and extent of Patrick's diocese, no one will argue that it extended overseas to include any part of Britain. Yet there can be no doubt that one main purpose of the *Epistle* is the excommunication of the murderers. How then does Patrick come to exercise his full powers as a bishop to excommunicate persons who (if we accept the Dumbarton theory) were not living in or even near his diocese? The normal procedure would have been to seek redress through the local bishop or bishops of the land in which the offenders lived. To interfere as crudely as Patrick is thought to have done in the diocesan affairs of another bishop would have been regarded as outrageous. Carney is reduced to desperate straits to save Patrick's good manners and to explain the problem away: 'It is possible that Patrick, being himself in difficulties with a number of powerful British ecclesiastics, felt unable to secure their help', and so acted on his own. Now, if Patrick had wanted to justify and intensify and multiply all the misgivings which some British clerics are thought to have felt about his mission to Ireland, he could have devised no better method than this. The excommunication by him of some members of their flock would have been one of the most heinous offences that a bishop could give to his fellow-bishops. I find it difficult to think that Patrick was guilty of any such crudely offensive and uncanonical act. The clear inference is that Patrick was himself the local bishop of the region in question and hence that Coroticus's normal residence was in Ireland. There is a very obscure passage in the *Epistle* which might be taken to have a bearing on this subject. The saint says to Coroticus's soldiers, 'I am not usurping. I have a part with those whom God called and predestined to preach the gospel among no small persecutions as far as the end of the earth, even if the enemy [i.e. the Devil] envies <us> by means of the tyranny of Coroticus', etc. No one can explain exactly what Patrick had in mind when he says that he is 'not usurping'. But if he meant that he was not usurping the powers and rights of neighbouring bishops, or of one of them, he is being extraordinarily offhand and devil-may-care. There is no word of apology or of justification or of explanation of why he was doing so, no explanation of his unmannerly and illegal action. If indeed he was referring to his stepping into the shoes of his neighbouring bishops, he would surely have felt obliged to give a more extended account than we find here of the circumstances which had led to his taking this action. Whatever the meaning of those words 'I am not usurping', I do not think that they have any bearing on the problem which we are discussing. So Patrick's action in excommunicating the criminals of Coroticus is in itself a strong and otherwise all but inexplicable indication that the murderers did not live in Britain or Caledonia: they lived in Ireland where Patrick was the sole bishop and alone had the right to excommunicate them.[8]

A number of considerations support this conclusion. In another passage he says of Coroticus that, unlike the Christians in Gaul, 'you rather slay them and sell them [your prisoners] to a foreign nation that does not know God'. But what would have been the point of complaining that the prisoners were being sold to a 'foreign nation' — he means the Picts — if they were already in the hands of the ruler of Dumbarton (or Cardigan) and his henchmen? To protest against the captors' selling them to a 'foreign nation' implies that the captors were not themselves a 'foreign nation': they were resident in Ireland. But the problem raised by this phrase disappears if British people in Ireland were selling the prisoners abroad to the Picts.[9]

If Coroticus lived overseas, is not the saint remarkably well informed about him? Patrick knows that he and his men are nominally Christian, that after returning home from the raid they used their spoils to ornament their homes, that they were selling their captives back to Ireland (an improbable piece of salesmanship, as we shall see) as well as to the Picts. But how could Patrick find out all that? On the day after the outrage he had sent a written protest to the marauders, which they received with crude guffaws. After an unspecified interval but certainly not a long one, he wrote the extant *Epistle*. How, then, did he know, for example, that in the meantime some of the prisoners had been sold off to the Picts? How did he know that the raiders had used the loot as ornaments? Had the bearers of his first letter overheard them discussing the matter? ('Don't you think a skull or two would brighten up the drawing room?') It is true that those who carried the first letter to Coroticus's men will have returned, but they doubtless did so without delay. They are not likely to have wasted time loitering about the raiders' camp in order to see what they planned to do with their loot and in order to pick up news. If they arrived there a day or two after the return home of the raiding party, they are likely to have left the raiders' camp no more than a day or two later still. In the couple of days which they may have spent in the camp, were the prisoners sold off to both Irish and Picts?

8 Carney, *The Problem*, p. 114. The quotation is from *Epistle*, §6 (255.7).
9 *Epistle*, §14 (257.13).

If so, it was a quick sale, evidently requiring little in the way of advertisement of the wares. Buyers must have materialised out of nowhere. And if the letter-bearers did not bring back news, are we to suppose that other travellers did so? But how long did that take? Was travel between Patrick's part of Ireland and Dumbarton a relatively common affair? If so, why should it have been common? On the other hand, if Coroticus and his men lived in Ireland — in a not very remote part of Ireland — there is no problem.

Now, Bury pointed out that Coroticus does not appear to have led the raiding party in person. That is why the *Epistle* is not addressed to him personally, although the writer addresses him directly, 'apostrophises' him, as we have seen, in one passage. The *Epistle* as a whole is addressed to his soldiers. But Coroticus had given the order for his men to carry out the raid, and to that extent can be said to have done the killing. But if Coroticus was not present in person and if his men had come from a distant overseas country, how did Patrick know the identity of the raiders and the name of their leader? How did he know to what address he ought to send his *Epistle*? We can hardly suppose that one of the killers paused in his work of butchery and, as he wiped his brow on his sleeve, informed the Irish survivors that his leader — 'His name is Coroticus, in case you want to know' — had unfortunately been detained at home by another engagement or perhaps by a slight indisposition but had happily been able to give the order for the massacre. In the circumstances, we may guess (since few of us have been in them), such conversations are probably unusual. It seems far more likely that Coroticus was a well known raider who had often molested parts of Ireland and that his raiders were a familiar and dreaded sight there. If Coroticus and his butchers normally lived in Ireland it is not unlikely that they would be known, perhaps all too well known, to Patrick and his followers, at any rate by reputation.[10]

This hypothesis — that Coroticus normally lived in Ireland — would also throw light on the raiders' sale of their prisoners to distant buyers. In a disorganised and collapsing world such as Patrick or indeed Homer describes — the sort of world which that great scholar H. M. Chadwick called a 'Heroic Age' — it is difficult to retain slaves near their place of origin and to exploit them there for long. Since they know the local language and are familiar with the local geography, and since their relatives are not far away, they can escape

10 Bury, *Life of St Patrick*, p. 192. For the other points made in this paragraph see *Epistle*, §2 (254.11), §12 (256.26).

from their bondage much too easily for their owners' liking. So they must be sold to far-off peoples, best of all to peoples who live overseas. Once they are shipped across the horizon, no one knows where they have been taken to, and so no one can hope to ransom them or rescue them, and they themselves can never hope to escape. In fact, Patrick seems to be the only slave in the history of the ancient world (in so far as we know) who, after being sold overseas, managed to escape from his owner, overcome the gigantic obstacles that confront every runaway slave, and rejoin his family at home. He refers to the extraordinary difficulties of such an escape only in a single monosyllable; and that perhaps is the reason why his modern biographers have hardly done justice to this achievement, a grim test of courage and resourcefulness. So it is improbable that Coroticus, if he had been living in Dumbarton or elsewhere in Britain, would have shipped his prisoners over to Scotland (or the like) immediately after the raid, only to ship them back again to Ireland later on, for in Ireland they could escape very much more easily than from among the Picts. Having once shipped them overseas, he would keep them overseas. Why go to the trouble and expense of fitting out a ship and sailing back again to Ireland? And having once reached Dumbarton, how did he advertise his wares to potential customers in Ireland? How did Irish slave-owners find out that there were slaves for sale in Dumbarton? It would hardly have been possible.[11]

It is interesting to note Patrick's remark that not only the prisoners who were sold to the Picts but also those who were sold in Ireland were sent to a great distance from the place where they had been captured and where no doubt they lived. In no other way could they have been retained in their slavery. But to be sold even to remote parts of Ireland did not appear to these men and women to be so hideous a fate as to be sold to the Picts. In fact, Coroticus's men did exactly what we should expect slave-raiders in Ireland to have done: they sold some of their prisoners to distant parts of Ireland and others to the Picts across the sea. But is this not what we should have thought that Coroticus would do if he had really been established in Dumbarton? Would he not in that case also have sold some of his prisoners to the Irish and others to the Picts? Might he not have sold off some of the captives to Irish customers while he was still in Ireland and then have sailed home with the rest of them? No: consider what this procedure would have entailed. It would imply that

11 *Confession*, §61 (253.9), *uix*.

the marauders stayed in or near the scene of the massacre until the news of the outrage reached distant parts of Ireland, until the slave-owners of those parts made up their minds to buy some new slaves to replenish their existing stock, and until they had time to travel to the scene of these events and pay for their purchases. We must suppose that the raiders stayed in that place, so far away from their homes in Dumbarton (according to the theory), all this time — perhaps several weeks — and felt themselves safe enough from counter-attack to do so. It seems an improbable risk. And furthermore, if Coroticus lived in Dumbarton or any other part of Britain, we should have expected him to sell his prisoners, not to Picts and Irish, but to Picts and Britons. If he lived anywhere in Britain it is hard to see why the Britons were not among his customers. If he lived in north-eastern Ireland, there is no problem. [12]

Patrick never mentions any physical difficulties in the path of those who were to deliver his letter to the soldiers of Coroticus. The letter may be stolen or it may be suppressed; but the writer does not seem to doubt that the bearer will reach his destination. We might have expected some reference to the dangers of a voyage across those treacherous seas which separate Ireland from Scotland if they had been relevant. Patrick does not even hint at them. To be sure, he seems able to communicate with the clergy in Britain, though we do not know how often he did so. But civilised life still continued in western Britain throughout St Patrick's lifetime, and travellers going there from the Irish bishop would know in advance what their reception was likely to be on arrival. To set sail for Scotland was a very different matter, and Patrick's letter-bearer would have been faced with a dangerous journey not only because of the treacherous currents of the North Channel but also from the treachery of men. But no such problem would arise if Patrick's messenger was simply making his way from one part of Ireland to another, close at hand. In that case, the question might be asked, Why did Patrick send a messenger instead of going himself in person to reprimand Coroticus face to face? No one can tell the answer to that question: a hundred reasons may have prevented him. But we do know what the answer is *not*: his failure to go in person was not due to any lack of physical courage. Patrick's courage is not in question.

I conclude that every mediaeval theory, or rather guess, about Coroticus being the ruler of Dumbarton or of some other part of

12 Sold far away: *Epistle*, §15 (257.23).

Britain cannot be reconciled with the evidence of Patrick himself and is therefore worthless and untenable. All the evidence (such as it is) points to his having been a Briton who had established himself as an irregular ruler, a 'tyrant', in Ireland. Anyone who rejects the thesis that he was a British 'tyrant' resident in Ireland will have to answer unanswerable questions, such as how Patrick could bring himself to excommunicate persons living in another British bishop's diocese, one that lay across the seas and had no point of contact with his own diocese. Why does the saint complain that the ruler of Dumbarton is selling his captives to a 'foreign nation' when Coroticus's own people were themselves (on this theory) a 'foreign nation'? How did Patrick come to be so well informed about the activities of Coroticus so soon after the raid if the tyrant lived across the sea? Indeed, how did he learn that the raiders were the followers of Coroticus rather than of some other miserable and murderous pirate? Why did Coroticus ship his slaves over to Scotland and then re-export them back to Ireland? Why did Patrick foresee no difficulties in having his letter delivered across the treacherous currents of the North Channel to Caledonia? Answer these questions without straining or forcing the evidence, and it may then become possible to believe in a Caledonian Coroticus. Possible, but even then there is no persuasive evidence. If the mediaeval evidence is worthless, and the genealogies the most worthless part of it all, then there is nothing whatever to connect Coroticus with Scotland, and the burden of proof — a back-breaking burden in this case — rests with those who accept the Caledonian theory. But in fact, all of these questions can be taken in our stride once we grasp that Coroticus's permanent address was in Ireland.

2. — *Patrick and the* Epistle

Let us agree, then, that Coroticus was a British 'tyrant' who had established himself somehow, somewhere in Ireland — probably in the north-east. The *Epistle* is a furiously angry attack on him for committing such a hideous crime, and it is also a moving lament for the dead Irish Christians. But in the middle of this letter Patrick has inserted a strange and at first sight unaccountable passage of autobiography, a passage which deals with his own position in Ireland. Why does he think that this is relevant to the condemnation and excommunication of the murderers? Here is what he writes:[13]

'Did I come to Ireland without God and according to the flesh? Who forced me? I am bound in the spirit not to see anyone of my kindred. Is it of myself that I feel a holy pity towards the nation which once took me prisoner and devastated the slaves and slave-women of my father's house? I was well born according to the flesh; I was born of a father who was a city-councillor. Why, I sold my noble rank — I do not blush for it nor do I regret it — for the good of others. In fact, I am a slave in Christ to a foreign nation because of the unutterable glory of the eternal life which is in Christ Jesus our Lord.

'And if my own people do not know me, a prophet has no honour in his own country. Perhaps we are not of the one fold, nor have we one God as father . . . It is not my grace but God who put this care in my heart that I should be one of the hunters or fishers whom long ago God predicted beforehand for the last days.

'I am envied. What am I to do, Lord? I am very much despised. Look, your sheep around me are mutilated and driven off as plunder by the aforenamed brigands, Coroticus giving the orders with foul motive. A long way from the love of God is he who delivers over Christians into the hands of the Irish and the Picts. Ravening wolves have devoured the Lord's flock which was growing excellently in Ireland thanks to the utmost care and attention; and the sons and daughters of Irish chieftains, monks and virgins of Christ — I cannot count them. Wherefore do not let the injury to the just please you: even as far as the dead it will not please you.

'What devout person would not dread to rejoice, or to enjoy a banquet, with such men? From the spoils of dead Christians they have filled their homes; they live off plunder. The wretched men do not know they are handing out a deadly poison as food to their friends and sons, just as Eve did not understand that she was handing death to her husband. Such are all those who do evil: they bring death on themselves as an eternal punishment.

'A custom of the Christian Roman Gauls: they send suitable holy men to the Franks and the other nations with so many thousands of *solidi* to ransom baptised prisoners. You, on the other hand, kill them and sell them to a foreign nation which does not know God; you are handing over the limbs of Christ as it were into a brothel.'

Patrick says here that he came to Ireland owing to the Holy Spirit, that it is a hardship for him, that he cannot now visit any of his kin,

13 The passage translated is *Epistle*, §10−4 (256.7−257.14). The word *ingenuus* could mean 'freeborn'; but Patrick is not concerned to say that he was free rather than a slave but that he was rich rather than poor. See *Thesaurus*, VII. 1545, 53.

and that he feels compassion for the Irish who did him so great a wrong in his youth. He was well born. At home in Britain his father was a member of the local gentry and a city councillor. But Patrick gave up everything for the good of others and does not blush to have done so, nor does he now regret it. 'I am a slave', he says, 'a slave in Christ to a foreign nation'.

Why on earth should he tell all this to a band of outlaws? What interest can they possibly have had in whether he had been rich or poor before he went to Ireland? Would they even know what a city-councillor was? And even though the brigands were Britons, in what way are autobiographical details relevant to his plea for the release of the prisoners or to his words of excommunication? And why the defensive note: 'I do not blush for what I have done, nor do I regret it'? If Patrick had addressed his *Epistle* to a bunch of Caledonians, this whole passage would be utterly unaccountable; but even if addressed to Britons, what is its meaning? Why should he dream of reporting such things even to a nominally Christian marauder living in Ireland? The passage only makes sense, I am convinced, if the saint is addressing, not simply an audience of Britons, but an audience of Britons who had themselves been carried off captive to Ireland against their will or who were descended from British captives or who had come to Ireland reluctantly or as refugees or at any rate in circumstances of hardship. They were now free. We do not know how they had become free if they had once been slaves. May not some at least of them have been nothing more than runaway slaves who had escaped from their Irish masters and by forming a strong and ruthless band had become impossible to re-capture? It seems improbable, for they were Christians, at any rate in name, and so are unlikely to have been agricultural workers or serfs who were the most likely people to have been carried off from Britain by Irish raiders. Again, we know from Salvian, writing in Marseilles about 440/1, that numbers of Romans were taking flight to the barbarians so as to avoid the corrupt Roman tax-gatherers. In the case of British refugees some may already have been in flight from before the Saxon invaders of their homes.[14]

But I am tempted to think that Bury, although he made Coroticus the ruler of Dumbarton, was on the right lines when he came to describe the followers of Coroticus. It is unlikely that a Roman writer of the fifth century would describe as 'soldiers' a random

14 Salvian, *De Gubernatione Dei*, V. 21–3.

collection of civilian outlaws who had grouped together to form a robber-band, an organised band of brigands. Bury accordingly remarks: 'The continuity of the rule of Coroticus with the military organisation of the Empire is strongly suggested by the circumstance that his power was maintained by "soldiers" . . . His soldiers may well be the successors of the Roman troops who defended the north of Britain' or some other region. That is very probable. It is not hard to think of circumstances which might have driven them to leave their homes and take flight to Ireland. The most obvious of such circumstances would be that the city-state or kingdom which they had helped to control in Britain had been overthrown by Saxon invaders or British rebels who had driven them overseas. They were now living under the command of their officer who had taken over the powers of whatever chieftain or sub-Roman official they had served under in Britain. So Coroticus was in fact a 'usurper', a 'tyrant'. This explanation of the position of Coroticus, which is mainly due to Bury, seems more convincing than any other which has been proposed. To be sure, it all hinges on Patrick's calling the men 'soldiers'. He also calls them 'brigands', but whereas it is not uncommon to call unruly soldiers 'brigands', it is decidedly unusual, if not unparalleled, to call a group of miscellaneous brigands 'soldiers'. Whoever they may have been, it is more than a little interesting that they claimed to be 'Roman citizens' and might be expected to feel stung if someone denied them their claim. Even the inhabitants of a province which had not been governed by Rome for several decades evidently took some pride to regard themselves as Roman citizens.[15]

However that may be, the context in which Patrick wrote this passage would be clearer if we supposed that Coroticus himself and the bulk of his followers were Britons who had been born in Britain, had grown up there, had lived there until fairly recently, knew about the administration of British cities, and were aware also of the standard of living which Patrick would have enjoyed as a landowner's son. And, knowing all this, some of Coroticus's men were cynical about Patrick and had ridiculed him and had thought him foolish to join them in living in Ireland when it was open to him to stay at home in a comfortable villa in Britain. Although they were themselves Britons, evidently it was not open to them to go back to their homes in Britain. Such a situation would perhaps explain why Patrick begins the *Epistle* by asserting with the utmost emphasis that it is for

15 Bury, *The Life of St Patrick*, p. 191f.

God's sake that he is in Ireland and that he has given up his country and relatives and even his life. Because he did so, 'I am despised by some'. He asks, 'Did I go to Ireland without God and in accordance with the wish of the flesh?' And again, 'My own people do not recognise me', and 'Men look at me askance . . . I am deeply despised'. These critics, I would suggest, are the followers of Coroticus. It is normally thought that these expressions of regret that his own people despise him refer to the criticisms which the clergy of Britain, or some of them, were making of him. But the *Epistle* is not on any theory addressed to British clergy in Britain or in what had once been Roman Britain; and why should Patrick defend himself in this context against criticisms put forward by ecclesiastics far away in Britain? For that purpose it would be hard to imagine a more grotesque context. And why should Coroticus, whether he lived in Caledonia or in Ireland or anywhere else, care one iota whether Patrick was or was not criticised by British ecclesiastics? If Patrick already knew that he was the object of criticism in Britain, why should he mention that fact in a letter to a murderous outlaw who had now nothing to do with Britain or its clergy, a man who can hardly have been noted for his interest in the life of the Church? Could any context be more bizarre for such a self-defensive argument? The context makes Patrick's arguments inexplicable if they are really intended for clerics at home in Britain. But if they are addressed to Coroticus's Britons — real Britons, not just nominal Britons — the case is different. Patrick's phrases quoted in this paragraph can only refer to criticisms advanced by British Christians living in Ireland, men who would gladly go back to their homes in Britain if only they had an opportunity of doing so, if only circumstances would make it possible for them to go, or who at any rate looked back wistfully to the Imperial province and to a life which no one in his senses would surrender voluntarily in order to exile himself in Ireland. They could not understand how a rich and comfortable Briton could throw everything away and come to live in a wild and dangerous country like Ireland *of his own free will*. They had gone there because — whatever the circumstances — they had no choice in the matter; but he had come although it was quite open to him to stay at home.

A further inference — this time a certain, undeniable inference — from his words is that the persons to whom Patrick is writing were to some extent acquainted with him and his circumstances, at any rate by repute. 'Did I come to Ireland without God and according to the flesh?

Who forced me?' Had there been some talk about his reasons for being in Ireland? It looks as though the outlaws had discussed him and had come to the conclusion that he was a fool to throw away all the advantages of his birth and instead of living in comfort in a British villa he had chosen to live in danger and hardship in Ireland. It may well be that when they attacked Patrick's neophytes, they knew what they were doing. They had not stumbled on the white-clad Christians by chance or accident. The raid was no chance windfall for overseas marauders who had marched inland in the hope of finding some worthwhile prey. To understand the situation fully, of course, we should need to know more than we can ever hope to know about Patrick's relations with the Britons in Ireland and especially about their attitude or varying attitudes to himself. At any rate, it would be unwise to draw inferences from this autobiographical passage in the *Epistle* about Patrick's relations with the church in Britain. The letter was not addressed to ecclesiastics living in Britain or to ecclesiastics living anywhere else. There were certainly few British ecclesiastics in the *entourage* of Coroticus who might have sent a copy of it to friends in Britain. There is no reason to think that the letter ever circulated in Britain or anywhere else in Patrick's lifetime. My own opinion is that he is unlikely ever to have made a copy of it. Since he was living in the last days of the world, as he believed, there was no point in building up an archive of his 'papers'. And he can hardly have expected Coroticus to send him a witty and point-by-point reply to which he would feel obliged to compose a rejoinder. It is not easy to believe that Coroticus had built up much of a reputation as a letter-writer. How then did the *Epistle* ever come to survive? I imagine that Patrick's emissaries brought back the copy which he had written with his own hand and that it was in due course stored up with such few documents as Patrick may have amassed. It was written so directly into a precise situation that there can hardly have been in the fifth century a public which would greedily devour it or even look at it twice. Certainly, it had nothing to do with Britain. When Patrick came to write the *Confession* he was obliged to answer criticisms which had been directed against him by certain British clerics (though we have seen reason to think that these did not reside in Britain). But the criticisms answered in the *Confession* were still in the future when he wrote the *Epistle*. We associate the two groups of criticisms from hindsight. In fact, they had nothing to do with one another. They were directed against Patrick by two wholly separate groups of

Britons, the one group in ecclesiastical office, the other lurking in the woods and hills of Ireland.

If we agree that Coroticus and his men were British refugees and outlaws living in Ireland, what can we learn about their style of life in that country? In fact, they were not skulking out of sight in some forest or cave: they seem to have lived in close touch with the people of their neighbourhood. Indeed, they could hardly have survived if they had cut themselves off completely from the other inhabitants of the country. Patrick is obliged to beg all Christians not to feast or drink or joke with them, not to flatter them, not to 'receive their alms'. That last phrase is interesting. It suggests that the brigands did not always keep all their loot to themselves: they would hand out largess to the people round about, including Christians. This largess, ill-gotten though it was, was by no means unwelcome to the recipients, and it could not be taken for granted that Christians would refuse to touch it. But in Patrick's eyes it was a deadly poison. At all events, it would be a mistake to think that Coroticus and his gang were oppressive to all the people round them. The saint unfortunately gives no hint whether these persons who came in friendly contact with the brigands were Irish or British or both — as we have seen, differences of nationality are of little interest to him. Certainly, many of them were Christian. What we should very much like to know is whether the outlaws lived solely by slave-raiding and by looting, whether they raided overseas (in Britain, say) as well as in Ireland, or whether they were also farmers, stockbreeders, fishermen, or the like as well, and whether they had brought wives and families with them or whether they had taken wives from among the Irish. Of two points we may be reasonably certain. The robber band probably lived in the north-east of Ireland from where the Picts were accessible: they would not have been accessible from Munster or Connacht or even from Donegal. And secondly, the raid on Patrick's neophytes will hardly have been the band's first operation. The machinery for disposing of the prisoners seems to have been already in existence. There is no hint that Coroticus had to organise his market on the spot or to send over an emissary, a 'salesman', a commercial traveller, to the Picts to see if there was a market for slaves in their country. So far as Coroticus was concerned, the whole operation went off very smoothly. No one, except the unfortunates who were kidnapped and their anguished relatives, would ever have given a second thought to the incident if the British missionary had not been in the vicinity of the crime.

CHAPTER NINE

Conclusion

Anyone who has some facility in Latin and who reads Patrick's account of, say, his escape from slavery and his journey with the ship's company will remember the story for the rest of his days. It is not because the saint writes like a great advocate, as Cicero wrote, or like a graceful philosopher of genius, as Plato wrote. No one could be further removed from the debating skill of the one or the charm and intellectual power of the other. On the contrary, technically Patrick is a very bad writer indeed. That is not open to dispute. Here is an example, admittedly an extreme example, of what he can do. When beginning his remarks about his career as bishop he writes: 'I shall tell briefly how the most holy God often freed me from slavery and from the twelve dangers wherein my life was imperilled, besides many ambuscades and matters which I am not able to express in words.' Not many Roman writers would have penned the sentence, 'I shall tell . . . matters which I am not able to express in words'. To make things worse, he never comes back to the 'twelve dangers', and we have no idea what they were. It has even been suggested that this was 'evidently a conventional phrase to describe his manifold difficulties.' But it is not conventional: it is unique. No one else says anything like it. Patrick does indeed tell us later on how he was held a slave for fourteen days, but we do not know what he has in mind when he says that God 'often' freed him from slavery. That is to say, he never redeems the promises which he makes here. But nothing in his writings is more awkward than his insertion in the story of his escape

144

from Ireland of the brief and almost incomprehensible reference to his second enslavement. This is so harsh and clumsy that it looks like a later insertion into the *Confession*, put in hurriedly when the work, or that part of the work, was already complete.[1]

What, then, makes the *Confession* such compulsive reading? I think it is the fact that Patrick can write with a degree of earnest, even burning, sincerity which is hard to analyse or even describe but which convinces us from the very first page that this man is utterly honest and truthful. One reason why he convinces us is that he seems to be addressing himself as well as us. As Christine Mohrmann put it: 'he not only wishes to tell and to explain to his readers certain facts of his life, but he is meditating in a sort of soliloquy, looking back on his life as a missionary and an apostle'. As we read, the possibility that he could knowingly deceive us, or that his critics were in the right and he in the wrong, never enters our minds. Such a possibility is out of the question: it is an impossibility. When he says that he went to Ireland to preach the gospel and not for his own personal gain, we believe him at once. We are never tempted to feel that he protests too much or that he merely wishes to outsmart his critics and to score debating points. What he says *must* be true.[2]

But that is not the whole story. It takes an effort to remind ourselves that a number of his fellow-Britons, men who probably knew him personally, who perhaps had even worked with him, did *not* believe him and did *not* admire him. On the contrary, they spread the view that he went to Ireland for gain. They succeeded in spreading this opinion so widely and winning so much belief for it, that they forced him to reply. The fact that he replied towards the end of his bishopric shows that the criticisms had been mounting for years and years until at last he answered them. The criticisms did not flare up in his early days as bishop and then suddenly die down again. It had been his intention to reply years before, but for fear of literary criticism he had refrained. He does not say why he changed his mind and decided to write at last, but one reason must have been that the criticisms continued to be made. He *had* to reply. It would be more than interesting to know whether, when the critics read the *Confession*, they recognised that they had been in the wrong, that their criticisms had been misplaced, that they owed Patrick an apology. But we must allow for the possibility that they were

---

1 See respectively *Confession*, §35 (246.2−4), §52 (251.4), §21 (242.3−7). For a brilliant picture of the character of St Patrick see Hanson, *St Patrick : His Origins*, pp. 198−209.
2 Mohrmann, *The Latin*, p. 2.

unconvinced and unrepentant. Critics of such long standing are unlikely to have changed their minds overnight. Who can tell?[3]

Patrick is a man of many faults. His extreme anguish at his lack of education is extraordinarily hard to understand. It cuts him off, he feels, from the landed gentry into which he was born. The rich and powerful, that is, for the most part the landowners, will scorn him, laugh at him, expose his ignorance if he should venture to write. The result was that for a long time he refrained from writing. This is out-and-out, crude class-consciousness, and it suggests that mentally in some respects he had never left Britain and the society of his youth, that he always judged himself by the standards of British landowners (clerical and lay), not by those which we should expect in an expatriate indifferent to the class-culture of his homeland. In these passages he is writing exclusively for educated Britons. To Irishmen his lack of a good Latin style was utterly irrelevant and meaningless. We can perhaps understand how this lack of the normal education might have pained a great Gallic nobleman of the circle of Sidonius Apollinaris, a man who was mixing daily with other such landowners, corresponding with them as a pleasant social duty. But why should it worry a man who was living outside the Roman world and its social life in a country where the very name of the 'rhetor' was utterly unknown? It is not easy to grasp the reason for it, but on this subject Patrick, as I have said, has nothing less than a chip on his shoulder. The strangest thing is that it is not at all certain that he *was* criticised on this score by anyone other than himself! And it leads him into a none too pleasant reaction when he tells how in the end — in spite of his handicap — he was preferred as bishop to the rich and educated men whom he envied. He is not far short of crowing over them! He wants to rub in their defeat, even to humiliate them (although that may be too hard an expression). At all events, his attitude as he tells how he was preferred as bishop to other members of his social class is not the most edifying page of his book. It contains no reference, for example, to the fact that those who appointed him disregarded what he thought to be his lack of a higher education and closed their eyes to any other faults which they may have noticed in him.[4]

Again, although he felt himself rightly or wrongly to be underrated owing to his lack of the higher education which was normal among the sons of landowners, he is not above remaining silent about two

3 *Confession*, §9 (237.13).
4 *Ibid.*, §10 (238.3−5), §12f. (238.23f.).

groups of people whom he ought, we may feel, to have mentioned prominently, no matter what was the purpose of his writing the *Confession*. He claims over and over again to have ordained a large number of clergy to serve his new converts: the clergy would baptise and encourage people who were in need of exhortation and who longed for it. But he never mentions one of these clergy by name, never hints at the specific services which any one of them — or all of them collectively — rendered him, never credits them with helping him or winning individual or collective successes on their own account. In the *Epistle* he does indeed mention one of his underlings, a priest, though he does not tell us his name. He reports two things about him: it was Patrick himself who had educated him since he had been an infant, and it was this priest who had carried Patrick's first (lost) letter to Coroticus. The priest, it might be said, plays a somewhat passive role in this report. He is hardly the leading actor! Patrick has upstaged him. But why does the saint refrain from giving us the name of one or two of his assistants or from singling out one or two of them for a word of praise and encouragement? It is inconceivable that he thought such a mention to be irrelevant to his theme or that it would detract from his own achievement. Did no assistant, no staff accompany him from Britain when he first came as bishop? If he did not land in Ireland alone, all by himself, a lonely figure on the windswept beach, were the services of his companions altogether negligible? Gerard Murphy suggested that 'no helper is mentioned (though all admit that Patrick had helpers); no convert is named; no mission district is described. The reason is clear. It was written for readers who knew the main facts.' That may be true, but, if so, it means that he wrote for virtually no one in Britain. Yet the remarks about his lack of education were written for no one except Britons! We have seen a possible answer to this dilemma: he wrote for Britons living in Ireland.[5]

His silence about his Christian predecessors in Ireland — Palladius and those who worked with him — is notorious. He has no direct, and only one indirect, reference to their work. The indirect hint is indeed indirect. He writes: 'For your sake I used to go among many dangers into the utmost parts, where there was no one beyond and where another person had never arrived to baptise or ordain clergy or confirm the people.' So there *may* have been other parts where someone *had* ordained clergy (which only a bishop could do). If this

5 *Epistle*, §3 (254.18); Murphy, 'The Two Patricks', p. 305.

is an admission that other bishops, or at least one other bishop, had been active in Ireland, it is not a very generous way of stating the fact! Worse still, in a couple of phrases Patrick would seem to deny the existence of such men altogether. He says emphatically that the people in Ireland 'who never had knowledge of God and always hitherto worshipped idols and unclean things, how they have lately been made the people of God,' a sentence which might be taken to suggest that there were also people in Ireland who *did* have knowledge of God. But if that is the implication, the work of those men who converted them could hardly have been more grudgingly admitted. Again, he mentions those who were opposed to his undertaking a mission 'among enemies who do not know God'. That could be taken to imply that there were Irish who *did* know God, but once again the implication (if that is what it is) is extraordinarily indirect.[6]

A number of scholars think it inconceivable that Patrick would fail to omit all reference to his predecessors, and so are reduced to supposing that Patrick carried out his work in Ireland *before* Palladius went there in 431. Esposito held this opinion partly because of Patrick's silence about Palladius. 'Do the Patriciological experts who . . . assert that Patrick must have come to a country already to a considerable extent Christian, wish us to believe that the author of the Patrician opuscula was a liar, who deliberately depicted Ireland as a wholly pagan country and suppressed all mention of his predecessor Palladius in order to be able to claim solely for himself the merit of having evangelised the country and the qualification of Apostle of Ireland?' If the *Confession* had been intended as a systematic autobiography, these questions would be embarrassing, and the answers to them unpleasant. Even as things are, the admirers of Patrick will wish that such questions could not be asked.[7]

The result of Patrick's silence about his fellow-workers (whatever its cause may be) is that we are left with the impression that the mission was a one-man show, that it all depended on Patrick and on him alone, and that all was achieved by him more or less single-handed, unaided. And this impression is not lessened by his statement that he would greatly enjoy a visit to Britain and his relatives and also a visit to Gaul 'to see the brethren' there. (Incidentally, it is absurd to suppose that this wish implies that Patrick had once sojourned in Gaul. He may have done so, but this wish tells neither

6 The quotations are respectively from *Confession*, §51 (250.25−8), §41 (248.6−9), §46 (249.25).
7 Esposito, 'The Patrician Problem', p. 152.

for nor against any such visit.) But Patrick feels that if he were to leave his mission in Ireland he might lose what he had achieved so far. In other words, all depended on his continuing presence among his flock. He dared not leave. If he did, his achievements might collapse like a house of cards. We know too little of the circumstances to be able to say whether the structure was really as frail as this prediction might suggest, whether one breath of wind would really lay it flat on the floor. We are driven to infer *either* that Patrick was one of those administrators who can delegate nothing, *or* that he has wittingly and clumsily suppressed the help which he received from others.[8]

The second group of persons whom we might have expected Patrick to mention with deep feeling is the enslaved Britons who had been carried off by Irish raiders as he himself had been carried off long ago. He had himself spent six years suffering the hardships of slavery in Ireland, and thousands of Britons must have been enduring the same fate, perhaps a very much harder fate, at any time during the period of his bishopric. Yet it was not to comfort enslaved Britons that he went to Ireland. He leaves us in no doubt about that. He went to Ireland to preach to the heathen Irish no matter what the personal risk and cost might be. But he has not a word to say about his fellow-Britons. They do not seem to have figured in his thoughts. And yet he knew of the efforts made by Christians in Gaul to ransom Christian prisoners from the Franks and the other barbarians. Although he was all too familiar with the loneliness and the fear which the British captives must have suffered, especially the women and, above all, the children, yet there is no evidence in his writings that any special concern for them ever entered his mind. And when he comes to speak of the results and achievements of his mission, he dwells on his successes among the Irish, not among the Britons. On the British captives whom he left behind he says not a word.[9]

Of course, the major conclusion at which he had arrived in connexion with his own slavery was that he and those who had been carried off with him had deserved their fate owing to their neglect of the commandments and of their bishops, a facile and misleading judgement, as we have seen. Secondly, he concluded that God had been so kind to him as a slave that he must repay God by 'confessing his wonders before every nation which is under the whole sky'. It is a simple religion, requiring no very profound thought. Hardship

8 *Confession*, §43 (248.24−6).
9 *Epistle*, §14 (257.10−2).

means that you have sinned; and if the hardship is not as hard as it might have been, thank God for his mercy! But this train of 'thought', while it perhaps satisfied and brought comfort to Patrick, may not have brought complete comfort to his fellow-Britons, toiling as slaves under the damp skies of Ireland. The new Christian was intent on his own personal salvation and was concerned to express his own personal feelings. If his words and his silences mean anything at all, they mean that Patrick was *either* indifferent to the fate of his British fellow-sufferers, *or* felt that their fate required no comment from him. Owing to their sins, they had deserved their fate.[10]

Again, when introducing his account of his work as bishop in Ireland, Patrick tells how God 'often' freed him from slavery and from the mysterious twelve dangers, to say nothing of many ambuscades, and so on. He does not set out to tell us of the dangers which threatened his colleagues: he will deal with his own personal dangers and with these alone. Does this mean that none of his priests and deacons was ever enslaved or sold or wounded or killed or even threatened? Was Patrick himself the only one who lived in peril? And so it is that throughout the whole *Confession* not a syllable hints at the appalling massacre carried out by Coroticus's soldiers. The newly baptised whom the soldiers of Coroticus cut down or sold as slaves have no place in this review of aspects of Patrick's bishopric. It can certainly not be that he regarded the massacre as a minor incident, a mere ripple on the placid surface of his life, a temporary setback of no permanent importance. His attitude was very different. Why then does he not refer to the tragedy? Is he concentrating on his own personal salvation, on his repayment to God for God's mercy to him in the days of his slavery, to such an extent that the massacre was in some sense a secondary reverse? We shall see in a moment that that was not the case.

Allied with this somewhat narrow outlook is his narrow conception of the aims of his mission. He aimed to convert the pagans, to bring them to the point of baptism, and, having baptised them, to move on to deal with persons who were still pagan. He might even leave new converts for his clergy to baptise and exhort, while he himself hurried on elsewhere. His aim, in fact, seems to have been to 'convert' the maximum number of pagans. It almost amounts to a counting of heads. Two or three times he tells us that the number of his converts amounted to 'thousands'. Sometimes it would seem that

10 *Confession*, §3 (236.6f.).

it was numbers alone which counted, not the results of conversion, not the effect on the lives of the converted. As he presents his case in the *Confession*, his mission set out to convert the greatest possible number of Irish people, and he spent decidedly less time on deepening their understanding of that to which they had been converted. Having converted one group (we might think), he rushes on to the next. So far as we can tell, little enough time was devoted to the ransoming of captives or to the relief of the sufferings which some of the converted were forced to endure.

But before we conclude that Patrick was the bustling, organising administrator whom we might have been tempted to infer from the *Confession*, we must turn again to the *Epistle*. It is exceedingly fortunate that the *Epistle* has survived, for the closing paragraphs of the *Epistle* show us another side of St Patrick. Nothing could be more human than his lament for the slain and the enslaved victims of Coroticus or than his joy as he expresses his conviction that the dead have now ascended into heaven. The *Epistle* leaves it beyond question that this was no narrow, egocentric, and stone-faced administrator but a man who cared profoundly for his followers. A French scholar was right to say of him, 'activité, énergie, esprit d'organisation, il avait des qualités de chef', or, as P. A. Wilson put it, 'I think we can safely say that he was a man whom many would feel was lacking in tact and diplomacy'. Perhaps, but the *Epistle* shows that he was far indeed from lacking humanity.[11]

So Patrick's shortcomings are plain and obvious. And yet we still cannot fail to admire him. It is a measure of his forcefulness that he can still make us respect him even while taking no steps to hide his weaknesses. Indeed, he is unaware that his lamentations about his having missed a literary education are unnecessary and unbecoming, especially if his book was intended to be read by (or to) Britons living in some hardship in Ireland. But it would not be quite accurate to say that he is wholly unaware of his limitations. He knows, for example, that some men criticised him for pushing himself forward, ignorant though he was in some respects and lacking in fluency. He does not deny the charge. Indeed, he all but admits it and half-justifies himself with a scriptural quotation about stammering tongues learning quickly (adapted from Isaiah, xxxii.4). Others criticised his self-confidence in launching himself into unnecessary dangers in Ireland. It looks as though some who knew him found him presumptuous,

---

11 *Epistle*, §16f. (257.27−258.22). See Hubert in Czarnowski, *Le Culte*, p. XIII, Wilson, 'St Patrick', p. 368.

too ready to push himself to the fore, and also too loud in declaring that God was in the habit of communicating with him directly in his dreams. On the other hand, when he writes, 'I was not worthy nor was I such that the Lord should grant this to his poor servant that after labours and burdens, after captivity and after many years he should grant me so much grace towards that nation, a thing which I never expected or thought of when I was a young man', we cannot write off his words as the expression of a false modesty. There is nothing false about it. [12]

So his personal behaviour came under fire. It looks as though he had some gift for arousing opposition and criticism, and the opposition to him continued to smoulder years and years after his bishopric had begun. It continued to be voiced even when he was an old man, not far from the end of his days.

When we try to see Patrick in his social context we have to confess that the task is impossible. To bring him to life, to re-animate him, we should have to view him against the background of the social life of Britain and of Ireland. It cannot be done. His background both in Britain and in Ireland is hopelessly lost. We cannot see him in his Irish context because so little is known of Irish society in the fifth century. We cannot even begin to guess at the impact which his activities are likely to have made on the various groups of which the Irish were composed — how he affected women as against men, slaves as against freemen, the tribal leaders as against their followers, and so on. Indeed, it is all but impossible even to formulate the right questions which we should ask about his probable effect on Irish society. So far as Ireland is concerned, Patrick exists in a vacuum.

He is hardly less isolated when we try to see him in his British context. We have no other British authors to throw light on the state of opinion, or on the general attitudes, of the British landed gentry at the relevant date. They were certainly capable of producing from their ranks such men as Pelagius, whose impact on the Western world in his own day was immense, and Faustus, the eminent bishop of Riez, so that intellectual life had by no means come to a stop in the later fourth and early fifth century; and it will not have come to an abrupt and total end through the whole of Britain in the following decades. Patrick himself speaks of Britons learned in the law (whether Roman law or canon law, is not quite clear) and in the scriptures, and a phrase in which he describes them is unfortunately

12 Respectively *Confession*, §11 (238.8f.), §46 (249.25f.), §15 (239.10−3).

corrupted in the Latin manuscripts in which his works have been preserved: it almost certainly implied 'learned clerics' rather than 'educated landowners' (though doubtless both types still existed). No doubt the British landowners' opinions and outlook were in essence identical with those of their opposite numbers in Gaul, on which we are relatively well informed; for, as we have seen, provincial differences were minimal in the Late Roman Empire. We may be sure, for example, that the task of converting the barbarians to Christianity was not an everyday topic of conversation among even the most pious of Britons. We have no evidence from Gaul to suggest that the idea of a mission to the barbarians would cause less hostility among the higher churchmen than Patrick's proposed mission aroused among his British colleagues. If any Gaul had indeed suggested undertaking such a mission outside the Imperial frontier, we may be sure that the bishops in general would have been as lukewarm about it as the Britons were. So far as we can tell, no Gaul ever did make such a proposal before Patrick's day, and so there was no occasion to discuss it in Gaul.[13]

But Patrick's are the only British writings to have survived from the mid-century, and they are the only writings to speak at length about contemporary Ireland. They do not explain the attitudes of contemporary Britons towards Ireland. Patrick's own opinions on the subject are far too individual to allow us to generalise from them. When he speaks of specific Britons he has in mind his own kinsfolk and, in a different context, some rich and educated clergy. But Britons in general, and political Britons, and Britons of no property have no place in his writings except on the one occasion when they were carried off as slaves. We cannot wholly account for this absence of the Britons from his writings simply by saying that 'national' feelings did not exist in his day. The fact is that his clerical critics probably held much the same views about society as he did, and so had no occasion to find fault with him on this score. Patrick may well have had opinions on the British peasants' life of drudgery, sickness, and starvation; but, if so, he says nothing of them. What could he say? He was or had been a considerable landowner himself, and neither he nor anybody else at the time knew of any remedy for rural poverty.

In fact, Patrick is more isolated, more outside and beyond comparison than practically any other Roman author. It would be hard

13 On Faustus see Hanson, *St Patrick : His Origins*, pp. 63 – 5. The learned clerics are in *Confession*, §13 (238.24), cf. §9 (237.14 – 7).

to exaggerate his isolation. Whether we date him in the first half of the fifth century or in the second half or in the middle, he certainly lived in what was by far the most catastrophic period of the entire history of Britain. At the beginning of the century Britain was part of the Roman Empire, outwardly peaceful, administered by a huge bureaucracy. At its end she was the scene of countless warring groups of Britons and barbarians, the British groups fighting each other as well as the aliens. The unity of the country had been destroyed, its literature silenced, even the Latin language as a spoken tongue all but extinct over the eastern areas of the island, city life dead. It might be thought impossible for any British writer, even if he were writing in Ireland, to succeed in shedding no light whatever on the disastrous times in which he was living. He must surely make *some* reference to these titanic events. Yet in this respect Patrick has come close to achieving the impossible. Of the collapse of Imperial rule, the invasions of the Saxons, the virtual extinction of the Church in the eastern half of Britain, the death of Bannaventa and all other towns, the desertion of the villas, he says not a single word. Our only surviving British writer of the sixth century, Gildas, refers back at least to the Great Persecution of the Christians under the emperor Diocletian and to the usurping Emperor Magnus Maximus (383 − 8), who had been elevated to the throne in Britain, and also to some harrowing events which occurred in a few years around the middle of the fifth century. But Patrick does not even do that. He never refers to an earlier time than his own except once: he knows that the Church had had its martyrs. There is no reason to think that he had Irish martyrs in mind, but no one can tell whether he had ever heard of Diocletian and the Great Persecution. We have seen that he never hints at the existence of Palladius or refers to the origins of Christianity in Ireland or to the interest taken in that island by Pope Celestine. He never mentions any of the popes, still less the fall of Rome to the barbarians in 410, an event which horrified the civilised world. For him there is no such thing as history, no history even of Christianity.[14]

But, of course, there is a great positive side to him. For example, he never claims to have perpetrated a miracle. The writers of the *Lives* of the saints of the early mediaeval period, including the writers of the *Lives* of Patrick himself, ascribe a superabundance of miracles to their subjects, telling how they healed the sick, raised the dead, and

14 Martyrs in *Confession*, §57 (252.6f.).

interfered with the course of nature in various ways, some of them ludicrous, as we shall see. This had been true of Christian propaganda from the earliest days. In early Christian literature nearly all the emphasis is on the superhuman qualities of Jesus, his powers of prophecy, of miracle-mongering, and his alleged resurrection from the dead. In assembling his first disciples, according to A. D. Nock, Jesus's impression of power was probably more important than the impression of love. It would be interesting to know whether the men to whom these miraculous achievements were ascribed by their biographers in early mediaeval times believed that they themselves had performed miracles. It is clear that some of them did indeed believe that they had wonder-working powers. Consider, for example, St Martin of Tours, the patron-saint of France, a very different figure from St Patrick, — coarse, brutal, and untainted by anything that might go under the name of 'thought'. We have no writings of his, but we know of him from Sulpicius Severus, who had met him personally. According to Sulpicius, a new convert to Christianity died so suddenly that there had been no time to baptise him. Martin ran up to the corpse weeping and howling. After working his spells over the corpse for about two hours, the dead man came to life and lived on for several years. In later days, by way of light conversation, he used to tell what had happened to him during the time when he had been dead. That is a subject which few of us are ever in a position to discuss: even Lazarus is not said to have held conversations of this nature. Now, it would be extraordinarily hard to imagine that anyone who knew St Patrick personally was ever able to ascribe such claims to him.[15]

In the later seventh century and after, writers who knew no more of Patrick than we do ascribed many miracles to him. But in his own writings he never claims to have worked a miracle. It is true that in that hungry march of twenty-eight days through the unknown wilderness he asked the captain and his starving crew to believe in the Christian God and assured them that He would send them food. In fact, they did not accept the Christian God, but nevertheless an appetising herd of pigs made its appearance and without loss of time was eaten. No one reading the passage where Patrick relates this incident could truthfully say that the saint is here asserting that he had done a miracle. Since the crew were not converted, the pigs, strictly speaking, ought not to have appeared at all and, having appeared, could

---

15 Nock, *Conversion*, p. 210. On Martin see Sulpicius Severus, *Vita S. Martini*, 7, 24. 4—8, 25. 7.

have claimed that in strict justice they had been eaten on false pretences. But pigs rarely argue on legalistic lines. At a somewhat earlier time, when Patrick first asked the captain to take him aboard and the captain angrily refused, Patrick went away and, as he went, he prayed. Before he had finished his prayer one of the crew shouted to him to come back and to go aboard the ship. Patrick in no way claims that the men's change of heart was due to his prayer just as he does not claim that the appearance of the pigs was an answer to his prayer. Perhaps he implies it. Perhaps not. He certainly does not claim explicitly that either event was miraculous, still less that he himself had worked a miracle.

Bury said that Patrick's achievement was threefold: 'He organised the Christianity which already existed; he converted the kingdoms which were still pagan, especially in the west; and he brought Ireland into connexion with the Church of the Empire, and made it formally part of universal Christendom.' All three of these claims would seem to be misplaced. The first and third of them must beyond question be credited to Pope Celestine and his emissary, Palladius. No one knows when Ireland was converted. Patrick no doubt made a start in the process: we know that at least once he was within sight of the Atlantic. But there is no reason to think that when he died Connacht was Christian. His greatest achievement and his greatest claim to originality lies in his decision, as a Catholic bishop, to leave the Western Roman Empire, to settle down for the rest of his life in a barbarian land, and to try to convert the pagans there to the Catholic variety of Christianity. So far as we know, his was the first organised mission to a country lying outside the Western Empire. But this feature of his work did not win him renown in later ages. Indeed, the significance of his activities outside the Empire was wholly forgotten. Even in Ireland Patrick seems not to have been remembered after his immediate associates had died. Throughout the sixth century we find no reference to him. If his name was remembered at all it was as the name of a venerable figure of the past whose achievements no one could now recall. We cannot tell what his reputation would have been if his two little books had not survived the fifth century. In my opinion, it would have been non-existent and his name would now be unknown. To that extent his most lasting achievement was not the conversion of 'thousands' of the Irish (whatever we are to understand by that figure) but the composition of the *Epistle* and the *Confession*.[16]

16 Bury, *The Life of St Patrick*, p. 212f.

CONCLUSION

In starting his mission outside the Roman frontier, or what had once been the Roman frontier, he was unique. No one helped him, though many tried to hinder him. But he left no model to future generations. He had no successors in the sense that no one learned from him: no one launched missions similar to his outside other frontiers in imitation of him. Later on men did indeed send missionaries outside what had once been the Western Empire, but they did so without knowledge of his work. They were not his debtors or his disciples. His books being lost or at any rate unknown, the originality of his work was also unknown.

Epilogue

Father John Ryan, S.J., wrote: 'Patrick died in what was almost a blaze of glory and lived on in the popular memory as a great national figure, a worthy companion of the heroes and the kings.'[1]

No doubt it ought to have been so, but as a matter of fact nothing could be further from the truth. Not a single writer mentions him until the seventh century. Those who converted the pagans, inside as well as outside the Roman frontier, were never regarded as heroes in the Roman and sub-Roman West, and more often than not their names were never recorded and never remembered. This is easy enough to understand when the successful missionaries were heretics, like those unknown and brave men who converted the Ostrogoths and the Vandals to Arian Christianity. When the heresy of Arius disappeared, its heroes vanished with it and we do not even know their names. But it is not so easy to understand when the missionaries were Catholic. Who was it, for example, who converted the Picts whom Patrick calls 'apostates' at the time of Coroticus's raid? Was it Ninian? If so, what do we know of Ninian? Nothing at all.

Nobody wrote a biography of St Patrick for a couple of hundred years after he was dead. In all that long time no one (so far as we know) described him as a preacher or as an organiser or as a miracle worker or as anything else. He was not remembered as an enormously successful missionary — because he was not enormously successful. At the time of his death Ireland was still predominantly

1 Ryan, 'The Traditonal View', p. 10.

Patrick's mission to the Irish
had only been a limited success
when he died, and since his
greatness was not appreciated by
the generation or two which
followed — they did not even
remember where his body was
buried — it is not surprising
that there are no early representations
of him. The earliest is probably
the medieval monumental slab
with a carved figure representing
St Patrick, from Faughart
churchyard, Co. Louth, and now
in the National Museum of Ireland.

pagan, aggressively pagan. His fellow-countryman, Gildas, writing in the first half of the sixth century, tells of the Irish raids on Britain, but he never hints that Christianity had won a footing among the raiders. Still less does he mention Patrick. It is not out of the question that Patrick was indeed wholly forgotten when those who had worked with him had died off — say, some thirty or forty years after his own death. It may be that his writings were preserved more by accident than by design. What is the fifth-century equivalent of 'an old box up in the attic' where so many valuable papers have been found in more recent times? Perhaps his two letters survived by chance in an old box up in some fifth-century attic or the like. It was only when his writings came to light that men began to talk of him, though knowing no more about him than they could infer from the *Epistle* and the *Confession*. They could not even find out where he had died or where his body was laid. But it would have been clear at once that he had been a man of exceptional piety, sincerity, and force of character, a man wholly out of the ordinary. And so he won a place of honour in the minds of Christians in Ireland even though all oral tradition about him had disappeared. These suggestions are, of course, guesswork; but if we do not form some theory of the kind — that his works came to light, or that they began to be copied about the year 600 — it is hard to see why he was so utterly forgotten for the century and a half or so which followed his death.

The first occasion on which he is explicitly named is in a letter written in 632/3 by an otherwise unknown Cummian addressing Segene, abbot of Iona. Cummian reports that 'our father Patrick' (*papa noster*) devised and brought with him to Ireland an Easter cycle. No one else at any date mentions that Patrick introduced a new Paschal system into Ireland; and Cummian says enough about this alleged Paschal system to suggest to experts on the subject that he was in all probability misinformed. In other words, Cummian is not known to have been aware of anything about Patrick except that he was a venerated but almost forgotten figure, that his name would give authority to a new Easter cycle, and that he had come to Ireland from abroad. On the other hand, about the year 590 the Irish St Columbanus had written from Gaul a letter to Pope Gregory the Great on the subject of Easter, but neither there nor anywhere else in his voluminous writings does he mention Patrick. It may not be a coincidence that it was about the year 600 — the date is very uncertain — that some scribe wrote out the manuscript from which all our knowledge of Patrick's writings is ultimately drawn.[2]

The vital change came in Ireland in the second half of the seventh century. It was brought about to some limited extent, but by no means wholly, by a campaign to establish the primacy of Armagh over the other churches of Ireland. My own view is that Patrick's writings were now available to literate Irishmen and that it was the strength of these two letters which compelled attention. Whatever the cause, we continue to find incidental references to Patrick such as the note in the late-seventh-century Book of Durrow in which the scribe asks Patrick's blessing and refers to him as 'priest', not as 'bishop', or that incidental mention of him in the second preface to Adomnan's *Life of St Columba* which, as Binchy points out, is 'much too casual and indirect to justify any claim that [Patrick] was already the object of special veneration'. In this work, written about the year 690, the author describes a certain St Mochta as a disciple of 'the holy bishop Patrick'. The writer assumed that his readers would understand the reference and would not need to be told who Patrick was. But it seems that his works were now widely read in Ireland, and it was now that full-scale books were devoted to him. We have a regular *Life* written by a certain Muirchu, perhaps the first biography of him that was ever written; and at about the same time there appeared a long catalogue of alleged actions of his by one Tirachan. Both Muirchu and Tirachan claim to have used written sources of information, but what the character of these sources may have been, no one knows. Muirchu begins his book with a great flourish in an introduction in which he undertakes 'to expound a few out of the many deeds of St Patrick, though having little experience, uncertain authorities, a faulty memory'. But the most that we can reasonably infer from this introduction is that there was at Muirchu's disposal a quantity of confused and unreliable stories. In his day there was no agreed outline, no standard version, of Patrick's life and achievements, and the means of drawing up a biography no longer existed. We can judge the value of his contribution to the study of Patrick's life by what he says and does not say about Coroticus. He knows the name of the villain but he is not even aware of the nature of the crime which his followers committed. To crown all, he believes that Coroticus ended his life by turning into a fox! It is no wonder that

---

2 Text of Cummian's letter in Migne, *Patrologia Latina*, LXXXVII, 969. See, e.g. Harrison, 'Episodes in the History', p. 311f., though contrast Wilson, 'St Patrick', p. 362. On the date of the archetype of our MSS of Patrick's works see Bieler, *Libri*, I, p. 29.

Macalister remarked that 'even when he narrates incidents that Patrick himself narrates, he shows what it is not too harsh to call an unconquerable bias toward inaccuracy'. That is, if anything, a charitable judgement. To say that a man changed into a fox is more than what most of us would call an 'inaccuracy'. O'Rahilly was not at all unkind when he wrote that 'possibly the only occasion on which he shows a glimmer of common sense is when he confesses in his preface that the task he has undertaken is far beyond his competence'.[3]

Tirachan wrote at about the same time as Muirchu in the last decades of the seventh century, and, while Muirchu's narrative is written with no obvious bias, Tirachan's memoir, at any rate in its second book, is aimed at maintaining the rights of Armagh. His book is not a regular biography, as Muirchu's aimed to be, but a collection of 'facts' about Patrick's mission. It includes, for example, a list of bishops whom Patrick is said to have consecrated. The list includes no fewer than 450 names in all, whereas scholars now agree that he consecrated not a single one! As MacNeill put it, 'careful study of that work will show that nothing written by Tirachan becomes credible by reason of being written by Tirachan.'[4]

It seems that towards the end of the seventh century all knowledge of Patrick's life and achievements, apart from what was mentioned in his two books, had long ago been lost. Although there did exist some written and many oral sources of what was claimed to be 'information', it was now too late to gather genuine accounts of his career and personality. Both Muirchu and Tirachan know some of the facts recorded by Patrick in his writings, yet even these they are all too well able to bungle. It is disputed whether either of them had first-hand knowledge of either work of the saint's; but at the least they had indirect knowledge of them.[5]

The conclusion must be that Palladius and Patrick form a sort of island. Of Irish Christianity before their time we know nothing at all, and for nearly two hundred years after them our ignorance is almost equally woeful. The careers of Palladius and Patrick are a sort of dim

---

3   For the Book of Durrow see the magnificent edition edited by A. A. Luce and others, I, pp. 17–24, with the photogrpah in II, fol. 247v. Luce thinks that the Patrick in question is someone other than the saint. Adomnan, *Vita S. Columbae : secunda praefatio*, 3a (ed. Anderson), p. 182; Binchy, 'Patrick and his Biographers', p. 169. For Muirchu's Introduction see Bieler, *The Patrician Texts*, p. 63; Muirchu on Coroticus, *ibid.*, p. 101; Macalister, *Ancient Ireland*, p. 171; O'Rahilly, Review of Bieler, p. 272. Hanson, 'The D-Text', p. 255f., has put it beyond doubt that Muirchu knew, directly or indirectly, the *Epistle*.
4   MacNeill, 'The Other Patrick', p. 313.
5   Binchy, 'Patrick and his Biographers', p. 65f., Hanson, art. cit.

lamp shining in otherwise unbroken darkness. We have seen that British Gildas says nothing of Patrick or of Christianity in Ireland. He was not mentioned at the Synod of Whitby in 664. What is even more surprising is that so great a man as Bede knew nothing of him. Bede is interested in the history of the Church in Ireland and reports in his *Ecclesiastical History*, published in 731, whatever he could learn of it. He reports, for example, the arrival of Palladius in 431 and gives a quantity of information about Irish Christianity in Britain and elsewhere; but of Patrick he knows nothing at all. The source of information about Palladius, of course, was the entry in the chronicle of Prosper. But it is hard to understand how it came about that Anglo-Saxon visitors to Ireland in the seventh and early eighth centuries or Irish visitors to Britain in that same period did not make known in Britain the facts about Patrick. Presumably at this date Patrick was not a talking-point and was rarely or never discussed. We could perhaps account for that state of affairs by supposing that Patrick's fame in Ireland still rested in the main on his two books, not on his actions; and that no copies of his books were available in Britain in and before Bede's day. On the other hand, the great outburst of writing about him took place in Ireland a generation before Bede brought out his *History*. On the Continent the earliest reference to Patrick is found before the time of Bede. It is a Latin couplet in what might be called a poem, composed or ordered by the abbot Cellanus of Péronne, who died in 706. The couplet claims that 'Gaul nourished him', which in fact Gaul did not.[6]

A huge red herring has been drawn across the path of Patrician studies by a theory that there was not a mere single Patrick: there were two of him, both active in the fifth century. But writers who speak of him before the year 700 know nothing of this fancy. They are never in any doubt: they speak of 'Patrick', not of the 'younger' Patrick or the 'older' Patrick, hairy Patrick or bald Patrick, black Patrick or red Patrick, or anything of the sort. They never suppose that their readers will wonder which of the two Patricks they are talking about. For them — for Muirchu, for example, and for Tirachan, and the others — there was one Patrick and one only. But not long after the year 700 there came into existence, for whatever reason, a double chronology of Patrick's life. The Irish annals tell of a Patrick who died in 457 or perhaps in 461 but who also died in 491 — or was it 492? Since neither chronology has any value at all, we

6 On Bede note Esposito, 'The Patrician Problem', p. 155 n. 56. On the Péronne couplet see Grosjean, 'Notes 7', p. 73, cf. Binchy, 'Patrick and his Biographers', p. 83.

need not ask whether one of the dates is to be preferred to the others. But inevitably the argument went that two chronologies meant two bishops, though men did not begin to believe in two Patricks until the middle of the eighth century. According to some, the older of the two Patricks was identical with Palladius, and as early as the beginning of the ninth century we find a reference to 'Paladius (*sic*) who was called Patrick by another name'; and the equation of Palladius and Patrick, according to Bieler, was the corner-stone of the modern Two Patricks theory. The fact was that while Patrick was remembered, Palladius was forgotten — and yet Palladius appeared in the chronicle of Prosper while Patrick did not. This discrepancy was resolved in either of two ways: *either* Palladius was identical with Patrick *or* Palladius' mission was an instant and total failure, and he disappeared from Ireland by 432, having only arrived there in 431.[7]

We find a small cloud of references to the 'two Patrick's, ranging in date from the eighth century until the present day. Zimmer accepted the identification at the beginning of this century; but the most famous discussion was that published in a lecture delivered in 1942 by T. F. O'Rahilly and often accepted later on, even by scholars so distinguished and normally so ungullible as Carney and Binchy. O'Rahilly's paper caused a tremendous flurry of excitement in Dublin, and one hothead went so far as to call it 'one of the most brilliant papers ever written on a point of Irish history'! And Binchy, for once, instead of attacking others (as he had been known to do) became himself the object of attack — and a vigorous attack at that. Bury, as so often, had taken the wise course: he dismissed the second Patrick as a mere 'phantom'.[8]

The later mediaeval *Lives* of St Patrick, written long after the time of Muirchu, contain an element of fancy. When I first obtained a copy of Bieler's splendid *Four Latin Lives of St Patrick*, I opened the book at random and read how 'three brigands stole a he-goat belonging to the blessed Patrick. Taking it away, they devoured it in secret; but this could not escape his notice. So the three of them came to the blessed Patrick wishing to swear falsely that they had not eaten the goat. So when they denied it, the animal itself shouted out loudly

7 Bieler, 'Interpretationes', p. 11. The three earliest references to the 'Two Patricks' are discussed by Binchy, 'Patrick and his Biographers', pp. 124—33. See Levison, 'Bischoff Germanus', p. 169f.
8 Zimmer, *The Celtic Church*, p. 39; O'Rahilly, *The Two Patricks* — 'one of the most brilliant papers', Murphy, 'The Two Patricks', p. 302. Binchy attacked by Shaw, 'The Myth'. Bury's opinion in *The Life of St Patrick*, p. 343.

from the stomachs of the three men as if it had said clearly: "Since you are not willing to confess to my lord the crime of theft which you perpetrated against me, I shall reveal myself" ', and so on. That a goat, even a he-goat belonging to St Patrick, should take part in an argument in Latin after being eaten by three separate individuals seemed so downright improbable that the temptation to read on was not irresistible. But Irish *Lives* of mediaeval saints tend to be like that: there are things in them which you could not easily believe.[9]

Of the stories about St Patrick which later became so widely told, the oldest is that relating to the treatment of the Irish people on the Day of Judgement. On that well known occasion (though I am not sure what is the evidence which has made its procedures so well known) lesser breeds may be judged by other authorities; but Patrick in the presence of Jesus will sit in judgement on the Irish. This prophetic information is first recorded in the seventh century, and doubtless has its adherents to this day.[10]

Centuries later we find the view that it was St Patrick who expelled the snakes from Ireland, and they have stayed expelled in spite of various twentieth-century humourists' attempts to introduce them. Unhappily, the old Romans a couple of hundred years before the days of St Patrick were aware that Ireland is snakeless. That fact is recorded by a writer called Solinus, who is thought to have lived early in the third century. Accordingly, it is not easy to believe in Patrick's achievement in this respect.[11]

Most famous of all perhaps is the belief that Patrick illustrated the nature of the Christian Trinity by comparing it to a shamrock. But there is no ancient or even mediaeval evidence that he did any such thing. We first hear of this story in the seventeenth century. At that time Irishmen were thought to dip shamrock in their whiskey from time to time (though that is not quite the same thing as using it to illustrate the Trinity). In point of fact the shamrock would be an even better illustration of Cerberus, the three-headed dog which, according to the ancient Greeks, guarded the entrance to Hades and made sure that, once you went in, you did not easily come out again.[12]

But the main interest of the Patrick-legend was pointed out by

9 Bieler, *Four Latin Lives*, p. 105.
10 Muirchu in Bieler, *The Patrician Texts*, p. 117, cf. *Liber Angeli*, §23 in Bieler, op. cit., p. 188.
11 Mommsen, *C. Iulii Solini*, p. 100. 8.
12 For bibliography on the shamrock see Bieler, *The Life and Legend*, p. 128 n. 10, to which add Forrestall, 'The Shamrock Tradition'. For some bibliographical material on Patrick in the Middle Ages, note Bieler, 'Vindiciae', p. 182—5.

James F. Kenney in his monumental book on the sources for the early history of Ireland: 'Because of the relatively large number of stages at which it has left permanent records, the Patrick-legend has a special interest as an example of the development of the acts of a mediaeval saint.' The process has not yet come to a complete stop. It is worth bearing in mind that in addition to the scholarly world of Binchy and Bieler, Carney and Hanson there is also a literary underworld where the faithful, or at any rate their leaders, write glowing passages of prose which are intended to uplift and edify their followers. True, they do not quite reach the levels attained by the author of that story of the three poachers and their incurably talkative goat. But, like him, they are prepared to throw evidence for their statements to the winds, and in place of evidence to use a quality which is much easier to handle — imagination. You need no footnotes and no references to ancient texts to bolster up your imagination: it is its own justification. This type of imaginative writing appears sometimes in unexpected places. There exists, for example, a worthy Irish journal called *Studies*, which has included many valuable essays on the subject of St Patrick. But if you rummage among the volumes published in the early 1960s, you will light on the following choice passage: 'The portrait that emerges from the *Confession* is that of a gentle and seraphic soul . . . What drew people towards him was an unmistakable sweetness and gentleness that comes from the anointings of the Holy Spirit. His eyes must have seemed (to those about him who had spiritual discernment) the eyes of a child, clear, wistful, ever kindling anew to the vision of the good God within. He was a child too in that radiant chastity that is one of the fruits of the Holy Spirit — not a strained and tense continence but the glow of an all-pervading chastity possessed in peace. He was a man on fire with God and men came to him for warmth.'

Beautiful — is it not? — and touching, especially that bit about his clear, wistful, infantile eyes, admittedly only visible to those who had spiritual discernment. No doubt the author of the passage which I have quoted is setting before his flock an ideal at which they may aim, though why he chose to call this ideal by the name of Patrick is not clear even to those with spiritual discernment. The significant point is that such passages of maudlin flapdoodle are still being written and — what is worse — are still thought worth printing even by the editors of reputable journals. It looks as though the legend of St Patrick may well have a future before it even now.

13 Kenney, *The Sources*, p. 326.

Appendix on Chronology

No feature of Patrick's life and writings has been discussed more frequently, with more warmth, with more flatly contradictory results, at greater or more boring length, or with more splutters of rage than — can you believe it? — his chronology! But most of the discussions have been vitiated by the tendency of the combatants to admit the evidence of mediaeval documents, especially that of the Irish annals. Thus, Macalister on page 169 of his book *Ancient Ireland*, famous in its day, emphasises that he will refuse to make use of all evidence except that of Patrick's own writings, for he is well aware of what he rightly calls 'the illimitable nonsense of which tradition is capable'. But turn the leaf and read his page 170, and you will find that he has already forgotten his sturdy resolution; for there, on the very next page after the one on which he proclaimed his brave intention, he accepts the year 441 as the date when Patrick was approved at Rome, as we learn from the *Annals of Ulster*. The evidence of those and all other Irish annals, where they claim to speak of St Patrick, is unacceptable.

Even D. A. Binchy has tumbled into error in this respect, though not so crudely as Macalister. He put forward a remarkable argument designed to prove that Patrick died in the closing years of the fifth century. A number of the saint's alleged disciples and associates are recorded in the Irish annals as having died in the period 480 to 549. There are about thirty of these men. Binchy admits that each of the dates of these men's deaths is in itself worthless, but taken collectively, he says, 'their combined testimony is most formidable'.

Unhappily, this argument breaches a rule of the Higher Mathematics. We all know that $0 \times 0 = 0$, but the Higher Mathematicians assure us that it is also true to say that $0 \times 30 = 0$ and neither more than 0 nor less than 0. If each of the dates is worthless, then all 30 of them are equally worthless and prove nothing about the date of St Patrick's death.[1]

'All difficulties concerning Patrick', writes James Carney, 'hinge upon his chronology.' If only it were so! But since we cannot place him in his political context, some may think rather that his exact chronology is a matter of limited interest. What difference would it make to our estimate of him if we discovered that his bishopric lasted from 435 to 445 or from 445 to 455 or from 455 to 465? Not a great deal. But it would certainly be of some interest to know whether he worked in the first or the second half of the century, for if he was active in the second half his silence about events in his native Britain is a puzzle. In formulating that question, by the way, I have arbitrarily assigned to Patrick a bishopric of no more than ten years. We shall see that the figure may not be improbable.[2]

1. — Relative Chronology

It is possible to draw a reasonable inference about Patrick's age when at last he became bishop of the Irish. At the time of his rejection by the seniors his confession of his youthful sin to his close friend lay thirty years in the past (and the sin itself perhaps as much as forty years in the past). Now, he had committed this sin when he was barely fifteen years of age. He admitted it to his friend before he became a deacon. In 384 Pope Siricius suggested that a deacon should be aged over thirty; and since Patrick, when he returned from slavery, had to make up an enormous leeway in matters of education, reading, training, and experience, he may well have been ordained as deacon when he was considerably over the age of thirty. After all, he had only returned to Britain at the age of twenty-two at the very earliest, and, if he spent a few years working in Gaul before reaching home, at the age of about twenty-five or twenty-six. Even after reaching home, he may have spent some time in relative idleness

---

1 Binchy, 'Patrick and his Biographers', pp. 111–5, cf. Murphy, 'The Two Patricks', p. 299, O Raifeartaigh, 'The Life', pp. 124–7.
2 Carney, 'A New Chronology', p. 24.

or at any rate inactivity before Victoricus appeared in his dream and told him that the Irish people were calling to him to come back to Ireland. Let us guess that he disclosed his sin to his friend when he was not less than twenty-five or twenty-six years of age. But this admission was thirty years in the past at the time of his rejection, and, if this line of argument is even approximately correct, it would follow that he was at the very least in his middle fifties when the seniors passed him over. The inference is that he was only appointed to the bishopric when he was aged sixty or thereabouts at the earliest. Even if he returned to Britain from slavery at the age of twenty-two and admitted his sin to his friend on the very day on which he landed in Britain — even if he called it out to his friend in the very act of jumping ashore from the ship which had carried him to his homeland — we could deduce that he was rejected at the age of no less than fifty-two; and when at last he became bishop he was in his middle or late fifties. That would explain why he says that he went to Ireland 'of my own accord' (as distinct from going there in the ship of the slavers) only 'when I was almost at the end of my strength'. When Patrick uses that phrase, he modestly exaggerates his physical weakness. He may indeed have been relatively advanced in years — say, at the least not much less than sixty — and it may have seemed rather late in the day to begin a missionary career. But as it turned out, he had more than ordinary strength still remaining to him when he was consecrated at last.[3]

Some scholars manage to make Patrick about ten years younger at the time of his consecration as bishop by supposing that the 'thirty years' elapsed *not* between the time when he admitted committing the sin and the time of his rebuff by the seniors, but between the time when he committed the sin and that same rebuff. Unhappily for any such theory, Patrick is explicit beyond all cavil that the thirty years elapsed after 'the word which I confessed before I was deacon'. No amount of special pleading can change that 'word' into the deed which the word denoted. What is also certain is that it is wildly misleading to say that Patrick 'was at least thirty' when appointed as bishop. Considering the amount of study — study of the Bible, if of nothing else — which he must have put in before being accepted for orders, there is no question of his being consecrated as bishop — or even as deacon, I imagine — when he was 'probably in his middle thirties'.[4]

3 Patrick, *Confession*, §28 (244.7).
4 Bieler, *The Life and Legend*, p. 69, rightly dated the thirty years from Patrick's admission,

There is nothing which need surprise us in these suggestions about Patrick's ripe age when at last he became bishop of the Irish. When he returned to Britain from slavery in his mid-twenties, he had only a schoolboy's education. As I have mentioned, it must have taken many years of hard work to acquire the general education of a potential bishop. At this date the Church demanded a fairly high standard of education in the upper grades of the clergy. And Pope Siricius had suggested forty-five or thereabouts as a suitable age for appointment to a bishopric. It would call for special pleading, I think, if we wished to argue that Patrick was consecrated as bishop when much under the age of fifty. I do not know why Carney regards it as 'quite unacceptable' to suppose that the saint might have been some sixty years of age before he went to Ireland as bishop. Theodore of Tarsus, after all, was consecrated as archbishop of Canterbury in 668 at the age of sixty-six and continued to function without becoming a senile dodderer until he was eighty-eight in 690. We must allow Patrick, then, an effective bishopric of not more than some ten or fifteen years or a shade longer, perhaps not so long. After all, he says himself that he went at last to Ireland only when his strength was already failing.[5]

2. — Absolute Chronology

At what date did the rejection of Patrick as bishop take place? On what occasion was he passed over for the bishopric? We must not suppose that it was in the year 431 itself and that Palladius was appointed on that same occasion in preference to him. Palladius was appointed in 431 not by any bishops or others who could be called 'seniors' but by Pope Celestine in person, and he may well have been elevated in Rome. Celestine knew Palladius. He had accepted Palladius's analysis of the situation in Britain in 429. It was at Palladius's instigation that he had appointed Germanus of Auxerre to go to Britain so as to combat Pelagian ideas there. There can be no

---

not from his commission, of the sin; but unfortunately he later changed his mind: see p. 66 n. 1 above. The problem is discussed by Hanson, *St Patrick : His Origins*, p. 135f. 'Middle thirties': Carney, 'A New Chronology', p. 35.

5 Education of the clergy: Jones, *The Later Roman Empire*, II, p. 924. 'Quite unacceptable': Carney, *The Problem*, p. 106. Theodore: Bede, *Hist. Eccles.*, IV. 1, V. 8 (ed. Plummer, I, pp. 202−4, 294f.).

question of Patrick's being in competition with Palladius for the appointment. So there is here a clear indication that Patrick was not the immediate successor of Palladius as bishop. One or more persons intervened. Presumably, when Palladius died or retired, Patrick hoped to become bishop, was interviewed for the appointment but was passed over. No doubt he eventually succeeded the person who was successful on this occasion of the 'test' or examination. So Patrick was at best the *third* Catholic bishop to go to Ireland. It is not out of the question, of course, that more than one bishop intervened between Palladius and Patrick, and that Patrick went to Ireland as late as the second half of the century. We cannot know how long a time elapsed after the rejection before he at last found favour.

We have seen that Palladius made his first appearance in history in 429 when he incited Celestine to send Germanus to Britain; and that he made his second appearance in 431 when he himself went to Ireland. His name is never mentioned again, and yet in a ghostly way he seems to make a third shadowy appearance in history even though his name is not mentioned in connection with it. He appears — if that is the right word — rather as the Invisible Man appears in the story.

Apart from his *Chronicle* Prosper wrote another work soon after the death of Pope Celestine on 27 July 432. The next pope, Sixtus III, took up his office on 31 July of that same year, and he had not yet had time to achieve much when Prosper published his new pamphlet. In it Prosper looks forward to the new pope's continuing the good work of his predecessors, though clearly he had not gone very far with it as yet. The pamphlet, then, appeared in 433 or 434 but not later. We can be more precise. At the beginning of the work Prosper says that the attack on the heresy of Pelagianism was begun under Augustine's leadership 'twenty years ago, or a bit more'. Now, Pelagius's opinions were first condemned at the Council of Carthage in 411, and Augustine began to write against them in 412. So 434 is the date at which Prosper was writing his pamphlet.[6]

Palladius was sent to Ireland in 431. We might have thought that he could hardly have made very much impression there by the year 432 or even 433. And yet something of a remarkable kind must have happened, for in 434 in his new pamphlet Prosper is able to report striking victories for the Church in Ireland. Here are his often-quoted words: Celestine 'by ordaining a bishop for the Irish, while he was eager to keep the Roman island Catholic, also made the barbarian

6 Prosper, *Contra Collatorem*, I, 2, XXI, 4 (Migne, *Patrologia Latina*, 51, 27). On this passage note Binchy, 'Patrick and his Biographers'. p. 142.

island Christian'. The words 'he was eager to keep the Roman island Catholic' refer to Celestine's efforts to defeat the heresy of Pelagius in Britain, the Roman island (a slightly out-of-date way of describing it), and to maintain the Catholic faith there. (Incidentally, he makes no claim that the pope was successful in this ambition.) But what does he mean when he says that Celestine 'made the barbarian island Christian'? He cannot mean that by the mere appointment of a bishop Celestine extended the jurisdiction of Rome over Ireland. That would be a ludicrous overstatement. It is certain, then, that news of a remarkable success did indeed reach Prosper in or just before 434. It is inconceivable that he would have invented it. If he had not heard some striking news about Christianity in Ireland he would have composed some other antithesis to make his point. After all, he was not obliged to refer to Ireland in summing up Celestine's papacy. Indeed, his reference to Ireland is something of an irrelevance. What he is mainly concerned with is that Celestine defeated the Pelagian heretics in their homeland, Britain. His subject is heresy. That the pope also converted much of Ireland from paganism to Christianity is a different matter. It is beside the point. It is a fact which adds nothing to his account of the struggle against Pelagius and his teachings, and it is these which are the central issue of the pamphlet. Indeed, by calling Ireland a 'pagan' country he goes some way — though by no means the whole way — towards contradicting his own statement in the *Chronicle* that there were sufficient Christians in Ireland to justify the appointment of a bishop there; and he could hardly have taken Ireland to be such a small island as to need only two or three years for its more or less complete conversion. Indeed, he is guilty of a gross exaggeration in another way. He gives the credit for Christian successes in Ireland to Pope Celestine, but in fact Celestine died on 27 July 432, only a year or two after the beginning of the Irish mission of Palladius. If Palladius won successes, he hardly won them so quickly as *that* would imply![7]

I have the impression that Prosper was slipping into his work a reference to some 'hot' news which, though not strictly relevant to the subject of his pamphlet, had just come to his ears and impressed him. And he phrases his antithesis in such a way as to suggest that his readers, too, would recognise the successes which he had in mind. If that is the case, it follows that events in Ireland were something of a talking point for the moment, though not a very prominent one,

7   The translation is from *Contra Collatorem*, loc. cit.

among educated men in Rome. The remarkable inference is that Palladius, arriving in Ireland in 431, to minister to the Irish Christians, immediately went beyond his 'terms of reference' (as we might say), became a missionary or supervised mission work among the heathen, and won instant and noteworthy successes for the Catholic Church, and that the fame of these successes spread immediately back to the Continent. In view of all this it is tempting to think that in his tract, *The Call of All Nations*, where he mentions ways in which Christianity crossed the Imperial frontier, Prosper had Ireland (and perhaps other places, too) in mind when he wrote these words: 'Christian Grace was not content to have the same frontiers as Rome, and Christianity has now subjugated many peoples to the sceptre of Christ's cross whom Rome did not conquer with her arms. Rome became greater under the lead of the apostolic bishopric by means of the citadel of religion than the force of <secular> power. As we know that some peoples were not adopted long ago into the association of the sons of God, so now also in extreme parts of the world there are some nations upon whom the Grace of the Saviour has not yet shone. We do not doubt that the time of their call has been arranged by the secret judgement of God, at which time they will hear and accept the Gospel which they have not heard.'[8]

It is not easy to see which places other than Ireland the author can have had in mind when he speaks of nations 'in extreme parts of the world' who were not Christian earlier but will become so in due course. The Christian religion had been spread in some measure to all the provinces of the Western Empire, but the author of the *Call* has in mind peoples who had never been overrun by the Romans. Ireland is the obvious example of what he is thinking about. The idea that Rome has occupied with her religion what she never won by her armies is also hinted at in a poem by Prosper: 'She grasps with her religion what she does not possess with her arms.' But before we draw too many conclusions about Ireland from these passages, it must be admitted the point had been something of a *cliché* in Roman writers since the second century. When Pope Leo the Great (440–61) used it, we do not know what exactly, if anything, he had in mind. Perhaps he intended it as nothing more than a mere morale-booster to keep the faithful happy. But it is hard to resist the conclusion that for Prosper it did have meaning: he is a shade more specific in the *Call* than the other composers of such *clichés*. At all events, so far

8 Prosper, *De Vocatione Omnium Gentium*, II, 16f. (Migne, *Patrologia Latina*, 51, 704).

as we know, the only persons who were actively trying to extend the Roman religion to areas which had never been part of the Western Roman Empire were busy in Ireland.[9]

The early mediaeval views that within a year of his arrival in Ireland Palladius died or was martyred or that he ran away or that he never went there at all, are baseless; and so is the bizarre opinion that he went, and had been instructed to go, not to Ireland at all but to what is now called Scotland! One opinion, not the wildest, is that Palladius on his arrival in Ireland instantly fell dead and was replaced by Patrick at such a high speed that Prosper published his chronicle in 433 without hearing of this dramatic event. That is to say, his chronicle was out of date even before he published it! In this way the traditional mediaeval date for Patrick's arrival in Ireland, 432, could be maintained. But since the traditional date is worthless, there is small gain in maintaining it! The fact is that, if Palladius had deserted through death or cowardice in 432, we should have to suppose that the decision to appoint a successor was taken, that the right man was found, that the right man travelled to Ireland, and that he won his impressive successes in time for news of his achievement to reach Prosper at latest in 434. All this would imply a speed at which such events could not possibly happen. The difficulties of travel inside the collapsing Empire, not to mention outside the Empire, would have seen to that, quite apart from the difficulty of making up official minds. And to suppose that Prosper had not heard of the death of Palladius when he wrote about making the barbarous island Christian is also inadmissible. Prosper was interested in Palladius. He mentions him not once but twice in his *Chronicle*, a far from common distinction; and Bury thought that he probably knew him personally. If Palladius had died within a year or two of his arrival in Ireland, we cannot believe that Prosper would have spoken of his achievements as though he were still alive. This would almost amount to suggesting that Prosper spoke of him as though he were still alive when in fact he knew that he was dead. That would be to accuse Prosper of deliberately and pointlessly misleading his readers; and that is out of the question. True, students of early Irish have often pointed out that the name 'Palladius' never took root in Ireland, and the man himself, if mentioned at all, is called by the Latin name 'Palladius' and never

---

9 For similar sentiments see Prosper, *De Ingratis*, 41f. (Migne, *Patrologia Latina*, 51, 97), 'quidquid non possidet armis, relligione tenet'; Augustine, *Enarratio in Psalmum XCV* (Migne, *Patrologia Latina*, 37, 1228), Leo, *Sermo*, LXXXII, 1; and for an earlier day see Tertullian, *Aduersus Iudaeos*, 1 (*ibid.*, 2, 650).

by any Irish adaptation of 'Palladius', and that he left no authentic Irish tradition of his life and activities. Anything that the Irish later on knew about him is derived exclusively from Prosper's notice of him in the *Chronicle* and not from any independent native tradition. We do not know the reason for this silence about him in Ireland: its importance could easily be exaggerated. But it seems a shade harsh, simply because he so quickly disappears into the mists of the Dark Ages, to call him 'the uncomfortable, embarrassing, and inexplicable Palladius'.[10]

From what we learn about Palladius's career it is possible to draw one crucial and, it seems, certain inference about St Patrick. It is that Patrick could not have been consecrated as bishop in Ireland before 435. Even if Palladius died in 434 at the very moment when Prosper was writing about him, it would still be difficult to infer that Patrick became bishop in 434/5, for we have seen reason to think that someone else — perhaps more than one person — intervened between the first bishop and Patrick.

But if that is all true, we are faced with yet another difficulty of great obscurity. This problem centres not on chronology but on those conversions of 431—4. The dates cannot be disputed. It is not in doubt that the bishop in those years was Palladius. Are we to conclude that a drive to convert Ireland had been started with success years before Patrick was appointed and was in full swing when at last — rather belatedly — he arrived on the scene? Had he missed the beginning of the great mission to the Irish? Had others been quicker than he in answering the call of those who lived beside the Wood of Voclut? It is not easy to visualise Palladius as a great missionary. His interest lay in heresy. On heresy he was an expert and was the adviser of the pope. Patrick, on the other hand, was the innovator. He had no interest in heresy. For him the central idea was the conversion of barbarians in Ireland, where God had shown him such mercy, as he believed. Conversion of the Irish was something which he had thought out for himself, something which he felt that he must explain and justify. And yet the vital facts here are (i) Patrick was appointed as bishop some years, let us say, after 434, and yet (ii) notable successes in converting the Irish pagans were won in the years 431—4. What are we to say about the relation between these two facts?

10 See Bury, *The Life of St Patrick*, p. 350. But Wilson, 'St Patrick', p. 366f., is among those who think that Prosper wrote this passage although aware that Palladius was in fact dead. For a good comment see O'Rahilly, *The Two Patricks*, p. 21. The quotation is from Carney, 'A New Chronology', p. 30.

Since the number of guesses which has been put forward in connexion with Patrick's life and writings falls not far short of infinity, one more will do little harm — provided we remember that it is nothing more than a guess. There is no evidence whatever to support it. It is simply a daydream.

We could account for these two facts, then, by supposing that after Patrick escaped from slavery he trained in Britain to become an ecclesiastic and in due course returned to Ireland, not in the first place as bishop, but as a deacon on the staff of Palladius — that is to say, that he went there as deacon in 431 (or even earlier) and it was at this time that his relatives offered him gifts to dissuade him from going. O Raifeartaigh rightly remarks that there was no reason why immediately on his return from slavery it should be necessary to beg him not to leave home again; but to offer him gifts when he had already been appointed bishop of the Irish would surely be a waste of time — and of gifts. 'The matter would only have arisen when, after some time at home, . . . he should have revealed his desire to depart, doubtless to study for the priesthood', or rather, as I am tempted to think, to return to Ireland as deacon. We might go on to suppose that Patrick had already formulated his new ideas on the subject of converting the Irish and on arrival went to work with no loss of time to win them to Christianity, and soon won some successes. We might further think that Palladius allowed this work to proceed and perhaps even encouraged it, though that would not have been a conventional attitude for a Gallic churchman to adopt. On this theory we can see how Patrick came to be in Ireland when the seniors considered him for the bishopric: he was certainly not in Britain at the time. We could also explain why he can say that he worked among 'you' since the time when he was a young man and how he had educated a priest — doubtless an Irish priest — 'from infancy'. We can understand why, when he was at last appointed as bishop, men already knew what use he intended to make of his bishopric and so were alarmed for his safety. Many possibilities open up before us, but since they would all be built upon sand, let us turn our backs to them and walk away, looking neither to right nor to left.[11]

---

11 Binchy, 'Patrick and his Biographers', pp. 111−5, cf. Murphy, 'The Two Patricks', p. 299, O Raifeartaigh, 'The Life', pp. 124−7, and others.

Further Reading

Modern study of St Patrick began in 1905 when J. B. Bury, a Co Monaghan man, published *The Life of St Patrick and His Place in History*. Bury was possibly the most learned historian produced by the British Isles in the twentieth century. He knew all the European languages except three; and his familiarity with the scholarly literature of Europe was unmatched. When he turned to Patrick he saw the saint and his career as an offshoot of Imperial Roman history, and he brought to bear upon him a fund of knowledge of the saint's Imperial background which few could rival. His procedure was to set out first a plain narrative of Patrick's life which anyone could read, and to follow it with 160 pages of closely printed and even more closely argued notes and appendices in which he justified the conclusions reached in his narrative. The result was such a work of scholarship as seemed to be the last word on Patrick, and it effectively killed the study of the saint for a generation. Except in details, it was thought, no one could hope to improve on Bury. He had written what would always be the standard life of Patrick.

But in 1962 it was shown that what Bury wrote was by no means the last word on Patrick. D. A. Binchy's paper, 'Patrick and his Biographers, Ancient and Modern', revealed, among much else, that Bury's book is vitiated from cover to cover by an error of judgement. Bury accepted the *Life* by Muirchu, the Irish annals, and other late documents as containing much reliable information about the saint, or at any rate as allowing many safe inferences to be drawn. He followed these sources to such an extent that, as Binchy's paper showed, enormous areas of his narrative must be written off, now that it is absolutely certain that the only source of true information about Patrick is Patrick's own writings. It follows that Bury's work gives the reader an old-fashioned view of St Patrick which few scholars would accept nowadays. Others had noticed that Bury was not to be trusted — James F. Kenney, for example, in his monumental book on *The Sources for the Early History of Ireland* had mildly commented on Bury's 'perhaps over-credulous examination of the sources' and remarked that Bury 'is over-lenient towards the received tradition' — but it was Binchy who put the matter beyond doubt.

In 1968 R. P. C. Hanson produced the comprehensive study of Patrick which is likely to hold the field for many a year, *St Patrick: His Origins and Career*. But it can only be read by those who know a good deal of Latin. Fortunately, Hanson produced a summary of his views for the Latin-less reader in his *The Life and Writings of the Historical St Patrick* in 1983. This book includes an English translation of Patrick's two little books.

As for the Latin text of Patrick's writings, in 1938 German barbarians drove Ludwig Bieler from his home in Vienna. After suffering much hardship he managed to take refuge in Dublin, to Dublin's great gain. He devoted the rest of his life to the study of the text of Patrick and of the later Patrician documents. He drew up a Latin text of the *Confession* and the *Epistle* with a commentary on the language. This text is unlikely to be improved on except in a handful of details. If his work on Patrick was intended as a return to the Irish people for giving him a home and a job in his hour of need, we may say of him what Homer says of one of his heroes, that he gave gold in return for bronze.

The text with French translation, introduction, and notes by Hanson and Cécile Blanc, published in Paris in 1978, is a little goldmine. It contains a wealth of information about Patrick, his life, his Latin, and everything else about him. It has the inestimable quality — not always appreciated by publishers — of being pocket-sized; and when I look at my battered copy of it, I recollect that it has travelled and been studied on hundreds of buses, scores of trains, two boats, and one aeroplane.

The reader who wants a plain Latin text with an English translation of Patrick and Muirchu could well read A. B. E. Hood, *St Patrick: His Writings and Muirchu's Life*. Unfortunately, this book contains an introduction by John Morris, which can only be described as lamentable. The reader's best course would be to skip the introduction, and read Hood's English translation.

It would be a shame, almost a crime, to end any book about St Patrick without a word of praise and gratitude for Ferdomnach. Ferdomnach was a scribe of Armagh who in 807 wrote one of the greatest of the mediaeval Irish manuscripts, that known as the Book of Armagh, which is now preserved in the Library of Trinity College, Dublin. The manuscript contains three groups of documents: (i) the *Confession* of St Patrick in a curiously shortened form along with Muirchu, Tirachan, and a number of additions, the Book of the Angel, etc., but not the *Epistle*; (ii) a New Testament, the only copy of the New Testament surviving from early Ireland, for the other great books, e.g. the Book of Kells, contain only the gospels; (iii) a number of Sulpicius Severus's writings about St Martin of Tours. Ferdomnach was fortunate in his editor. In 1913 John Gwynn produced a 'diplomatic' edition of the Book of Armagh. This is a wonderful example of book production, and it should if possible be examined. You will not fail to admire it. The text shows something of the beauty of Ferdomnach's work, and it is preceded by an introduction of marvellous learning and judgement — and, not least, of enthusiasm. 'Here, then,' writes Gwynn, 'we have before us the writing of a choice Irish scribe, a consummate artist in calligraphy; which, though 1097 years old, is for the most part as legible as if written yesterday.' (That figure 1097 can now be changed to 1178).

The Irish Manuscripts Commission also produced a collotype edition of the Patrician part of the Book of Armagh, with an introduction by John Gwynn's son, Edward, in 1937.

Bibliography

ANDERSON, A. O. & ANDERSON, M. O., *Adomnan's Life of Columba* (Edinburgh 1961)

ANDERSON, W. B., *Sidonius: Poems and Letters*, 2 vols. (Harvard & London 1936, 1965)

BARLEY, M. W. & HANSON, R. P. C., *Christianity in Britain A.D. 300—700* (Leicester 1968)

BATESON, J., 'Further Finds of Roman Material from Ireland', *PRIA* 76 C (1976) 171—80

BATESON, J., 'Roman Material from Ireland: A Reconsideration', *PRIA* 73 C (1973) 21—97

BETHELL, D. L. T., 'The Originality of the Early Irish Church', *JRSAI* 110 (1981) 36—49

BIELER, L., 'A Linguist's View of St Patrick: Remarks on a Recent Study of St Patrick's Latinity', *Eigse* 10 (1961—3) 149—52

BIELER, L., *Four Latin Lives of St Patrick* (Dublin 1971)

BIELER, L., 'Interpretationes Patricianae', *IER* Series 5, 107 (1967) 1—13

BIELER, L., *Libri Epistolarum Sancti Patricii Episcopi* in *Classica et Mediaevalia*, 11 (1950) 1—150 and 12 (1951) 79—214, re-printed as a book in 2 vols. (Dublin 1951)

BIELER, L., 'Muirchu's Life of St Patrick as a Work of Literature', *Medium Aevum* 43 (1974) 219—33

BIELER, L., 'Patrician Studies in the *IER*', *IER* Series 5, 102 (1964) 359—66

BIELER, L., 'Patriciology: Reflections on the Present State of Patrician Studies', *Seanchas Ardhmhacha* (1961—2) 9—36

BIELER, L., 'St Patrick and the British Church', in BARLEY, M. W. & HANSON, R. P. C., *Christianity in Britain A.D. 300–700*, 123–30

BIELER, L., 'The Christianization of the Insular Celts during the Sub-Roman Period and its Repercussions on the Continent', *Celtica* 8 (1968) 112–25

BIELER, L., *The Life and Legend of St Patrick* (Dublin 1949)

BIELER, L., 'The Mission of Palladius', *Traditio* 6 (1948) 1–32

BIELER, L., *The Patrician Texts in the Book of Armagh* (Dublin 1979)

BIELER, L., 'Vindicianae Patricianae: Remarks on the Present State of Patrician Studies', *IER* Series 5, 79 (1953) 161–85

BINCHY, D. A., 'Patrick and his Biographers: Ancient and Modern', *Studia Hibernica* 2 (1962) 7–173

BINCHY, D. A., Review of K. Hughes, *The Church . . .* in *Studia Hibernica*, 7 (1967) 217–9

BINCHY, D. A., Review of K. Jackson, *Language and History in Early Britain*, in *Celtica* 4 (1958) 289

BINCHY, D. A., 'St Patrick's "First Synod" ', *Studia Hibernica* 8 (1968) 49–59

BREEZE, David J. & DOBSON, Brian, *Hadrian's Wall*, 2nd ed. (Harmondsworth 1978)

BROOKS, N. (ed.), *Latin and the Vernacular Languages in Early Mediaeval Britain* (Leicester 1982)

BROWN, P. *Augustine of Hippo* (London 1967)

BURY, J. B., *The Life of St Patrick and His Place in History* (London 1905)

CAPPUYNS, M. 'L'auteur du "De Vocatione Omnium Gentium" ', *Revue bénédictine* 39 (1927) 198–226

CARNEY, James, 'A New Chronology of the Saint's Life', in John Ryan (ed.), *Saint Patrick* (1958), 24–37

CARNEY, James, *The Problem of St Patrick* (Dublin 1973)

CHADWICK, H. M., *Early Scotland* (Cambridge 1949)

CHARLES-EDWARDS, T. M., Review of N. Brooks, *Latin and the Vernacular Languages* (1982) in *Journal of Roman Studies* 74 (1984) 252–4

CHARLES-EDWARDS, T. M., 'The Social Background to Irish *peregrinatio*', *Celtica* 11 (1976) 43–59

COURTOIS, C., *Les Vandales et l'Afrique* (Paris 1955)

DE STE. CROIX, G. E. M., 'Early Christian Attitudes to Property and Slavery', *Studies in Church History* 12 (1975) 1–38

DIVJAK, J., *Epistolae S. Aureli Augustini, CSEL* vol. 88 (1981)

DUMVILLE, D. N., 'Kingship, Genealogies, and Regnal Lists', in SAWYER, P. H. & WOOD, I. N. (edd.), *Early Medieval Kingship* 72—104

DUMVILLE, D. N., 'Some British Aspects of the Earliest Irish Christianity', in Ni CHATHAIN & RICHTER, M. (edd.), *Irland und Europa*, 16—24

ESPOSITO, M., 'The Patrician Problem and a Possible Solution', *IHS* 10 (1956—7) 131—55

EVANS, A. J., 'On a Votive Deposit of Gold Objects Found on the North-East Coast of Ireland', *Archaeologia* 55 (1894—7) 391—408

FARIS, M. J. and others, *The Bishops' Synod ('The First Synod of St Patrick'),* (Liverpool 1976)

FARRELL, A. W. & PENNY, S., 'The Broighter Boat: Re-Assessment', *Irish Archaeological Research Forum* II part 2 (1975) 15—28

FORRESTALL, James, 'The Shamrock Tradition', *IER* Series 5, 36 (1930), 63—74

FRERE, Sheppard, *Britannia: A History of Roman Britain,* (London 1974)

GALLETIER, E. (ed. and transl.), *Panégyriques latins,* 3 vols. (Paris 1949—55)

GRATWICK, A.J., 'Latinitas Britannica', in BROOKS, N., *Latin and the Vernacular Languages* (Leicester 1982) 1—79

GREENE, D., 'Some Linguistic Evidence Relating to the British Church', in BARLEY, M. W. & HANSON, R. P. C., *Christianity in Britain 300—700* (Leicester 1968) 75—86

GROSJEAN, P., 'Notes d'hagiographie celtique, 6—14', *AB* 63 (1945) 65—130; 'Notes . . . 19—22', *ibid.*, 70 (1953) 312—26; 'Notes . . . 27—36', *ibid.*, 75 (1957) 158—226

GROSJEAN, P., 'S. Patrice à Auxerre sous S. Germain', *AB* 75 (1957) 158—74

GWYNN, John, *Liber Ardmachanus: The Book of Armagh* (Dublin 1913)

HALM, Carolus, *Sulpicii Seueri Opera, CSEL* 1 (Vienna 1866)

HANSON, R. P. C., *St Patrick: A British Missionary Bishop,* Inaugural Lecture (Nottingham 1965)

HANSON, R. P. C., *St Patrick: His Origins and Career* (Oxford 1968)

HANSON, R. P. C., 'The Date of St Patrick', *Bulletin of the John Rylands Library* 61 (1978/9) 60—77

HANSON, R. P. C., 'The D-Text of Patrick's *Confession*: Original or Reduction?' PRIA 77 C (1977) 251—6

HANSON, R. P. C., *The Life and Writings of the Historical St Patrick* (New York 1983)

HANSON, R. P. C. & BLANC, Cécile, *Saint Patrick: Confession et Lettre à Coroticus* (Paris 1978)

HARNACK, A., *History of Dogma*, vol. 5 (London 1898)

HARRISON, K., 'Episodes in the History of Easter Cycles in Ireland', in WHITELOCK, D. & others, *Ireland in Early Mediaeval Europe* (Cambridge 1982) 307—19

HAVERFIELD, F., 'English Topographical Notes', *English Historical Review* 10 (1895) 710—12

HITCHCOCK, F. R. M., 'The Confession of St Patrick', *Journal of Theological Studies* 8 (1907) 91—5

HOOD, A. B. E., *St Patrick: His Writings and Muirchu's Life* (London and Chichester 1978)

HUBERT, H., Introduction to S. CZARNOWSKI, *Le Culte des héros et ses conditions sociales: St Patrice héros national de l'Irlande* (Paris 1919)

HUGHES, K., *Early Christian Ireland: Introduction to the Sources* (London 1972)

HUGHES, K., *The Church in Early Irish Society* (London 1966)

JACKSON, K. H., *Language and History in Early Britain* (Edinburgh 1953)

JACKSON, K. H., 'Some Questions in Dispute about Early Welsh Literature and Language', *Studia Celtica* 8/9 (1973/4) 1—32

JONES, A. H. M., *The Later Roman Empire, 284—602: A Social, Economic, and Administrative Survey* 4 vols. (Oxford 1964)

KENNEY, James F., *The Sources for the Early History of Ireland: Ecclesiastical*, 2nd ed. by L. Bieler (New York 1966)

KENT, J. P. C., 'From Roman Britain to Saxon England', in R. H. M. DOLLEY (ed.), *Anglo-Saxon Coins* (London 1961)

LEVISON, Wilhlem, 'Bischof Germanus von Auxerre und die Quellen zu seiner Geschichte', *Neues Archiv der Gesellschaft für ältere deutsche Geschichtskunde* 29 (1904) 95—175

LINDSAY, W. M., *Isidori Etymologiae*, 2 vols. (Oxford 1911)

LUCE, A. A., *Euangeliorum Quattuor Codex Durmachensis*, ed. with introductory matter by LUCE, A. A., SIMMS, G. O., MEYER, P. & BIELER, L., 2 vols. (Olten, Lausanne, Freiburg in-Br., 1960)

MACALISTER, R. A. S. *Ancient Ireland* (London 1935)

McGANN, M. J., 'A Reconsideration of Some Linguistic Evidence', in FARIS, M. J., *The Bishops' Synod*, pp. 23—7

MACMANUS, Damian, 'A Chronology of the Latin Loan-Words in Early Irish', *Eriu* 34 (1983) 21—71

MacMULLEN, Ramsay, *Christianizing the Roman Empire* (Yale 1984)

MACNEILL, E., *St Patrick* (Dublin 1964)

MACNEILL, E., 'The Hymn of St Secundinus in Honour of St Patrick', *IHS* 2 (1940) 129—53

MACNEILL, E., 'The Other Patrick', *Studies* 32 (1943) 308—14

MALASPINA, E., 'Patrizio e i *dominicati rethorici*', *Romano-barbarica*, 4 (1979) 131—60

MARCUS, G. J., 'Irish Pioneers in Ocean Navigation of the Middle Ages', *IER* Series 5, 76 (1951) 353—63, 469—79; 81 (1954) 93—100

MARKUS, R., 'Gregory the Great and a Papal Missionary Strategy', *Studies in Church History*, 6 (1970) 29—38 = MARKUS, R., *From Augustine to Gregory the Great* (Variorum Reprints 1983) chapter 11

MIGNE, J. P., *Patrologia Graeca*, 161 vols. (Paris 1857—66)

MIGNE, J. P., *Patrologia Latina*, 221 vols. (Paris 1844—64)

MOHRMANN, Christine, *The Latin of St Patrick* (Dublin 1961)

MOMMSEN, T., *Chronica Minora* 3 vols. (Berlin 1891—8)

MOMMSEN, T., *C. Iulii Solini collectanea rerum memorabilium* (Berlin 1895, reprinted 1958)

MOMMSEN, T., *Iordanis Romana et Getica* (Berlin 1882)

MÜLLER, Carolus, *Fragmenta Historicorum Graecorum* 4 vols. (Paris 1874—85)

MÜLLER, Karl, 'Der heilige Patrick', *Nachrichten von der königlichen Gesellschaft der Wissenschaften zu Göttingen: phil-hist. Klasse* (1931) 62—116

MURPHY, Gerard, 'The Two Patricks', *Studies*, 32 (1943) 297—307

NASH-WILLIAMS, V. E., *The Early Christian Monuments of Wales* (Cardiff 1950)

NERNEY, D. S., 'A Study of St Patrick's Sources', *IER* Series 5, 71 (1949) 497—507; 72 (1949) 14—26, 97—110, 265—80

Ni CHATHAIN, P. & RICHTER, M., *Ireland and Europe* (Stuttgart 1984)

NOCK, A. D., *Conversion* (Oxford 1961)

O'BRIEN, M., 'Miscellanea Hibernica', *Études celtiques* 3 (1938) 362—73

O'MEARA, J. J. & NAUMANN, B., *Latin Script and Letters* (Leiden 1976)

BIBLIOGRAPHY

O'MEARA, J. J., 'Patrick's *Confessio* and Augustine's *Confessiones*', in O'MEARA, J. J. & NAUMANN, B., *Latin Script and Letters* (1976)

O'MEARA, J. J., 'The Confession of St Patrick and the Confessions of St Augustine', *IER* Series 5, 85 (1956) 190−7

O'RAHILLY, T. F., Review of L. Bieler, *The Life and Legend of St Patrick*, *IHS* 8 (1952/3) 268−79

O'RAHILLY, T. F., *The Two Patricks* (Dublin 1957)

O RAIFEARTAIGH, T., Review of Hanson, R. P. C. & Blanc, C., *St Patrick: Confession et Lettre à Coroticus*, *IHS* 21 (1978) 219−24

O RAIFEARTAIGH, T., 'St Patrick's Twenty-Eight Days Journey', *IHS* 16 (1969) 395−416

O RAIFEARTAIGH, T., 'The Life of St Patrick: A New Approach', *IHS* 16 (1968/9) 119−37

O RAIFEARTAIGH, T., 'The Reading *nec a me orietur* in Paragraph 32 of St Patrick's Confession', *JRSAI* 95 (1965) 189−92

PATON, W. R., *Polybius: The Histories*, 6 vols. (London & Cambridge, Mass. 1954)

POWELL, D., 'The Textual Integrity of St Patrick's Confession', *AB* 87 (1969) 387−409

PRAEGER, R., *The Way That I Went* (London 1937)

PRUDENTIUS, ed. and transl. M. Lavaronne, 3 vols. (Paris 1943−8)

RYAN, J., 'A Difficult Phrase in the Confession of St Patrick', *IER* Series 5, 52 (1938) 293−9

RYAN, J. (ed.), *St Patrick* (Dublin 1958)

RYAN, J., 'The Traditional View of St Patrick', in RYAN, J., *St Patrick* 10−23

SAWYER, P. H. & WOOD, I. N., *Early Mediaeval Kingship* (Leeds 1977)

SHARPE, Richard, 'St Patrick and the See of Armagh', *Cambridge Mediaeval Celtic Studies* 4 (1982) 33−59

SHAW, Francis, 'Post-Mortem on the Second Patrick', *Studies* 51 (1963) 237−67

SHAW, Francis, 'The Linguistic Argument for Two Patricks', *Studies* 32 (1942) 315−22

SHAW, Francis, 'The Myth of the Second Patrick', *Studies* 50 (1961) 5−27

SIDONIUS, see ANDERSON, W. B.

SOZOMEN, *Historia Ecclesiastica*, ed. J. Bidez, *Die griechischen christlichen Schriftssteller*, vol. 50 (Berlin 1960)

SULPICIUS SEVERUS, see HALM, Carolus

THE IRISH MANUSCRIPTS COMMISSION: *Facsimiles in Collotype of Irish Manuscripts, vol. 3: Book of Armagh: The Patrician Documents*, with an introduction by Edward Gwynn (Dublin 1937)

THESAURUS LINGUAE LATINAE (Leipzig 1900—)

THOMAS, Charles, *Christianity in Roman Britain to A.D. 500* (London 1981)

THOMPSON, E. A., 'Barbarian Raiders and Roman Collaborators', *Florilegium* 2 (1980) 71—88

THOMPSON, E. A., *St Germanus of Auxerre and the End of Roman Britain* (Woodbridge 1984)

THOMPSON, E. A., 'St Patrick and Coroticus', *Journal of Theological Studies* New Series 31 (1980) 12—27

WHITE, Newport J. D., '*Libri Sancti Patricii*: The Latin Writings of St Patrick', *PRIA* 25 C (1905) 201—326

WHITELOCK, D. and others, *Ireland in Early Mediaeval Europe* (Cambridge 1982)

WILSON, P. A., 'Romano-British and Welsh Christianity: Continuity or Discontinuity?' *Welsh History Review* 3 (1966/7) 5—21, 103—20

WILSON, P. A., 'St Patrick and Irish Christian Origins', *Studia Celtica* 14/15 (1979/80) 344—80

WINTERBOTTOM, M., *Gildas: The Ruin of Britain and Other Documents* (London & Chichester 1978)

ZIMMER, H., *The Celtic Church in Britain and Ireland*, translated by A. Meyer (London 1902)

INDEX

adolescens, 39 with n. 4
Adomnan, 126f., 160
Africa, 110; pagan tribes in, 62; invaded by Vandals, 131
Agamemnon, xiv
Alans, 24
Ambrose, St of Milan, on celibacy, 7; on barbarians, 64; on patriotism, 111
Annals of Ulster, 166
Antonine Wall, 130
Apollinaris, see Sidonius
'apostrophe', 116f., 134
Arians, Arian heresy, 36, 158; missionaries of, 62f.; author on conversion, 63; of Rugi, 63
Armagh, xiii, 160; unmentioned by Patrick, 94. See Ferdomnach, Book of Armagh
Armenia, 89, 91
Armorican Jew, Patrick thought to be, 10
Asia Minor, 59
Attacotti, 64
Augustine of Hippo, 13, 60; on celibacy, 7; on slavery, 29 n. 16; attacks Pelagians, 53, 55, 170; unmentioned by Patrick, 54; Prosper on, 56; on pagan African tribes, 62
Augustine of Canterbury, 83f., 90
Austria, 83
Auxerre, xiii, 36, 66. See Germanus
Auxilius, 76

Bannaventa, 1f., 4, 9, 92; in Britain, 12; Whilton Lodge and, 10; identification of, 10f.; why does Patrick mention? 11f.; estate at, 101

Barbarians, regarded as sub-human, 63f.; Romans flee to, 139
Bede, 162
Berniae or Burniae, 1, 9, 12 n. 9
Bernicians, 127
Bishopric of Patrick irregular? 49, 51f.
Black Sea, 59
Boniface, Pope (418–22), 55
Book of Durrow, 160, 161 n. 3
Book of Armagh, 178
Bristol Channel, 10
Britain, Britons, Bannaventa situated in, 12f.; in 409 Roman power ends in, 9; raided by Picts, 10; alleged desert in, 26; did Patrick escape to? 25f., 31; Pelagianism in, 36; Patrick absent from, 38; alleged synod in, 39 n. 4; Latin in, 40, 41 n. 5; Germanus in, 53; British/brutish, 64; British bishops appoint to Irish see, 76; travel between Ireland and, 76, 134, 136; thought to have financed Patrick, 97, 100; coins in, 97; grain removed from, 97; Patrick as bishop wished to visit, 148; learned scholars among, 115f., 152f.; British history unmentioned by Patrick, 154. See Celtic
British Christians in Ireland, 56, 60, 91, 117; scattered over Ireland, 120f.; born in Ireland, 60, 110, 123; pagans in Ireland unmentioned, 110; slaves in Ireland unmentioned, 149
'British' Isles, 113
Broighter, Co Derry, 23f.
Burniae, see Berniae

'Caledonian Forest', 25

186

Family of Patrick, 1f., 8, 27, 36f., 77, 105, 175; slaves of, 3
Faustus of Riez, 152
Ferdomnach, a scribe of Armagh, 178
Foghill, Fochoill, 16, 17 n. 1
Forth, Firth of, 129
Franks, conversion of, 62; their prisoners ransomed, 100, 138, 149
Friend, Patrick's false, 13, 38, 68f., 73f., 86; dream concerning, 46, 74; motives of, 75; seniors and, 75, 107f.; chronology of, 167

Gaul, Gauls, Patrick may have escaped to, 25f., 28, 31; not resident in, 28f.; Pelagians expelled from, 35; become Latin-speaking, 92; ransom prisoners, 100, 138; eat heartily, 110; as beer-drinkers, 110f.; Patrick wished to visit, 148. See Franks
Genealogies, limited value of, 128
Georgia, 89
Germanus of Auxerre, xiii, 36; sent to Britain, 53, 57f., 169f.; but not by Gallic bishops, 72
Gildas, on Irish raiders, 6f., 159; on Irish and Pictish ships, 24; Latin of, 37, 41; silent on Pelagianism, 54f.; on Vortiporix, 112; refers to historical events, 154; silent on Patrick, 159, 162
Gloucester, 26
Gobi desert, 26
Goths, 59; Christian prisoners among, 63, 65, 90
Gregory the Great, Pope (590–604), 55, 90, 159
Gregory the Illuminator, 89

Hadrian's Wall, 10 with n. 8
Helios (the sun) in Patrick's dream, 48, 50
Hengist, 130
History absent from Patrick's writings, 154
Homer, 13, 177

Iberians, 89
ingenuus, 138 n. 13
Innocent, Pope (401–17), 55
Iona, 159
Ireland, Patrick resident in before bishopric, 39, 68; Christians in before 431, 60; British Christians in, 60f.,

64f.; Pelagianism unlikely in, 57, 64; travel between Britain and, 76; dangers of, 87f.; Roman influence on, 87f.; pagan when Patrick died, 159
Irish influence on Patrick's Latin, 41 with n. 5; Patrick's knowledge of, 91; Christians before 431, 56, 171f.; Christian organisation before 431, 61; held wives in common, 64; lack of knowledge of Latin, 81; people's knowledge of Roman Empire, 92; not Romans, 11f.; pre-literate, 113; alleged settlers in Wales, 52, 129; Christians won by Palladius, 171
Iserninus, 76
Isidore of Seville, 64
Italy, Pelagians expelled from, 55
iuuentus, 39 with n. 4

Jerome, St, 15; on celibacy, 7; on Pelagius, 52; on the British cannibals, 64
Jew, Patrick thought to be a, 10
Jordanes, historian, 64
Judges, Irish, 95, 98f.
Julian Caesar, 97
Julian of Eclana, 55

Kalahari, 26f.
Kent, 10, 90
Kerry, Co., 85
Killala, 16
Kings and their sons, 87, 102; Patrick's attitude to, 89, 95

Land, market value of, 101f.
Latin language, Patrick's knowledge of, xv, 36f., 40, 42f., 74; in Britain, 40, 41 with n. 5; Christian terms in Irish, 61 n. 10, 113; little known in Ireland, 113f.
Leinster, 51
Leo I, Pope (440–61), the Great, xiii, 172
Lérins, xiii
Lincoln, 10
Lives of St Patrick, mediaeval, 163f.
London, 10, 26, 92
Lupus, bishop of Troyes, 53
Lyons (Lugudunum), 11

Magnus Maximus, Emperor (383–88), 154
Marseilles, see Salvian